TRAILED

TRAILED

One Woman's Quest to Solve
the Shenandoah Murders

KATHRYN MILES

ALGONQUIN BOOKS OF CHAPEL HILL 2022

Published by
ALGONQUIN BOOKS OF CHAPEL HILL
Post Office Box 2225
Chapel Hill, North Carolina 27515-2225

a division of
WORKMAN PUBLISHING
225 Varick Street
New York, New York 10014

Design by Steve Godwin.
Maps by Margot Carpenter, Hartdale Maps.

Library of Congress Cataloging-in-Publication Data

Names: Miles, Kathryn, [date]– author.
Title: Trailed : one woman's quest to solve the Shenandoah murders / Kathryn Miles.
Description: First edition. | Chapel Hill, North Carolina : Algonquin Books of
    Chapel Hill, 2022. | Includes bibliographical references. | Summary: "An account
    of the unsolved murder of two women in Shenandoah National Park, by a journalist
    with unprecedented access to all key elements of the case, and a story that reveals
    the challenges of wilderness forensics and the failures of our justice system"—
    Provided by publisher.
Identifiers: LCCN 2021057136 | ISBN 9781616209094 (hardcover) | ISBN 9781643752938
    (ebook)
Subjects: LCSH: Williams, Julie, –1996. | Winans, Lollie, –1996. | Murder—Virginia—
    Shenandoah National Park—Case studies. | Shenandoah National Park (Va.)
Classification: LCC HV6533.V8 M55 2022 | DDC 364.152/3097559—dc23/eng/20220103
LC record available at https://lccn.loc.gov/2021057136

10 9 8 7 6 5 4 3 2 1
First Edition

For Camille and Suzanne,
who saw us through

Border Woman
Walls her own lands
With her own soul
In communion
With her own spirits

Between two lands is where my heart is.
The land is not mine any less than
It is yours.
I am me you are you. And we are we.

Stop and listen.
Flow and ebb with me.
I bleed. I breathe. I live.

—JULIE WILLIAMS, *journal entry*
  December 12, 1995

Author's Note

TRAILED **IS BASED ON FOUR YEARS** of reporting, which includes reviewing court transcripts and motions, archival news stories, and scholarship, along with the author's interviews with over a hundred sources. All dialogue rendered in direct quotations was either independently verified or recorded. Dialogue in italics has either been paraphrased for the sake of clarity or because it is based on a person's recollection and cannot be independently corroborated. Whenever possible, I have used the full names of individuals. In some cases, where people have reasonable expectations of privacy, I have opted to identify them only by their first names. In a few cases, people have asked to remain anonymous because of safety concerns or fears of reprisal. In those cases, I have changed their first names. These changes include the name of my partner at the time, who has asked to be referred to by his nickname, Ray.

This book includes multiple references to violence, including sexual assault and murder, that some readers may find upsetting or otherwise triggering. Every effort has been made to approach these subjects with sensitivity and respect.

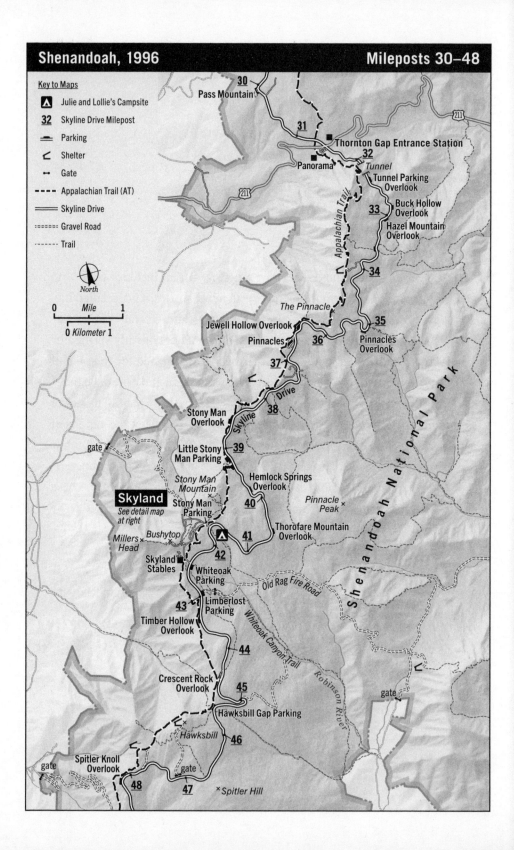

Key to Maps

⬛ Julie and Lollie's Campsite

32 Skyline Drive Milepost

🅿 Parking

< Shelter

⊷ Gate

- - - Appalachian Trail (AT)

═══ Skyline Drive

:::::: Gravel Road

------ Trail

North

0   *Mile*   1

0 *Kilometer* 1

30
Pass Mountain

31

⬛ Thornton Gap Entrance Station

32
⬛ Panorama
Tunnel
Tunnel Parking Overlook

33
Buck Hollow Overlook
Hazel Mountain Overlook

34

The Pinnacle

Jewell Hollow Overlook
Pinnacles

35
Pinnacles Overlook

36

37

Drive

38

Stony Man Overlook

Skyline

39
Little Stony Man Parking

Hemlock Springs Overlook

Stony Man Mountain

Pinnacle Peak ×

Skyland
See detail map at right

Stony Man Parking

40

Bushytop

Millers Head ×

Thorofare Mountain Overlook

41

42

Skyland Stables ⬛
Whiteoak Parking

Old Rag Fire Road

43
Timber Hollow Overlook

Limberlost Parking

Whiteoak Canyon Trail

44

Robinson River

Crescent Rock Overlook

45
Hawksbill Gap Parking

gate

Hawksbill

46

Spitler Knoll Overlook

gate

gate

48

47
× *Spitler Hill*

Shenandoah National Park

211

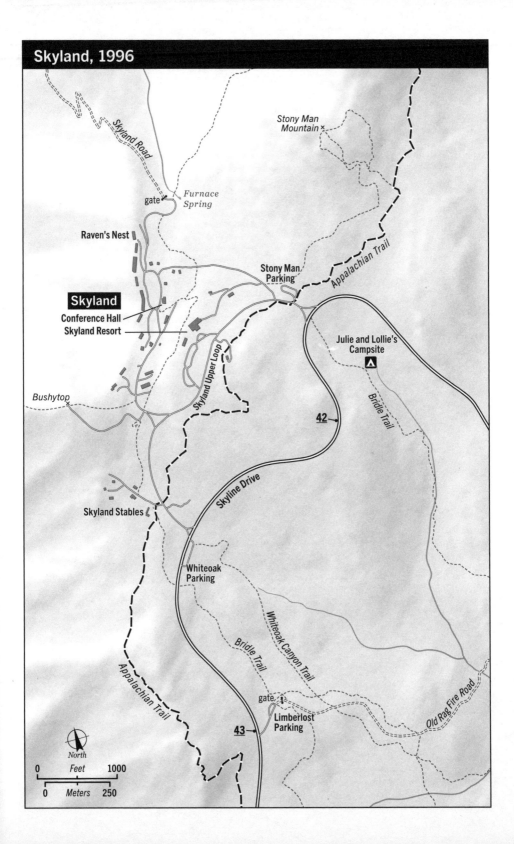

Skyland, 1996

Skyland Road

Stony Man Mountain ×

gate
Furnace Spring

Raven's Nest

Stony Man Parking

Appalachian Trail

Skyland
Conference Hall
Skyland Resort

Julie and Lollie's Campsite

Skyland Upper Loop

Bridle Trail

Bushytop

42

Skyline Drive

Skyland Stables

Whiteoak Parking

Whiteoak Canyon Trail

Bridle Trail

Appalachian Trail

gate

Old Rag Fire Road

43

Limberlost Parking

North

0   Feet   1000

0   Meters   250

TRAILED

Preface

THEY MUST HAVE BEEN FOLLOWED. That's the thought I return to after all these years.

They must have been tracked as they left the Skyland lodge and stepped across Skyline Drive, the well-traveled backbone of Virginia's Shenandoah National Park. He—for murderers are almost always *hes*—must have been prowling Skyland's parking lots and public areas, hoping he'd find the right target. Perhaps he studied the two young women as they lounged in the grass outside the lodge, oblivious as they consulted a map or warmed themselves in the afternoon sun. Maybe he bumped into one of them as she was leaving the restroom or grabbing a drink in the taproom. Something about their countenance and mannerisms must have caught his eye, made him decide he'd found what he had been hunting for.

He was calculating and confident. He would have thought little about following the women as they left the lodge area and descended that lonely, overgrown path. He must have felt emboldened once he realized how easy it was to hide there. Spring had come early to the Shenandoah Valley. Up near the lodge, grass had already become meadow: blades waved high and were bowed over by seed; wildflowers stood in ostentatious clumps. Along the Bridle Trail, the gnarled stems of mountain laurel and rhododendron had erupted in glossy, deep leaves, creating a sea of dark shadows. Towering above them, a canopy of wizened hickories and chestnut oaks made the corridor feel close and tight, blocking everything but the immediate present from view. The foliage was so thick, in fact, that days later searchers looking for the women would repeatedly walk past their hidden campsite without even noticing their brightly colored tent.

But not him.

He must have hung close, stalking them as they turned off the trail and bushwhacked back to their campsite. The roar of the nearby stream would have masked the sound of his footfall as he drew near. And even if the women had time to scream, he knew no one else could hear them.

JULIANNE "JULIE" WILLIAMS and Laura "Lollie" Winans were skilled back-country leaders. By May 1996, they'd each led dozens of trips: orchestrating ten-day expeditions in unforgiving landscapes like Minnesota's Boundary Waters and New Hampshire's White Mountains and taking inner-city women and their children on their first camping experiences in urban parks and recreation areas. Just one semester separated Lollie, age twenty-six, from a college degree in outdoor leadership at Unity College in Maine. She was confident, egoless, and a unique combination of gregarious and fiercely protective: always glad to meet you but also cautious to trust. Julie, twenty-four, had already traveled the world, volunteering in hardscrabble communities in South America, sifting through archaeological sites in Greece and Italy, surveying some of our most remote wilderness areas. She was quiet, big hearted, self-assured.

They'd met the previous spring while working at a world-renowned outdoor program for women. They'd also fallen in love there. But this was 1996: the same era when the US Supreme Court determined that antisodomy laws did not violate the Constitution and when voters in Colorado approved measures to declare homosexuality abnormal and perverse. It was also two years before Matthew Shepard was beaten and left to die in a coarse prairie field dotted with sagebrush and a year after the Olympic diver Greg Louganis sparked panic in public pools across the country after announcing he was both gay and HIV-positive.

Julie and Lollie were all too aware of the repressive zeitgeist of that time. And so that new, crazy love they felt was also something they kept almost entirely private. Out in the world, they traveled as good friends—just two young women who happened to share a passion for wild places.

That passion was what had taken them down Shenandoah National Park's Skyland Meadows Bridle Trail in May 1996. Located just two hours from our nation's capital, Shenandoah National Park feels a lot more remote. On a map, its 196,000 acres of forest look like a lizard sprawled along the narrow ridge of Virginia's Shenandoah mountains. Slicing through the middle of this long stretch of green is Skyline Drive—the only significant paved road in the park. During the height of the summer season, Skyline Drive is thronged with visitors, who flock to its postcard-perfect overlooks, resorts, and picnic areas. But get a mile beyond the drive on either side, and the park can seem as wild as any remote western landscape.

Decades earlier, the Bridle Trail had been well used: a thoroughfare for the nearby Skyland resort's stables, a place where parades of families were led on trail rides day after day. In time, stable managers decided crossing busy Skyline Drive was too dangerous for novice riders, so they relocated their horse trail behind the resort complex. In the years following, Virginia's abounding foliage—first serviceberry and interrupting ferns, then tickseed, wild blackberries, and poplar shoots—began to overtake the path. The trail slipped off park maps entirely. By the time Julie and Lollie arrived, all that remained was an unimpressive concrete marker on the edge of the park's main road. No bigger than a Civil War gravestone, it floated half-submerged in a tangle of grass and weeds.

Despite the overgrown terrain and lack of obvious markers, Lollie and Julie somehow found their way to the hidden Bridle Trail trailhead. Weighed down by overstuffed backpacks, they slowly descended eastward. A quarter mile down the steep path, they, along with Lollie's golden retriever mix, Taj, turned left and bushwhacked two hundred yards through the understory. There, they reached the northern fork of the Whiteoak Canyon Stream. The women set up their tent, stacked their heavy packs one upon another. They hung their water purifier; draped the tent's blue-and-yellow rainfly and staked it to the ground. They were so far hidden even the bright nylon of that rainfly would have seemed barely a whisper through all the early-season growth: maybe a resting goldfinch or jay, if you noticed it at all.

He noticed. And he came prepared. He brought with him gloves, along with duct tape and at least one weapon. He bound and gagged the women, then separated them. He left Lollie in their tent. He brought Julie, along with her sleeping blanket and pad, to the edge of the creek. When he was done with them, he killed both women with a single, unhesitating knife stroke to their throats. And then he disappeared, seemingly without a trace.

PART I

1

MORE THAN CHRISTMAS, RAMADAN, OR YOM KIPPUR, Earth Day was the high holiday at Unity College, a small environmental studies college located in the foothills of central Maine. For several weeks each April, the campus celebrated with drum circles and shaman workshops, adventure races and hydroturbine construction contests, bike parades and recycled pageants.

I first arrived at the college in late August of 2001. It was my first teaching job after graduate school. I was twenty-seven, nervous, and certain that I needed to appear as cerebral and donnish as possible. Luckily for me, Unity College stood for none of that.

To some visitors, the college seemed like a glorified summer camp. To me, it was more a throwback to 1960s idealism, a place where students proudly wore their beliefs writ large and thought nothing about cutting class to chain themselves to logging equipment or to follow a blood trail after shooting a deer.

Everything about the college was homegrown. The school itself was founded in 1965, when a printing snafu meant that the town of Unity, located about three hours north of the Maine–New Hampshire border, was omitted from the multipage atlas of the state. Outraged by the oversight, town elders launched a campaign to forever put Unity on the map. For reasons unknown, they settled on a new college as the best way to do so. An abandoned chicken hatchery became the school's first official building. To it, they added a cinder-block gymnasium and an all-purpose building laid entirely by volunteers. The library was stocked by donations received at the town's demolition derby, which that first summer offered free admission in exchange for two books.

Unity College's environmental studies focus evolved out of necessity, mainly because the campus had plenty of outdoor spaces and not much in the way of classrooms or technology. But by the time I arrived to teach, it had become a bona fide leader in the field.

Even then, the campus population was small: about five hundred students and thirty faculty members. Pet dogs roamed the woodlot, waiting to be reunited with their humans during lunch breaks. The main hangout on campus was the Tavern: a kind of rumpus room with couches and foosball, a pool table, and a massive projection television and screen that covered the back wall. The Tavern also had the only beer taps in town: with the closest bar twenty-five miles away, early school administrators decided it was just safer for students to drink on campus. Before evening classes, students and faculty alike would all hang out there over Tater Tots and pints of PBR, talking about energy efficiency and disc golf and which singer-songwriter would be playing that week. Then, at the appointed time, we'd trudge up to our classroom and assume a tiny modicum of academic hierarchy.

I loved everything about it.

By April 2002, Lollie Winans had been dead for almost six years. But she was everywhere on that small campus. In 1997, the year after Lollie's death, Unity administrators erected a massive stone fireplace in the college's welcome center and dedicated it in her memory. The college also endowed a women's leadership award in her name. Throughout campus, in framed photos and posters, she was often up front and smiling, forever memorialized in the ambitious wilderness trips she had once led or the campus-wide dances she'd attended.

Like a lot of Unity students, Lollie had taken a meandering route to campus. She spent her childhood in Grosse Pointe, Michigan. The town, one of the richest in the nation, had been built with old Ford money. Not the Model T variety but rather from the descendants of John Baptiste Ford, who amassed a fortune during the late nineteenth century making soda ash and lye. That wealth multiplied a hundredfold when he entered the emerging world of chemical production.

Lollie was born directly into Ford's massive inheritance. Her mother, Laura, for whom Lollie was named, graduated from Miss Porter's School in Connecticut, returned to Grosse Pointe, and married John Winans, a stockbroker. They established themselves at Wingford, one of the Ford family's grandest compounds. There, Laura bred Labradors and volunteered with local gardening clubs. She and her family entertained friends at the guesthouse and spent weekends gunkholing on *Galatea*, Laura's 140-foot motor yacht. In the winter, they'd decamp to Arrow Y, Laura's Arizona cattle ranch, complete with cowboys and plenty of ponies for anyone who wanted to play the part. Proud Republican donors, her parents served as board members for everything from desert galleries to ladies' riding clubs to Ducks Unlimited, a philanthropic group of hunters and conservationists. They reveled in their assured spot in the society pages.

Even as a young kid, Lollie felt like everything about this curated life was bullshit. At the age of five, she requested a tent so she could abandon her estate bedroom for the back lawn. She attended University Liggett School in Grosse Pointe Woods and tried playing field hockey there. But team sports were never her thing, and she had absolutely nothing in common with the other students, save for the ability of their parents to pay a hefty tuition bill. Life at home had also become unbearable. Her parents divorced, and her father quickly remarried, then moved to Boca Raton with his young wife. Lollie's mother brought home a new spouse as well. Lollie would later reveal—and only to a few of her closest friends—that that's when the sexual abuse started. According to those same friends, she tried once—and only once—to tell her mother what was happening in her bed. The response she got was harsh enough to never try again. (Laura Winans and her second husband divorced after Lollie's death. Laura died in 2011; he died a few years later. Shortly thereafter, Lollie's father was diagnosed with Alzheimer's disease).

According to Lollie's surviving friends, she dealt with the abuse by doing everything she could to escape Grosse Pointe. She found summer camps in the Blue Ridge Mountains where kids stayed for weeks, not days. She sent away for boarding school brochures and lobbied her mother to let her attend. She and Laura eventually compromised on one: Garrison Forest School in suburban Baltimore. Lollie liked little about the place. She made fun of the squash courts and polo team, the fashion collectives and pageant girls. But Baltimore was also a decent plane ride away from Grosse Pointe, and that was the kind of distance Lollie needed to feel safe. There, hundreds of miles away, she could bury the trauma deep down and try to act like a normal teenage girl.

Somehow, after graduation, Lollie found her way from Garrison to Sterling College, a tiny school in the equally tiny town of Craftsbury Common, Vermont, that offered an associate's degree in environmental studies. Once a private high school, the college had found a niche for itself, first offering a kind of gap-year work experience: a place where wealthy kids who had struggled at prep schools could file down some rough edges by working on the school farm, hewing trees on the adjoining woodlot, and completing winter expeditions in the mountains of northern Vermont. Their motto was (and is) "Working hands, working minds."

Wilson Hess was dean of students when Lollie arrived at Sterling in 1989. He was certain the place, with its strict rules, would never work for her. She'd immediately fallen in with a group of hard-partying older students who were notorious for divining every chink in the administration's precepts: from using recreational drugs to flouting curfews and any attempts to limit sexual activity. Fearless, Lollie would scope out remote wooded spots for late-night parties at locations so secret revelers still won't reveal them. On weekends, they'd change into their best tie-dye shirts and peasant skirts, then make clandestine drives to catch Phish at the University of Vermont. There was never coffee (way too corporate and *the man*). Instead, it was hand-rolled cigarettes and Mexican beer and at least one guitar. Sometimes someone would show up with weed or mushrooms. Any and all of this was cause for expulsion. But no one, not even Wilson Hess, could administer the punishment that kind of behavior warranted—at least not to Lollie.

"Lollie was always like, 'Rules aren't something I do,'" he says today.

After a disastrous and volatile visit from her father that first year, Hess began to understand why. There was so much dysfunction in that relationship—an observation confirmed by the school counselor. And even if it hadn't been apparent that Lollie had real challenges at home, Hess and others probably would have found a way to save Lollie from certain expulsion anyway. She was just so . . . likable . . . with this tremendous life force that filled every room.

At Sterling, she and the other first-year students spent their time pulling carrots and beets. They learned to use an ax and maul to split wood and start a fire. They lugged water and built lean-tos. In December, they set out for a weeklong wilderness trip. Temperatures fell below zero, and snow blew most of the time. Lollie adored every minute of it. Hess says that expedition was a real epiphany for her and that she returned to campus with a new sense of purpose and drive. After graduating from Sterling College with an associate's degree in 1991, Lollie and two of her classmates moved into the Woodbury House: a ramshackle place with cedar shingles, a tin roof, and a perfectly massive front porch, all located just steps from the Sterling campus. They hung hammocks and bought mismatched yard-sale chairs. Inside, they decorated with political broadsides decrying technological oppression and capitalism; they hung blocky posters printed by the nearby theater group, Bread & Puppet, espousing cheap art and the brilliant resistance inherent in growing flowers.

That first summer, Lollie planted the tiniest of gardens—just four feet square, with a couple of limp basil plants and a struggling tomato. But when the first blossoms appeared, you'd have thought she'd just watched her first child be born. Each time a friend would visit, she'd drag them over to her garden, always calling them by their last name as she ordered them to ooh and ahh: *O'Brien, check out this amazing cucumber*, she'd insist. *No seriously. I grew it.* She became a vegetarian, a devoted follower of *Diet for a New America,* the best-selling book that espoused a radical return to environmentalism and an end to industrial agriculture. Most weekends, Lollie and her roommates hosted ragtag parties that brought together all manner of local residents. They'd find Lollie in the kitchen, a bottle of Corona in her hand, talking jam bands. Or in the living room, making terrible bets on poker hands she knew she would lose.

Eventually, she settled on her life's passion: leading sexual assault survivors like herself on wilderness expeditions as part of their healing process. That led her to Unity College, where she pursued a bachelor's degree in outdoor recreation and leadership, or what we now call adventure therapy. In 1994, Unity folks referred to the program as "outdoor rec." These were the students kicking around Hacky Sacks, practicing their balance on slacklines strung between trees, and wearing stinky polypro gear and secondhand Patagonia before it was cool. In a program of about twenty or thirty students, Lollie was one of just three women. At first, she was deeply intimidated by the coursework: her classmates had already led multi-ascent climbing trips and paddling expeditions in Class V whitewater. They were certified in wilderness rescue and backcountry navigation. Some of them could actually get around by looking at the stars.

That first semester at Unity, she mostly sat back and didn't say much. In time, say her friends, Lollie's personality started to shine through. People grew to adore her—that dry, biting wit; the fact that she would always drop anything and give people her undivided attention whenever they were in need.

Lollie's parents provided little financial support, so the limited money she had came mostly from odd jobs. When she wasn't working, she wanted more than anything to be with her people. On random afternoons, Lollie would load up her limping VW microbus with friends and strangers and anyone else who happened to be around. Then she would drive to the nearby quarry, blaring the Allman Brothers or the Grateful Dead, singing her fool head off. At outdoor gatherings, she'd sit on the trunk of a car, wearing patched jeans and her trademark John Lennon glasses, playing harmonica. Or she'd dance and dance and dance, spinning circles for hours. She planned ambitious hikes and persuaded her best girlfriends to come along—regardless of what they'd been up to the night before. When no one was around, they'd pull off their T-shirts and sports bras, snapping a couple of nervous photos of their topless selves from behind. Later, they'd look at the developed photos as proof they were free. And in most of them, Lollie was the centerpiece. That's just the way it always was, her friends say now: if their circle of friends was a wheel, Lollie was the hub. They were content to be her spokes.

Part of what Lollie's circle loved the most about her was her humility. She was unassuming and hated affectation in any form. She didn't talk about her family and would change the subject when anyone asked. Not even her closest friends had any idea she came from unbelievable wealth—that she would one day inherit millions. To her friends, she was just Lollie, with her beat-up VW van and busted-up sneakers that you'd hear coming from a mile away—that ridiculous *swack* of a half-unglued rubber sole hitting the pavement before the rest of the shoe.

If you knew what to look for, there were signs of Lollie's inner struggles: the way she never wanted to skinny dip at the quarry; the resentment over the awkward false poverty her parents had put her in, purportedly to teach her responsibility. She tried to make light of it, to make it part of a mindfulness practice or life dedicated to antimaterialistic ideals. She'd buy a cookie and leave it on her dashboard for weeks, saying she was waiting for just the right time to eat it. She'd collect bottles and cans at reggae festivals to make sure she had enough gas to get home.

Money that she did find, she'd spend on the people she loved—glass suncatchers for her friends (they still have them, more than twenty-five years later). Giant waffle cones at an ice cream parlor. In return, she had this sincere way of being shocked and delighted and shy whenever anyone reciprocated, cupping her hand over her mouth, as if to contain the surprise and joy that someone cared enough to think of her.

She brought her golden retriever mix, Taj, with her everywhere: *This is Tajey Winans*, she'd say. *She is very pleased to meet you.* She continued to call everyone else by their last names. She was an unapologetic train wreck and sometimes a total pain in the ass. She ate the last of the provisions on a trip. If you were sharing a tent with her, she'd always make you go out and check on creepy noises at night. But she was the one who could make everyone else laugh on a particularly terrible or grueling hike. When rain soaked through a food bag, making everything a soggy mess, she'd invent bawdy songs about what you could do with your mush. Off trail, she'd do anything—*anything*—for you, whether it was getting you to the hospital in the middle of the night or listening for hours while you talked about the worst moment in your life. And she was always glad to do it. Because, for the first time ever, Lollie knew she'd found her family in that tight-knit Unity community.

ALONG WITH THE tangible memorials to Lollie, far more poignant were the indelible memories she'd left in those who had known her. Many of Lollie's closest friends remained in the greater Unity area. They served on campus and town committees; they dropped in on classes and played pickup floor hockey games with the rest of us on long winter evenings. My faculty colleagues had served as her advisers and professors. They'd adored Lollie when she was alive and struggled mightily with the viciousness and scars surrounding her death. In the weeks and months immediately after Julie and Lollie were killed, federal law enforcement agents had descended upon campus, wanting to know every detail about Lollie's private life. They subpoenaed her academic and medical records and compelled counselors to open their files. They implied friends and classmates committed the murders, which sowed suspicion and sliced deep rifts that have yet to heal.

And through it all, there was the quiet reminder that a strong, competent leader had been brutally murdered doing what she most loved. For members of the Unity community, bound by a shared passion for the wilderness, trying to make sense of the violence that had occurred there came with its own emotional challenges. This was particularly true for many of the students who identified as female. In the spring of 2002, the campus still suffered a serious gender gap, with a seven-to-one ratio of male-to-female students, and none who outwardly identified as transgender or nonbinary. Those studying conservation law were repeatedly reminded that barely 13 percent of all rangers and other law enforcement officers within the Department of the Interior were women. Of those female rangers, a full three-quarters reported experiencing job discrimination; over half said they had been sexually harassed by colleagues and supervisors. Students in other majors would return from expeditions sponsored by leading outdoor leadership schools angry and humiliated that they'd been made to rock climb on pitches with names like Gang Bang or paddle whitewater rapids dubbed One Last Bitch or Flogging Faggots. A disturbing number of female students completed internships in the field only to report their own exposure to sexual harassment and assault and the helplessness they felt to combat it.

The cumulative effect of these experiences added an aura of somberness to class discussions and many of the major events on campus.

In a lot of ways, the annual monthlong Earth Day celebrations held on campus every April offered an emotional salve—a chance for our tight-knit community to celebrate the return of spring and one last chance to let off steam before final exams and what, for many students, would be stressful summers spent conducting field research or leading backcountry trips across the American wilderness.

That opportunity to let loose was particularly welcome in 2002. Like every other campus in the United States, ours had been rocked by the tragedy of September 11. Students were angry, confused, and fearful. Several were in the National Guard and Reserves, well aware their deployment could be imminent. Others had lost friends and family members in the twin towers. We were all on edge, wondering what the Patriot Act would mean both for academic freedom and the privacy of townspeople who depended on our institution's library for internet and access to news. That same season, one of the campus community's favorite restaurants, which was owned by a much-beloved Pakistani family, was forced to close after repeated acts of vandalism and threats against the family. Suddenly, the rise in racially and ethnically motivated hate crimes across the country, which had seemed abstract to many of our students, had been made incontrovertibly real.

By the time the second week of April rolled around, we were all ready to take a break from public events and return to the shared passions that had brought us to this little rural college. That Sunday morning, April 7, the maple-sugaring club hosted its annual pancake breakfast. Afterward, students raced down the campus's main throughfare in go-carts made of recycled materials and questionable design. Early the next morning, a Passamaquoddy healer led a medicinal plant walk through the college forest, followed by a meditation and sweat lodge ceremony. Sidewalks were festooned with chalk art; trees were hung with paper stars and homemade dream catchers. Spirits were high.

Probably, then, we were all a little distracted that week. Few of us were paying close attention to the ongoing congressional investigations into the intelligence failures surrounding 9/11; nor were we talking about Attorney General John Ashcroft's very public announcement of indictments concerning the 1993 terrorist bombing of the World Trade Center. However, we all noticed when, on Wednesday, April 10, 2002, Ashcroft announced to a live-television audience that the murder of Lollie Winans and Julie Williams had finally been solved. Federal prosecutors, he said, had indicted Darrell David Rice, a thirty-four-year-old computer programmer from Maryland's Eastern Shore, in connection with the murders. Rice, said Ashcroft, had known mental health issues and was currently in prison for another crime in Shenandoah National Park: in 1998, he had pled guilty to assaulting a female cyclist in the park the previous summer. Ashcroft made it clear he thought that were it not for the gumption of that cyclist, she may have suffered the same fate as Julie and Lollie. Because of the perceived severity of that 1997 crime, a federal judge had insisted Rice serve a fourteen-year sentence for attempted kidnapping and sexual assault.

The murders of Lollie and Julie, continued Ashcroft, were particularly grievous because Rice had intentionally targeted the women based on their sexuality. As a result, and in addition to the four counts of murder, Rice would also be the first person tried under new enhanced sentencing measures that allowed prosecutors to seek the death penalty in federal hate crimes cases. *It was a most appropriate punishment*, Ashcroft continued. The 1996 Shenandoah killings, he insisted, were a clear example of the worst kind of hate crimes this country has witnessed.

As part of his official remarks that day, the attorney general revealed that he had met with both the Williams and Winans families just prior to his press conference. He held up the Williamses and Winanses as an emblem of the collective grief we'd all been experiencing in the months since 9/11: "These families have suffered what Americans now know all too well," Ashcroft lamented. "Just as the United States will pursue, prosecute, and punish terrorists who attack America out of hatred for what we believe, we will pursue, prosecute, and punish those who attack law-abiding Americans out of hatred for who they are. Hatred is the enemy of justice, regardless of its source. We will not rest until justice is done for Julianne Marie Williams and for Laura 'Lollie' Winans."

And there it was: some strange but powerful link between the Shenandoah murders and the tragedy of September 11. The implication seemed to be that, by executing Darrell Rice, we as a nation could somehow begin to heal from the loss of nearly three thousand people seven months earlier.

Many Americans celebrated Ashcroft's announcement of Rice's indictment. A spokesperson for the National Gay and Lesbian Task Force said that the Shenandoah case was a "sad reminder of the pervasiveness of hate crimes" and that she was "relieved" closure was on the horizon for the Williams and Winans families. News of the indictment was picked up by every major media outlet, many drawing the same parallels between the murders of Lollie and Julie and the rapid rise in Muslim-targeted hate crimes in the wake of September 11. That week in April alone, more than fifteen hundred newspaper stories were dedicated to Ashcroft's announcement and a renewed interest in the murders.

For the Unity community, that coverage both reignited grief and produced a collective sigh of relief. Lollie would never be brought back. But the judicial system had done its work, and we could at least trust in the integrity of the process. After five years of waiting, the person who had taken so much from so many people would finally be brought to justice. And for many of us, I think, Rice's indictment had also brought a sense of hope: that we might get answers about why he had targeted Lollie and

Julie, that the subsequent trial and conviction would provide some tangible proof that the crime was a tragic but bizarre one-off, that the woods could be made safe again.

Any temporary peace afforded by the indictment was soon interrupted. Within days of the attorney general's announcement, the press swarmed the campus. Writers from glossy magazines called my colleagues all hours of the day, asking prying questions about Lollie's previous relationships, what the world had lost in her death, and how we all felt knowing that her murderer had been caught. We learned quickly that there were no right answers to such questions. And that answering them again and again did little to help mitigate the complex emotions held by a small community. But the reporters kept at it, eventually shifting their focus to Darrell Rice himself. They asked what we knew of him, if we had any idea where his hatred for women and homosexuals had begun. They asked if Lollie might have flaunted her sexuality in front of him or somehow egged him on.

Not a single one of them asked if prosecutors had the right person.

2

BY 2016, I HAD LEFT UNITY COLLEGE; however, the murders of Julie Williams and Lollie Winans continued to haunt me. On June 1 of that year, exactly twenty years after the bodies of the two women had been found at their remote campsite, the FBI issued a strongly worded press release, asking for any information that may lead to the successful prosecution of the case. The choice of language in that press release—*information that would assist law enforcement with convicting the person(s) responsible for the double homicide of Laura Winans and Julie Williams*—seemed noteworthy to me. Most such releases ask for assistance in the arrest and prosecution of a suspect. Limiting that verbiage to a conviction seemed to suggest they already had the person in custody—or, for whatever other reason, they didn't need to make an arrest.

As it turned out, in 2004 the feds had quietly dismissed their case against Rice, citing insurmountable challenges that included contradictory DNA evidence. But rather than dismissing the case outright, the Department of Justice had evoked a legal concept known as *salvis iuribus*, or "without prejudice," which allows prosecutors to retry their case against a defendant at any time, and one that is often used because procedural or technical errors have occurred in the case. Rice had served his sentence for the 1997 assault on the cyclist and was released from prison in 2007. By then, it appeared as if any attempt to prosecute the murder of Julie Williams and Lollie Winans had stalled altogether.

The June 2016 FBI press release made no mention of those events. But the same day it was issued, the Washington, DC, NBC affiliate ran a televised interview with Adam Lee, then the senior supervising agent at the Richmond FBI field office. The station's bureau chief asked Lee point-blank if Darrell Rice remained a suspect. "Though I can't speak about any individual in the case," Lee responded, "I can tell you that nobody has been exonerated in the case."

I watched the clip several times online, wondering if Lee's response was really a big knowing wink about Rice's guilt, delivered in PR speak, or if the agency did not know who had killed the women. By then, I'd carved out a niche for myself as a journalist covering backpacking and our nation's long and scenic trails: paths like the Appalachian and Pacific Crest Trails that span hundreds or even thousands of miles and captivate the imagination of many. I'd written about heroic, record-setting speed hikes and heartbreaking disappearances and deaths. As soon as I'd read that June 2016 FBI press release and watched the subsequent interview, I contacted my editor at *Outside* magazine and proposed a long-form story about the unsolved case. He agreed, and soon after, I scheduled my own preliminary interview with Adam Lee.

"This is still an open and pending investigation," Lee told me. "It's very unusual to describe a twenty-year-old case as active, but it still is. We want to enlist the public for tips and leads, that sort of thing."

He added that theirs was a particularly challenging investigation, because of both the location and the joint jurisdiction.

"Usually, most of our crime investigations are in urban environments. They're very controlled crime scenes," said Lee. "With Shenandoah, the scene is very expansive and organic. You have wildlife activity and thousands of witnesses potentially transiting through. Also, we're accustomed to having exclusive jurisdiction in violent crime investigations. But in this case, because it was on federal land, we were sharing that with Park Service investigators. This kind of deep forensic work is not what they really do."

Even that early in my reporting, Lee's statement struck me as odd—if not a clear example of one federal agency throwing another under the bus. In my interview notes, I put a series of question marks next to his quote—my own personal shorthand for assertions that seem dubious or demand further attention.

In that same interview, Lee emphasized the fact that evidence, particularly DNA evidence, had been collected from the crime scene. He said he was particularly hopeful that emerging techniques in DNA analysis would help advance, and eventually resolve, the case. But what he returned to again and again in that hour-long phone call were variations on the same statement he had made in the NBC interview: *I want to be very clear here: no one has been exonerated in this case.*

The implication seemed clear: like no small number of true crime and outdoor enthusiasts, the FBI still believed Darrell Rice had murdered Lollie and Julie; they just lacked enough evidence to overcome the procedural hurdles that had stymied his first trial.

That thesis had become the basis for what the editorial staff at *Outside* and I had agreed would become my deep-dive feature article: I'd detail what was known about the murders and subsequent investigation, and I'd explore the difficulty in solving backcountry cases and why Adam Lee was so confident this decades-old case could soon be closed. I figured it would be a descriptive but fairly straightforward narrative based on the women's biographies and the FBI's renewed interest in the case. And if I'm being completely honest, that approach to the story felt safe: I figured I could pay homage to the lives of Julie and Lollie and help raise awareness about the ongoing case while also skirting what was particularly graphic or emotionally disturbing about their deaths. Instead of coming to terms with that aspect of the story, I could retreat to the safety of science and a profile on criminal investigation work.

What I had not yet begun to unpack was just how personal the story of Julie Williams and Lollie Winans had become for me. There was the Unity connection, yes. But it was also more than that. Growing up in several small midwestern towns, I spent most of my childhood with no real exposure to violence, save for what appeared in the movies carefully selected by my parents. Then, in my sophomore year in high school, a friend's mom was kidnapped while getting into her car at a mall in a nearby city. Her assailants wanted the vehicle, and she was collateral damage. They shot her in the head and left her for dead in a barren cornfield. Miraculously, she survived. But that incident had made me perennially fearful, even in our little rural town. I learned the rituals too many other women already practiced: always scan the parking lot when leaving a store. Drive around the block before parking outside your house. Press your keys between the webbing of your fingers in case you must defend yourself against an attacker.

That next fall, at age sixteen, I took a job as a junior reporter at the region's daily paper. At school, I felt awkward and self-conscious, having long since slipped between the cracks of different cliques and social groups, without coming to rest in any of them. Among the professional editors and journalists at the paper, I was enviably precocious and quickly embraced as the valued spokesperson of a rising generation. I relished the sense of belonging that new status created, certain I'd finally found my tribe. The person tasked with training me was twenty-four and about to leave for college. Our flirtation began almost immediately and was mutual. He courted me with giant pink plastic baby bottles and stuffed animals, poking fun at my age. I thought the gifts were weird, but I was also hugely flattered by the attention. On New Year's Eve that year, he invited me to the house he shared with his father. I had the flu and the roads were icy, so my parents wouldn't let me drive. He begrudgingly picked me up in his dad's Camaro and drove me to his house. We began to fool around, which seemed okay to me, but I also knew I wanted it to stop there. I told him no, that I wasn't ready to have sex, but he kept going. The pain that followed pinned me with a blinding flash. I covered my mouth to try to muffle the strange animal screams I could hear myself make, for fear that I would wake up anyone else who happened to be in the house. When he finally finished, he told me to get dressed and then he drove me home. Neither of us said a word. A few days later, he called to say he didn't want to see me again.

In the weeks and months that followed, I told no one what had happened. Initially, it was because I felt like a failure: I'd wanted so badly to belong to this older, more sophisticated set, and clearly the encounter proved I wasn't up to snuff. I also felt certain there must have been something very wrong with my body to have made the sex so painful, and I was mortified by how much blood I'd left behind. Later, I felt ashamed I'd put myself in a compromising position by going to his house in the first place and figured I probably deserved it. I compensated by throwing myself into a series of relationships with a whole spectrum of wildly inappropriate people. When that failed to make the memories go away, I began retreating within myself.

By my junior year in college, I was anorexically thin and living an ascetic existence only a medieval hermit could appreciate. A philosophy major, I had become enamored with big ideas and the comforting belief that any objective Truth could be proven through logical argumentation. That fall, 1995, I went on my first backcountry camping trip—a requirement for an environmental literature course I was taking. By way of preparation for the expedition, I'd borrowed an old cotton army sleeping bag from my dad and a massive external-frame backpack from my roommate. I bought a box of oat cereal, filled a couple of water bottles, and joined my classmates for the three-hour drive into Missouri's Ozarks. It was a miserable weekend: I was underdressed, ill prepared, and bad tempered. But sometime during that first night, as I shivered in the thin bag, I also fell in love. I wanted to be good at this thing—like the handful of students who stayed up late into the night, sipping tea from their stainless-steel mugs, lounging with ease in their nylon camp chairs.

The next morning, I was up before dawn. I rekindled our dying fire and surveyed the little encampment we'd made. There was something so pure and almost holy about the scene: the slow rise of daylight, the quiet of the woods, the closeness and serenity of our little tent village. For the first time in a long time, I was at ease, convinced of our collective safety and freedom. By the time my classmates stirred, I had the fire blazing. It felt good to be of use and to do honest work. Later that morning, we summited a starkly picturesque mountain. Our professor and I were the first to reach the top. He was a Romantic who'd long ago fallen in love with the wisdom of philosophers and poets like Henry David Thoreau and Ralph Waldo Emerson. There on the summit, as we waited for my classmates to join us, he gave me a knowing look that seemed to say, *See what I mean?* All I could do was nod in agreement.

After that experience, I returned to the trail again and again, a little more competent each time. I bought a pack that actually fit. I learned how to stuff the heaviest items down low, to conserve space and pounds. I could also set up a tent in the dark and light a cookstove in the rain. The woods had become my living, breathing nursery. My body grew strong and assured scrambling over rocks or up steep terrain. I found comfort in the truths of the trail: water flows down; blazes always show you the way; no matter how tired you are, you can still keep walking.

Once in grad school at the University of Delaware, I spent every possible weekend and academic break on the Appalachian Trail, or AT, which spans the Appalachian Mountains from Georgia to Maine. For me, everything about that place was profound. I relished the history of the seventy-year-old footpath, envisioned as "America's trail," a way to make wilderness accessible to all. With each footfall, I contemplated that sense of history and the fact that I was somehow connected both to everyone who had walked the path before me and every other backpacker currently making their way on a twenty-two-hundred-mile bridge that connected landscapes and experience along the spine of this continent's oldest mountains.

I began to learn the culture and the language of the place as well. "Thru-hikers" were those audacious souls attempting to hike the entire trail in one trip—usually a four-month slog that left them battle-weary, calorie-deprived, and otherwise wizened. "Flip-floppers" were also trying to complete the trail in one go, but they began their hikes at Harpers Ferry, West Virginia, the trail's halfway point, hiked either north or south to one terminus and then returned to Harpers Ferry to complete the other half. Both groups were trail royalty. They gave each other names like Yoda and Trash Panda and Coca-Cola Jones and proudly referred to themselves as "dirtbag hikers." I, on the other hand, was a section hiker—out for three days or a week or two. In the caste system of the trail, I was just one rung above the widely reviled day-trippers, who by and large seemed to know nothing about trail etiquette and gummed up popular sections with their rambling pace and cheerful conversation.

The trail itself is set up such that a hiker will reach an Adirondack-style shelter or three-sided lean-to about every twenty miles, an average day's walk for an experienced backpacker. Accommodations in the shelters themselves are rough: on nights during peak season, hikers will pack in and sleep shoulder to shoulder, often with smelly, farting strangers. If a shelter is crowded, thru-hikers get precedent, followed by flip-floppers. The rest of us are expected to pitch our tents nearby and try to stay out of their way as they rearrange gear, fill water bottles, and eat a spoonful or two of gruel before falling asleep, exhausted but prepared to do the same damn thing the next day. When not in striking distance of a shelter, most hikers set up "stealth campsites": hidden spots picked by weary backpackers because they are far enough off the trail to escape notice or attention from a passerby.

During waking hours, the AT shelters also serve as the primary means of communication on the trail. Local trail clubs will often post notices there, alerting backpackers to washouts or dried-up springs or who to call for a ride into town. Those offering the rides are called "trail angels": hiking club members or sympathetic retirees or former thru-hikers who offer little acts of service intended to make a thru-hiker's slog more enjoyable. Maybe they'll leave a coveted banana on a pack or set up a cooler with beer and soda at a road crossing. Some wander up to shelters with cookies or ice cream bars. Others will even set up charcoal grills at trailheads and hand out burgers as emaciated thru-hikers shuffle by. All these types of gifts are known as "trail magic."

As a section hiker, I wasn't supposed to partake of any trail magic. Unlike the thru-hikers who, to keep their packs as light as possible, pare down their essentials to the absolute minimum and were often surviving on peanut butter and pouches of tuna fish, I could pack heavy and bring along extravagances like fresh vegetables and a book or two—what hikers call luxury items. I could also dally wherever I chose and would often spend long lunches lounging at a shelter.

Even today, with the ubiquity of cell phones, thru-hikers will stop at nearly every shelter to sign the logbook there. Often, they'll leave notes for other hikers a day or two behind them, offering to rendezvous with them in the next town or providing some good-natured trash talk about their pace. They'll write raunchy limericks and rhyming poetry complaining about ticks or rain or the heat; they'll mention which hostel has bed bugs or the biggest breakfasts. If they encounter a bear or someone who seems unbalanced or potentially a threat, they'll record that, too. In the late 1990s, these logbooks were hikers' only means of communication with one another: the one lifeline connecting them in an expanse of otherwise lonely wilderness.

On my own hikes, I loved nothing more than spending an hour or so flipping through the pages of these logbooks, reading the ever-growing narrative of that season. Over the course of longer trips, I'd develop a fond familiarity with the hikers who always had something clever to write or those who were so slow it seemed like they might never finish. Sometimes I'd overtake one of them a few days in; it always felt a little bit like finally meeting a favorite author or TV personality.

In November 1998, I began a multiday hike on a rocky section of the AT near Pennsylvania's Tuscarora State Forest—about 120 miles west of Philadelphia. Early on a Friday morning, I parked my car at a popular trailhead, donned my pack, and huffed my way up a steep thousand-foot incline. That time of year, the trees had already lost their leaves, and the days were getting short. Late in the afternoon, I stopped at the Thelma Marks Shelter, just a brief climb from the trail town of Duncannon, Pennsylvania.

One of the original Adirondack shelters along the trail, Thelma Marks had never been grand. Built of low-slung stone with a rusting metal roof, it was dark and mouse infested, stuffy in the summer and drafty the rest of the year. The shelter log was filled with vitriol for the place: otherwise chipper thru-hikers complained of having their worst night's sleep on the trail at Thelma Marks; others insisted the place was haunted and refused to stay at all.

About fifty yards away from the Thelma Marks structure, trail crews from the Appalachian Trail Conservancy had been at work constructing a newer, airy shelter. When I arrived, the new place was about half-finished, and the tools left about made it clear that construction was ongoing. I'd yet to see another human that day and contemplated setting up camp for the night so that I could offer them a hand.

About fifteen minutes later, a volunteer trail worker returned to the site to pack up his carpentry tools for the day. We chatted for a bit, and I lamented the fact that one of the original trail shelters was being replaced.

We have to, he told me.

I looked at him, not understanding.

You know, he said, awkwardly now. *Because of the murders.*

No. I didn't know. I had no idea that, eight years earlier, a drifter and wanted man named Paul David Crews had shot to death twenty-six-year-old thru-hiker Geoff Hood, then raped and fatally stabbed Hood's girl-friend and hiking partner, twenty-five-year-old Molly LaRue. Crews had then stolen their gear and left both hikers to bleed to death where I now sat eating my snack.

That brief exchange with the trail worker changed my life in ways both large and small. Never once had I thought I was in danger hiking the trail. Yes, I hung my food in bear bags and traveled with a first-aid kit and always checked the weather before ascending a ridge. But I had also come to believe the trail was populated entirely by like-minded people—an oasis of egalitarianism and mutual consideration. I never felt safer than I did pitching a tent or sharing a shelter with other hikers, whether I knew them or not.

That evening, as the sun began to set, I shouldered my pack and tried to put some distance between me and the Thelma Marks Shelter. I knew I couldn't sleep where two people had been so brutalized. As it turned out, I couldn't sleep farther down the trail either. Late into the night, a thunderstorm roared through the forest, knocking down limbs and illuminating the sky. With every flash of lightning, I was certain I saw the figure of a killer outside my tent. The next morning, I decided I'd had enough. I packed my things and returned to my car.

Back on campus, I studied everything I could about Molly LaRue and Geoff Hood, two of the six people who had been killed on the AT proper by that time (the number has since grown to eight and does not include individuals like Julie and Lollie who were killed near the AT or on abutting side trails). I read about how Molly and Geoff had met and fallen in love taking kids into the backcountry at a Christian camp. About how they managed to befriend everyone they met on the AT with their easygoing affability and penchant for bad rhymes. I read accounts of how Paul David Crews, already wanted for murdering a Florida woman, had made his way to Duncannon, hoping to disappear on the trail and avoid capture.

Perhaps most chilling of all was a book I discovered, Claudia Brenner's *Eight Bullets: One Woman's Story of Surviving Anti-Gay Violence*, a firsthand account of the attack just off the AT in Pennsylvania's Michaux State Forest that killed Brenner's partner, Rebecca Wight, and seriously wounded Brenner. Unbeknownst to either woman, they had been followed by Stephen Roy Carr, a local man, as they hiked down a spur trail and began setting up camp next to a remote stream. Carr repeatedly fired his .22 caliber rifle at the women. One bullet pierced Wight's liver, a fatal shot. Brenner was shot five times: one bullet passed through her arm; the others lodged in her head and neck. Miraculously, she managed to walk for over three hours, mostly in the dark, until she was eventually able to flag down a passing car.

Something about Brenner's narrative cut even deeper. It was all too easy for my mind to make reading her book a vicarious experience—to place myself on that same section of trail, to imagine what it was to be hunted and even shot while alone in the wilderness. That first research blitz, three years before I wound up at Unity, was also the first time I learned of Julie Williams and Lollie Winans and their deaths in late May 1996. At least in terms of age and interests, we had been contemporaries, and I idolized them both from the start. Everything about them just seemed so self-aware, so self-possessed. From photos and published narratives about the women, it was clear they were experienced backpackers. Without knowing it, they were also so impossibly cool, not to mention a little intimidating with their breezy confidence, their corded leather necklaces and tied bandannas, their scuffed boots. It was inconceivable to me that they and others could have been killed in the backcountry. They should have owned that place. If they couldn't, I wondered, then who could?

I SPENT THE fall of 2016 researching the Shenandoah murders and the multiyear investigations they had prompted for *Outside* magazine. All my Freedom of Information Act (FOIA) requests for information about the case had been denied by the FBI. But the Richmond office seemed interested in the idea of an article showcasing their work. Collaborating with their public affairs liaisons, I had hatched a plan that involved a visit to both the crime scene and the FBI's forensics lab. The idea was that I'd be able to observe and report in real time the key assertions made by Adam Lee: namely, about the particular difficulties in investigating backcountry crime and the advances in DNA science he believed could solve the 1996 case. What followed were weeks of lengthy email exchanges between me and various representatives of the FBI. In the midst of it all, I returned to visit my family in central Illinois for the holidays.

Christmas Eve, I holed up in my childhood bedroom, pleading my case for full access to the investigation with public affairs officers at the FBI Richmond field office and the bureau's main forensics lab at Quantico Marine Corps Base. Amid a string of conference calls and emails, I could hear first my parents, nephews, and sister-in-law down in the kitchen, cycling their way through every known Christmas carol while frosting cookies, and, later, a stream of family friends stopping by for early cocktails and snacks. I felt terrible for keeping hardworking civil servants from their own family gatherings. *Christmas Eve is not a federal holiday*, the patient public affairs folks kept reminding me as I apologized for the millionth time for ruining their Christmas cheer.

But I was also hell-bent on making this story work. The fact is that it wasn't just the friends and family of Julie and Lollie who had been traumatized by their brutal deaths. It was also thousands of individuals like me who identify as female or queer or any other marginalized identity that makes them potential targets in the wilderness. More than a few people have told me that the murder of Julie and Lollie ended their time in the backcountry, that even though they'd never known the two women personally, news of what had happened to them was scary enough. I could empathize with that. Maybe, if I could tell the story of what really happened to them and who was responsible, I could ameliorate some of that collective pain and help make the woods feel safer for all of us.

I knew full well the weight of that task. For while it may be tempting to say that crimes like the murder of Julie and Lollie are isolated incidents, statistics prove otherwise. It is true that reported crime rates in our nation's parks, forests, and deserts are, for the most part, lower than they are in cities and even some small towns. But that tells only part of the story. Julie Williams and Lollie Winans were two of eight women and girls killed in the rural Shenandoah Valley over the course of just fourteen months. In 1996, they were also two of fifteen reported homicides in our national parks. That same year, thirty other people reported being raped, and 158 reported aggravated assault, all in the wild and scenic places conceived of as "America's best idea." (These crime statistics have remained fairly constant since 1996. In the past five years, seventy-three people are known to have been murdered and 1,257 violent crimes have been reported in federal wilderness areas, which include land maintained by the National Park Service [NPS], the US Fish and Wildlife Service, and the Bureau of Land Management.)

Some Department of the Interior leaders downplay these statistics, pointing to the fact that our national parks alone receive about three hundred million discrete visits each year. It's true, but it's also skewed data. That figure of three hundred million tallies the total number of people entering a park gate, so there's a lot of duplication. (Say, for instance, that my partner and I visited Acadia National Park, drove into the town of Bar

Harbor for lunch, and then returned for a late afternoon hike in the park. Say the two of us then woke up the next day and did the same thing. That would be logged as eight visits total.) The overall visitation number also doesn't account for how long someone stays in the park or whether they even get out of their vehicle.

What is perhaps more troubling is the systemic underreporting of crimes in our wild places. As federal and private watchdog groups have noted, the NPS and other federal land management agencies have a long history of not fully documenting illegal activities, including violent crimes. In a 2002 study, rangers revealed that they didn't report crime information in order to "protect their image" or because "no one ever asked them to." The authors of the resulting report concluded that the collective failure to maintain and study crime information was a serious and ongoing problem within the Department of the Interior and that most senior park administrators were unaware of the crime rates at their parks. The superintendent of one national park told inspectors that he disregarded the crime statistics for his park, saying he did not believe they were a "true measure of risk assessment." Instead, he said he favored using customer service surveys, in which visitors indicated they felt our national parks are safe. Another superintendent said he disregarded known crime statistics in his park because he believed those figures were "not worth the paper they were sent in on."

Follow-up reports found that the NPS and other Department of Interior agencies failed to rectify the underreporting of crime stats. Officials argue there are multiple explanations for this deficiency, including budget constraints that prevent them from employing enough rangers to effectively monitor and report crime. In fact, as many as twenty-eight parks conceded that they didn't report crime figures because they had no law enforcement rangers to report them. In other wilderness areas, such as in many of our national forests and recreation areas, responsibility for investigating crimes actually falls to state and local authorities, who may not forward data to the federal government. In the case of the NPS, only about a quarter of its 393 units have adopted any kind of standardized incident reporting system. The rest use their own ad hoc programs or none at all.

The statistics that are recorded also only reference those incidents that clearly occur within delineated national park, forest, or wilderness areas, so they don't include crimes that occur in forests and deserts just outside of park borders, nor do they account for crimes in places like state parks, state forests, or locally conserved land. They also don't include the people who disappear from parks without a trace. Most of these cases fly under the radar—so much so, in fact, that the NPS can't even say for sure how many people have gone missing on its eighty-four million acres of public land.

And let's be honest. Even if the true number of murders in our wilderness areas is the annual figure actually reported, it is still way, way too many. Think about it this way: Eighteen million people visit Disneyland every year. If I told you that, on average, three people are murdered in that park every year, would you think twice about taking your kids? I would.

Although the FBI does not keep statistics on gender and backcountry crime, my own archival research finds that the majority of reported murder and rape victims in our national wilderness areas are female, despite both the fact that we still constitute the minority of backcountry users and that national murder rates are skewed overwhelmingly toward male victims. Nevertheless, the list of female victims killed in the backcountry continues to grow. It includes women like Meredith Emerson, twenty-four, who was abducted in 2008 just after she and her dog completed a hike on Georgia's Blood Mountain, part of the AT. Her kidnapper, Gary Hilton, had already murdered two other female hikers, along with an elderly couple who had been camping in a national forest, when he came upon Emerson. He held her hostage in his van for three days, threatening her with a knife and beating her repeatedly. He eventually tied her to a tree and bludgeoned her to death before decapitating her.

After he was arrested, Hilton told police he targeted Meredith Emerson "because she was a woman." They asked if he had any second thoughts or regrets about murdering her. He admitted he did.

"You gotta remember," he said. "We had spent several good days together by that point."

With assertions like Hilton's, it's hard to see how this phenomenon is not a gender problem.

As part of my preparation for the initial article on Lollie and Julie, I'd spent the tail end of 2016 reading every account of similar violence I could find. One such book was Terri Jentz's *Strange Piece of Paradise*, a narrative of her twenty-year search for the man who had repeatedly stabbed her and her cycling partner while they slept in their tent while overnighting in a remote Oregon state park. Their attacker left them both for dead with critical stab wounds before running them over with his truck and fleeing the scene. No one has ever been arrested for the crime, and Jentz understandably wanted to know why.

As I waited for word from the FBI that Christmas Eve, I contacted Jentz. She told me she's always believed that she and her roommate were attacked because of their gender, because they'd dared to break a cultural taboo by cycling and camping alone. Residents in the rural Oregon county where she was assaulted told her the only women who would dare to do such things must be prostitutes—or women who act like it. We talked that day about her research for the book and where it had taken her. In the end, she said, she'd arrived at one sobering conclusion: "Far too often, women are prey in our culture," she told me. "And there are more guys than we'd like to admit who go out in the wilderness to hunt them."

3

IN FEBRUARY OF 2017, I was at last granted an audience with scientists at the FBI's main laboratory, along with the field agents handling the murder investigation. I departed for Virginia on the last day of that month. The military had just begun requiring all visitors to present Real ID–compliant driver's licenses to gain entry on its bases. Maine, where I live, hadn't converted to the license requirement yet, and I realized midflight I'd forgotten to pack my passport. Frantic, I texted my Quantico public affairs contact using the plane's Wi-Fi. She wrote back almost instantaneously: *Don't worry about it. If the marines give you any hassle, just tell them you're here to see the FBI.*

Once on base, and past the bemused members of the Marine Corps Military Police, who clearly did not share this belief in the FBI's supremacy, I was greeted by my public affairs contact, along with the FBI's senior DNA scientist and two of her research geneticists. The scientists seemed genuinely perplexed by Adam Lee's claims that innovations in DNA forensics were about to advance investigations into the murder of Julie Williams and Lollie Winans. *Yes,* they confirmed as we settled around a conference table, *advances in DNA replication now mean positive matches can be made on just trace evidence—as little as a few cells.* But that technology had been used for years now and was helpful only if Lee and his agents had reason to believe those cells still existed within the crime scene evidence. *Yes, innovations using single nucleotide polymorphisms, which reveal genetic variations in our DNA, suggest that we might one day be about to determine a person's sex, race, ethnicity, and even their hair, skin, and eye color based on a few cells, but it will be decades before the FBI lab embraces that kind of testing.* Besides, they said, it wasn't clear to them how that might solve this particular case.

We were all at a little bit of a loss, then, as to what role the lab could serve in advancing Lollie and Julie's case. Nevertheless, the foursome amiably answered my questions about DNA testing and showed me around the facility. We toured one of their main DNA labs, which looked surprisingly like a high school science classroom with its rows of tables and microscopes. The scientists then stopped in a hallway where colorful posters hung so that they could explain the DNA analysis process.

Prior to about 2009, almost all forensic DNA testing was done by examining mitochondrial DNA (mtDNA), a small portion of DNA found in a cell's cytoplasm. The first type of human DNA to be sequenced, mtDNA contains 16,569 base pairs composed of different proteins. In the early 1980s, a British biochemist and geneticist named Alec Jeffreys determined that the combinations of proteins in those base pairs create a pattern distinct to immediate family members—almost like a collective fingerprint. In 1986, British law enforcement approached Jeffreys in 1986 about the unsolved murder of two teenage girls. In the two years since the teens had been raped and murdered, the case had grown cold. An enterprising detective had learned of Jeffreys's research and wondered if it could be used in their case. Jeffreys agreed and conducted a full analysis of the semen found on the girls. The police then asked every male resident of their village—about five thousand men in all—to contribute a DNA sample of their own. Subsequent lab analysis eventually found their murderer. A year later in the United States, Tommie Lee Andrews, a serial rapist, became the first American convicted based on mtDNA evidence and testing. "But analyzing the samples was tedious, and it really only helped if you had a known suspect you could compare it to," one of the FBI scientists explained to me, still pointing at the posters. In 1989, Virginia became the first state to create a DNA database, populated by convicted offenders

who had been compelled to provide their DNA. A federal database—the
Combined DNA Index System, or CODIS—was created shortly thereafter,
also containing only the DNA of convicted offenders, unidentified bodies,
and DNA taken from victims or found at some crime scenes. As a result
of these advances, thousands of cases have been solved, but the probability rates of mtDNA matches have remained statistically problematic, with
the chances of two people having the same genetic fingerprint sometimes
as high as one in two hundred. Forensic analysis itself has become more
sophisticated, however. Today, crime lab work has largely shifted away
from mtDNA in favor of other approaches such as short tandem repeat
(STR) DNA testing, which can reduce the likelihood of two unrelated
people matching to about one in a billion.

To demonstrate how DNA analysis works, the scientists brought me
to a viewing window, where we watched as a technician laid down butch-
er-block paper to collect any trace evidence, then opened a box labeled
with a particular case file. He removed a stained backpack and other
items, then carefully swabbed the brim of a red baseball cap, collecting
skin cells and depositing the swabs into test tubes. Behind him sat a large
refrigerator and freezer, along with what looked like a cobalt-blue micro-
wave called the EZ1 DNA Investigator Kit, which purifies and reproduces
DNA samples (you can purchase your own online for just $536).

"There's still a real art to this," one of the research biologists explained
to me as we watched. "Someone is still visually inspecting the evidence
and deciding what to test. Where do we sample? What do we cut?"

Getting a single swab took that lab technician at least fifteen minutes.
Processing the sample would take hours more. In 2021, the average national
turnaround time for a single lab result hovered between 150 and 180 days.
Meanwhile, the FBI lab receives hundreds of thousands of requests for
testing from agents each year, a volume of requests they cannot possibly
fill, and which has only exacerbated already serious delays. Crime labs
across the country suffer from massive case backlogs; the Department of
Justice estimates there are currently around 500,000 backlogged requests

for forensic analysis, while an estimated 170,000 DNA samples from crime scenes haven't even been tested at all, many of which are DNA samples taken from rape kits. What did that mean, I wondered, for decades-old cold cases like Lollie and Julie's? Would their evidence ever get retested?

The scientists shrugged. "You can't just open up your vaults and retest everything in them," one of them told me. "We just don't have those kinds of resources. Besides, even if we wanted to, we're not the ones who get to open that vault. The lab exists in support of the field. All we do is examine what they tell us to."

Another of the scientists nodded her head in agreement. "And with each completed retest, there's less of the sample to preserve for later examination," she added. "Test a piece of evidence again and again, and eventually there's no evidence left to test."

AFTER LEAVING QUANTICO, I checked into a motel just outside of Richmond. The room was quiet and lovely, and I was exhausted from the day, but sleep eluded me. I felt agitated about my trip to the FBI lab: the science geek in me relished the opportunity to be with smart geneticists, getting a backstage look at how research is done. That no one there seemed to know what advances Adam Lee was counting on to help close Lollie and Julie's case or whether there'd even be an opportunity to use those advances troubled me. I'd gone into this project thinking I would be telling the story of how progress was finally being made in this important case. I began to worry that maybe the case just couldn't be solved—that federal authorities had done all that they could. That seemed a particularly bitter pill for the many people desperate for answers.

Lying there in that dark hotel room, I also couldn't shake the gravity of the next day's itinerary and how it would feel to spend hours at the scene where Julie and Lollie had been murdered. Like a lot of people, I've enthusiastically given myself over to the voyeuristic fascination of the true crime industry: I've binge-watched premium channel series and shows, listened to the podcasts, and gobbled up magazine articles about how one terrible thing or another could have occurred in a place no one expected. But here's the thing about those sorts of shows and stories: they are as aseptically presented as meat in a grocery store. Ratings standards and broadcast regulations usually strip these programs of what is most grotesque about violent crime: the blood and feces and battered tissue; the awkward and often humiliating ways bodies come to rest. They rarely dwell on the invasive interrogation into a victim's most private and vulnerable places: the physical exams, the combing through diaries and emails, the lights that are shone not only into every vulnerable aspect of their personal lives but also those of everyone they have loved. Instead, popular depictions of violent crime curate a sanitized experience for the consumer—a few blurred shots of blood splatter at a crime scene; a body bag solemnly loaded into a medical examiner's van.

The reality of criminal investigation has no such filter. And what it depicts leaves an indelible mark on those who are willing to look: plucked samples of a victim's pubic hair; the autopsy photos depicting their naked bodies, their eyes milky and blind, once beautiful lips frozen in a rigored sneer. We might get a glimpse of such things in fictional TV dramas, but the understanding that we're actually looking at actors or wax figures or cow intestines somehow makes the visceral starkness of it okay. It's another thing entirely when what you are dealing with is the private life of a real person who never, ever, wanted you to see them that way.

Investigating a violent crime—even one twenty years old—is difficult for the people who remain, too. So few people are granted an intentional death and an opportunity to really get our emotional affairs in order. Most of the time, we never know when we'll last see someone or have a chance to say goodbye. Our parting memories can be filled with regret over harsh words or petty squabbles or missed opportunities. None of the people in Julie and Lollie's circles had any idea they would lose them that May. And for many, there are deep wounds not only about the loss of these two individuals but also from unresolved issues or words and conversations. Embarking on this story would mean asking people to dredge up that hurt as well.

I woke up the next morning feeling the weight of all those considerations. I dressed for the field and checked out of my hotel long before I was expected at the Richmond FBI office. It was the first day of March. Back in Maine, a blizzard was raging. But here in central Virginia, spring had arrived along with all the splendor wrought by magnolias and cherry blossoms.

It took some doing to find the Richmond FBI field office building, which is tucked between an industrial cleaning equipment warehouse, an auto repair place, and an Asian spa. One story tall, with mirrored windows and no arches or embellishments, the building housing the FBI's offices had been rendered almost invisible by its lack of anything architectural. Only the traffic barrier and black Palisade fencing surrounding this property suggested that anything of note might occur there.

Once inside the compound, I met up with Dee Rybiski, the division's public affairs officer, and Scott, a senior evidence response team agent who asked that I only use his first name. The three of us climbed into a massive black Chevy Suburban with tinted windows, and we headed out. As we sped westward on I-64, the landscape quickly became rural. Neither Scott nor Rybiski seemed to notice the SUV's radio, which hopped between Bruce Springsteen and a Christian preacher. Instead, Rybiski invited me to begin my interview. Scott cheerfully agreed. A former navy helicopter pilot with a strong jaw and enormous biceps, he looked right out of central casting. After they age out, many navy pilots go work for the commercial airlines. Scott explained that he, instead, went to the Federal Law Enforcement Training Center. Part of his curriculum included a two-week course on crime scene investigation, which covered such topics as processing blast areas, excavating mass graves, and documenting fingerprints. From there, he joined the Richmond office's Evidence Response Team (ERT). One of the first in the country, Richmond's ERT was formed in 1995. The program itself was conceived shortly after the 1993 bombing of the World Trade Center, which killed at least five people, injured more than a thousand, and left a massive hundred-foot crater in the center's underground parking garage. More than three hundred FBI investigators spent weeks combing through the rubble, looking for clues.

That, Scott tells me, is the typical kind of work the FBI envisioned for the ERT: serving on joint terrorism task forces, investigating plane crashes, that sort of thing. Most of their investigation of violent crime is in built, urban environments. Wilderness scenes, he said, present a whole set of different challenges.

"We're hardly ever the first ones on the scene. We're arriving six, eight hours later—sometimes even more," he said. "In the meantime, evidence outside can blow away, get washed away, be affected by weather. And then there are the environmental conditions. You don't know who else has been at the crime scene, whether that's humans or animals. So you're also dealing with a potential scatter pattern that could go on for a mile or more."

ERTs also receive next to no training about the particulars of backcountry investigations. "They're a different beast altogether," Scott conceded.

To understand why, he said, consider the Department of Justice's codified protocols for homicide investigation, which were issued just a few months before the 1996 Shenandoah murders. These procedures mandate that investigators should begin by documenting the crime scene's building name and address. They should then determine the entry and exit point of the crime scene and check door handles, telephones, windows, and light switches for latent prints. After that, they should be sure to collect witness statements from neighbors. None of these steps make any sense in the backcountry.

Even getting to the crime scene can seem all but impossible. Conditions and weather are big factors there as well. Some field offices, like Denver's, are staffed by agents proficient in mountaineering, rappelling, and other backcountry skills, but most agents don't have such special training. If a crime scene is down a crevasse or tucked deep within a slot canyon, the agents might not be able to reach it. And if weather conditions prove threatening or particularly precarious, supervisors might decide not to send them for days or weeks, if at all. In the meantime, rain can wash away blood or erase a fingerprint, particularly if the area is experiencing warm temperatures and high humidity. Plus, said Scott, "it's next to impossible to lift fingerprints from porous surfaces like boulders or trees."

And then there's the difficulty ERTs have in determining what even constitutes evidence in the backcountry. Say a victim appears to have been killed by blunt force trauma on the side of a mountain, offered Scott. A rock could have been used as a murder weapon. But which one? The deceased individual is surrounded by thousands of them. Do you pick up each one and look for blood or hair? And if it rained the day before, what's the likelihood you'd even see any evidence, assuming you managed to pick that one rock out from all the others?

When talking about solved murder investigations, law enforcement officials and scholars often refer to their "clearance rates": the number of cases solved in any given year. Nationally, clearance rates have been declining steadily over the past fifty years. They are particularly low for wilderness crimes. A study completed by Washington, DC's Justice Research and Statistics Association reveals, at least in part, why that is. They found that murder cases are more likely to be solved when the crime occurs in private residences or bars and stores rather than in open public areas. Those cases are also more likely to be closed if detectives arrive at the crime scene within a half hour of that crime being reported and if those investigators are followed by the prompt arrival of medical examiners and crime lab technicians. Other factors for success include the rapid interviewing of witnesses, the careful securing of the scene, and the swift retrieval of a murder weapon.

"Good luck doing any of that out in the woods," Scott concluded.

ABOUT AN HOUR after we departed the Richmond field office, Scott pulled our SUV into a multiuse office building on the outskirts of Charlottesville. Inside, placards for medical labs and child support enforcement offices directed visitors to the various floors. We headed, instead, to a cramped office space with the lights already out. There, Jane Collins, who has served as the lead FBI agent in Julie and Lollie's case since early 2000, greeted us with a Diet Coke in one hand and the handle of a small roller-board suitcase in the other. If Scott is straight out of central casting, Jane is anything but: salon-perfect blond hair, pink nail polish, skinny jeans. The only thing giving her away as an FBI agent was the pistol holstered at her hip. We said our hellos and agreed that we'd follow her to Shenandoah.

Once inside the park, our little caravan was joined by a cadre of park rangers. Among them was Tim Alley, fifty-seven, the original lead law enforcement ranger in the case. Since retired and working as a private detective, Alley was dressed that day in cargo pants and a navy blue fleece pullover commemorating the seventy-fifth anniversary of the park. With his thick goatee, short cropped gray hair, and reflective Ray-Ban sunglasses pushed back on the top of his head, he looked as much like a high school football coach as he did a longtime law enforcement ranger—a persona further enforced by his gruff colloquialisms. Within just a few minutes of chatting, he was referring to the NPS as the "park circus" and Lollie and Julie as "our girls." I liked him right away.

The group of us briefly consulted maps, and then our caravan, now five vehicles long, made its way northward on the park's fabled Skyline Drive. We were headed for Skyland, the park's largest and most well-known resort complex. Widely considered the crown jewel of the Shenandoah, the twenty-seven-acre Skyland resort includes dozens of freestanding cabins and blocks of rooms and suites, along with conference buildings, an amphitheater and horse stables, and lodging for about sixty-five staff members (mostly dishwashers, cooks, and waitstaff but also groundskeepers, stable hands, and maintenance workers). The AT crosses right through the property, making it a favorite stop for backpackers.

At the center of it all sits the Skyland lodge itself, a sleek stone and wood building with panorama windows and sweeping views of the valley. On a summer weekend, the place is hectic: there's a coffee bar with takeaway sandwiches and salads; the main dining area often has wait times of well over an hour. The pub, which opens in the late afternoon, hops with live music on the weekends. And then there are the restrooms with rows and rows of stalls, and the gift shop and plush couches and coffee tables stacked with coffee-table books dedicated to the park.

In the summer and fall, Skyland can feel as crowded as any major airport; however, few visitors venture to the park in early spring, when snow is still common and the trees bare. The lodge is shuttered until late March, as are most of the other amenities here. So it's no real surprise that the Stony Man parking lot, located just north of Skyland at mile 41.7 on Skyline Drive, was empty when we arrived. We parked, and once outside our vehicles, the group seemed somber, standing in a tight circle, making small talk about the weather.

A few minutes later, we left the parking lot on foot, crossed Skyland Drive, and then descended down the remnants of the Bridle Trail. Without this crew, I doubt I ever would have found the overgrown path: even without the camouflaging effect of summer foliage, the trailhead was all but invisible.

Walking beside me was Tim Alley, who was quick to note that he'd heard I live in Maine. He told me he grew up on a small island there, and within just a few minutes we'd found a handful of shared acquaintances, including his first cousin, whom I had first met when we were both competing in a trail marathon. Tim graduated from the University of Maine in 1980 and immediately began his career as a park ranger. In 1986, he was one of the law enforcement rangers working on the NPS's Colonial Parkway, which connects historic Jamestown, Williamsburg, and Yorktown in eastern Virginia. That same year, Cathy Thomas and Becky Dowski, a young lesbian couple, were found in Cathy's car, just off the parkway. Both women's throats had been slit. The impact of working that case, Alley told me, had left an indelible mark. "The whole crime investigation thing was relatively new for all of us," he said. "We were still trying to find our way." The mere presence of law enforcement rangers, he continued, was something the NPS was still very much trying to get used to by the time Lollie and Julie were killed.

It wasn't until the late 1970s that the Department of the Interior began distinguishing between two types of rangers: interpretive, who are responsible for programming and education, and law enforcement rangers, who are cops with all the powers of state police officers. It took another twenty years to establish hiring and training rules for the latter. Even today, most visitors to our national parks don't realize that there are two types of rangers. That lack of understanding creates all kinds of public confusion—and ultimately adds to the perils of the job, already considered one of the most dangerous in all of law enforcement. Between 1990 and 2020, eight FBI agents and six park rangers were killed in the line of duty, a staggering number when you consider that FBI agents outnumber rangers by a scale of ten to one.

The rangers walking alongside us on the Bridle Trail that day agreed that the murders of Julie Williams and Lollie Winans only intensified concerns for their own safety. "The terribleness of this crime changed our collective view of the woods and our profession," one ranger told me. "It took a place we all loved and filled it with horror. I don't think any of us will ever really get over it."

I was listening, but I was also distracted by the racing of my heart as we got closer to the spot where Lollie and Julie had set up camp.

I've always been agnostic about notions of the afterlife or the presence of ghosts and spirits, but I do believe that violence leaves some kind of metaphysical trace. The AT thru-hikers who stopped long enough to write in the Thelma Marks Shelter log noted that phenomenon again and again. Maybe it was just the power of suggestion. Maybe they saw what other hikers had written before them, and those words became their own, new reality. Or maybe they'd read about the place before setting out on their hikes and were anticipating a sinister feeling. I don't know.

But here's what I do know: as apprehensive as I was, as predisposed as I was to find something terrible and sad and stained about the place where Julie and Lollie died, I felt none of that. To the contrary, their little stealth campsite was undeniably beautiful. Even in the austerity of early March, when the canopy is bare and the forest floor is packed with dank and decomposing leaves, it is a lovely, peaceful place. The former tent site itself is the only level patch of ground in the area. It is surrounded by a horseshoe of trees that makes the place feel like a secret oasis. The only noise is the brook, running fast and strong with snowmelt. Had I been backpacking here, I would have selected this site for myself and thought I had hit the lottery.

When Julie and Lollie arrived here in May 1996, the ground would have been soft with early ferns and new grass. The spot was the perfect size for their tent and gear, along with room to set up a small outdoor kitchen and a place to sit and eat or write or just think the day away. The northern fork of the White Oak Run flows right alongside, so water for cooking and drinking was in easy reach. Best of all, because it was a back-country spot, there was no sign announcing the place, no fire ring or pic-nic table. Just a delicious patch of ground tucked in the woods, with the comforting gurgle of a river's headwaters nearby.

Today, no cross or drying wreath marks this site as the place where Julie Williams and Lollie Winans were murdered. The only memorial is a small scatter of brightly colored rocks that once formed a peace symbol on the ground not far from where Julie's body had been found, a tribute left by her friends to commemorate her love of geology, and one that the intervening years have begun to dismantle. Standing there studying those stones from around the world and the scene that con-tained them, I struggled with the cognitive dissonance of admiring a place where something so unspeakably awful had occurred. I did not know Julie or Lollie. I cannot speak for them, nor do I want to seem so presumptuous as to say what they may have felt or thought. But maybe, just maybe, when two selfless, joyful, beautiful humans die in a place, what is left behind is not the agony of their deaths but the brilliance of their lives.

AS PASTORAL AND lovely a spot as the women's final resting place was, neither the investigators nor I could figure out how Lollie and Julie found that little patch of ground in the first place—or how their killer knew they were there. "It doesn't make sense that someone went down this trail randomly looking for someone to kill," said Tim Alley. You'd go over to the next trail, Whiteoak, which is much busier, or you'd stay on the AT. Some interaction occurred that brought the killer here. I am a true believer that something went on between them."

Bridget Bohnet, the backcountry ranger responsible for patrolling this section of the park in 1996, nodded in agreement. "This trail was never very popular. And after we moved the horse rides, it no longer served any real purpose. By 1996, it was basically nonexistent," she said. "You'd really have to study the map to even know it was there."

Bohnet said the few people she ever saw on the Bridle Trail during her regular patrols were day hikers looking for shortcuts from Old Rag Mountain, or Skyland employees looking for a place to party—mostly to play games like Dungeons & Dragons after a long shift. A couple of miles down the trail from the women's campsite, two small cabins sit tucked back from the Old Rag Fire Road, basically a gated double track used by park maintenance employees and rangers. In late May 1996, the cabins at the base of the trail were occupied by college-aged women working for the Student Conservation Association. *Could someone have come upon Lollie and Julie while returning from a visit to those cabins?*

"Maybe," said Alley with a shrug. "But doubtful. We interviewed those girls for what felt like hours. They would have mentioned it."

I asked who else would have known the trail and campsite were here. Could someone have recommended it to Julie and Lollie? Alley gave an emphatic no to that as well.

"Years earlier, when I was a seasonal ranger, I lived in one of the cabins at the base of the trail," he told me. "No one ever came down there. Ever."

Bridget Bohnet agreed. "No one would ever suggest this trail because no one ever went down it. Not many people even knew about it."

We spread out a copy of the Appalachian Trail Conservancy topographical map Lollie and Julie were carrying with them when they died. On it, the Bridle Trail isn't even labeled: it's just a narrow, easily overlooked line. Topo maps are valuable to hikers in part because they illustrate relief, which is to say elevation gain and loss, with contour lines. The closer the lines are to one another, the steeper the terrain. With even the most minimal understanding of how a topo map works, it would have been abundantly clear that the chance for a good stealth campsite would have been much better on the other side of Skyline Drive, behind the Skyland lodge and back by the AT, where the terrain was far more level. *So how and why would Julie and Lollie have ended up here?*

"We always assumed it was their last night in the park," Alley said. "Their car was parked just a couple of miles from here. Maybe they just wanted an easy night before heading out."

I tried to ask a question about Darrell Rice's possible involvement in the crime, but Dee Rybiski, the FBI public affairs officer, interrupted to remind us all that this is an open case and, thus, the particulars cannot be discussed. Everyone but Rybiski seemed to find that frustrating, if not a little absurd. We were standing, after all, at the scene of a murder. We had come here deliberately to unpack that murder. At her request, I began to channel all my questions through her. It felt a little like talking on a landline telephone with an international delay. I'd ask my question, we'd all wait for a nod or a shake of Rybiski's head to know if the others could answer, and then they'd funnel their response back through her.

"Tell me about the campsite," I ventured. Rybiski looked ready to censor but said nothing.

So the rangers walked me through where they found the tent and the packs, where they assumed the women had just begun cooking dinner.

"I can still see the dog food. I can see their pot of uneaten couscous," one told me, tearfully. "It was all sitting right here, overflowing with rainwater."

Many months later, I'd see in that emotional assertion the simultaneous power and frailty of human memory. After looking at dozens of crime scene photos, I'd come to understand that there was no dog food, no uneaten couscous sitting in a pot and drenched with rainwater. But that didn't make that ranger's memory any less real for him, nor did it mitigate the tangled briars of emotion he so clearly still felt these many years later.

Our walk back up the trail was mostly silent. By then, I'd run out of questions I could get past Rybiski. Tim Alley and Jane Collins, who had said little the whole trip, seemed visibly saddened by the return to the murder scene. The others had their hands stuffed in their pockets, heads down. Violence clearly leaves other kinds of traces, too.

"I still live it every day," Alley admitted to me as we made our way back to Skyline Drive. "I decided early on that my real employers were the Williams and Winans families. I still believe that. It haunts me that we haven't closed this for them—and for the girls."

We walked in silence for a few minutes. Then he asked me about my interest in the case.

I told him I'd spent years backcountry hiking and picking stealth campsites exactly like the one we just visited. If I had stumbled on it, I would have thought myself the luckiest hiker in the park. I also would have believed I was the safest person in the world.

"You're a backpacker?" Tim asked.

I nodded.

"Solo?"

"Yes," I said. "Or at least I used to be."

"Bear spray? Handgun?"

"Huh?"

"What do you pack?"

"Oh, right," I said, finally understanding. "Nothing but my gear."

He shook his head. "Just you and your big smile in the wilderness?"

"I guess."

We both thought about that for the rest of the short walk up to the parking lot.

Once back at the vehicles, Alley offered to show me the site of a long-gone concession stand on the far side of the parking lot. We stepped away from Rybiski and the others. Just out of earshot, he handed me his card.

"Call me," he said. "I'll tell you everything I know."

4

JULIE WILLIAMS HAD PROMISED HER ROOMMATE, Derek, that she would be moved out of their second-floor apartment by the end of the month. College friends, they'd spent time together in Washington State just after graduation. Afterward, she had gone to work as an intern at Big Bend National Park, and Derek had eventually made his way to Vermont. Not long after Julie and Lollie fell in love, the two women found themselves faced with the prospect of managing a long-distance relationship. Lollie still had a year and a half of schoolwork at Unity; Julie was toying with the idea of graduate school but hadn't committed to any program yet. They agreed Julie had the most flexibility in her life, so she decided to move in with Derek. That fall, the old friends found a second-floor apartment in Richmond, Vermont, about fifteen miles outside of Burlington. It seemed like the perfect compromise: just five hours from Unity, and with enough social and cultural opportunities that Julie wouldn't feel completely dependent on Lollie and her world at the college.

Now, with just one day left in the month of May, Derek was pissed. Julie and Lollie had left for Shenandoah twelve days earlier, and Derek hadn't heard from them since. Before she left, Julie managed to box up some of her things, but when or how she intended to move them remained to be seen. If they wanted to get their security deposit back, the two roommates would have to clean the place, too. As far as Derek could tell, Julie had blown off multiple appointments and social plans that week as well.

Derek phoned Julie's dad in Minnesota. *Time was running out on their move*, Derek said. *Messages wondering where Julie was were piling up on their answering machine, too. What was he supposed to do?*

A second-generation funeral director, Tom Williams had spent a lifetime learning patience and quiet compassion when faced with the emotions of others. He could tell Derek was angry, and Tom assured him that Julie would be back any time now. It wasn't like her to miss an appointment. Even less so to leave a friend in the lurch.

Later that night, Tom and his wife, Patsy, a longtime registered nurse, revisited the call. It had been over a week since they'd heard from Julie: not entirely out of the ordinary—particularly when she was on a trip. But still. Something about Derek's call didn't sit right.

Julie had grown up in St. Cloud, a town of sixty-eight thousand people in the center of Minnesota. Patsy and Tom had raised their four children in a close-knit middle-class neighborhood defined by tidy ranches and two-story colonials perched on perfectly square blocks. Neighbors entered one another's house with a simple *hello* instead of a knock. They took turns hosting block parties and Christmas get-togethers. In the summer, kids played kick the can until the streetlights came on. During the school year, those same kids spent weekends skating at the roller rink, the girls sporting white bell bottoms to catch all the neon lights. They had sleepovers and pajama parties and stayed up late in basement rumpus rooms, watching *Raiders of the Lost Ark* and *Star Wars* and *The Outsiders* over popcorn and cans of Tab. Families regularly caravanned to Vikings games; the kids passed the backseat time with slug bug and staring contests.

Life couldn't have been idyllic in all those three-bedroom homes, but whatever abuse or neglect might have happened stayed locked behind closed doors. And at the Williamses' house, you could always count on the doors being open. Tom and Patsy just had a way about them that made every kid in the neighborhood feel like they belonged.

The family spent a lot of their summers and vacations at their extended family's shared cabin on one of those classically deep, clear Minnesota lakes. There, Julie, her siblings, and scores of cousins fished and swam and told ghost stories on the back deck. They toasted marshmallows and stuffed themselves with sweet corn and fried walleye.

Back in St. Cloud, the Williamses' lives revolved around their faith and their church. In many ways, that community was Julie's second home. She belonged to her Catholic church's youth group, as did most of her closest friends. She attended school, first at the neighborhood parochial grade school and then at Cathedral High School, where she always toted a Bible in her backpack. She'd argue theology with anyone who would listen, sometimes getting so heated she'd storm away.

After the church choir director heard Julie strumming a guitar, she asked Julie to perform at Sunday services. Julie tried it once or twice but didn't like the spotlight. She was quiet, a true introvert: hilarious and often goofy when you knew her, but far more comfortable sitting back and watching any social interaction when among strangers. Growing up, tennis and basketball courts were her safe spaces—places where she could do and be without having to say much. She was a natural athlete, but she had also been a perfectionist, regularly lobbing balls against the garage door until her parents couldn't take the noise any longer.

Julie's grade school teachers repeatedly approached Tom and Patsy about promoting their daughter a grade or two, but they resisted: more than anything, the Williamses wanted their children to have a normal childhood with normal friends. Besides, Julie loved being the smart kid, her hand first in the air to answer a teacher's question, always knowing she had the right answer. At night, she'd write in her journal about her accomplishments, her big universal questions, and what might hover beyond the cosmos. She wanted to know everything. Makeup, clothes, and teen magazines never did much for her. As long as anyone could remember, Julie's real passion was geology. She'd harvest chalk from the ground behind her garage for hopscotch games; on the school playground, she was always rooting around for new quartz specimens when other kids were horsing around. Her friends didn't really get the obsession, but they also saw why it was the perfect relationship: *Julie was shy; rocks are quiet,* one told me recently.

In high school, geology was complemented by Julie's growing commitment to social justice. She took enough Spanish courses to become fluent and would regularly volunteer to translate for Latinx women at shelters and police stations. She founded advocacy clubs and traveled to Bogotá, Colombia, for her senior project. She could have been valedictorian, were it not for her catastrophically bad grade in speech class: an A–, punishment for giggling every time she stood up in front of the class.

After high school, Julie enrolled at Carleton College, a small liberal arts school about an hour south of Minneapolis. There, she majored in geology. Her professors adored her. She challenged them in class and wore T-shirts bedecked with science jokes only rock jocks would get. OVERDRESSED FOR THE ORDOVICIAN, read one. During school breaks, she traveled across Europe, participating in geoarchaeology digs at ancient Roman settlements. Along the way, she'd phone home from weekend trips to Salzburg and Prague with stories about chatting up Peruvian musicians or splurging on a flamenco dress she knew she'd never wear. Back at home, she spent her summers in the wilderness: leading canoe trips one year; checking hunting and fishing licenses on tribal lands in northern Wisconsin; and conducting water-quality testing on the shores of Lake Superior. She took more mission trips, working with women and children in Madrid's alleyways and tiny villages in the Huasteca region of Mexico. *A one-woman Peace Corps,* people began calling her.

A one-woman Peace Corps doesn't leave their roommates hanging—at least, not in the way Derek was describing. Tom and Patsy decided they needed to alert the authorities. But who? The sheriff's office seemed a logical place to start. Which one? Shenandoah National Park straddles eight different counties, each with its own jurisdiction. Tom made a best guess and dialed a dispatcher. *Not our area,* she told him. *Try the park.* By then, it was nearly midnight. After what seemed like endless rings, Williams

finally got a tinny recording that listed the business hours for park headquarters and no other numbers. Troubled, he went to bed.

First thing the next morning, he tried again and was transferred to a
ranger on duty. The ranger, in turn, reported Williams's call to his supervisor, who initiated a lost- and missing-person's file. The two rangers
agreed that if the women didn't turn up by nightfall, they'd launch a more
thorough investigation the following day. In the meantime, they issued an
ATL, an "attempt to locate" call for all on-duty rangers.

Friday, May 31, 1996
9:30 a.m.

Shenandoah National Park was struggling. A host of environmental
challenges—damage from acid rain and a recent gypsy moth infestation,
along with the worst air quality of any national park—stretched the park's
already thin resources. The park's built infrastructure was faring little better, with a twelve-million-dollar maintenance backlog that had resulted
in leaking pipes and roofs, broken down equipment and vehicles, and
outmoded equipment. Similar budget deficits meant programming cuts,
closed sections of the park, and furloughed staff.

Shenandoah was not the only national park struggling that season.
By the end of 1995, the entire park system was in the midst of its worst
ever budget squeeze. As a result, all fifty-four of the biggest parks were
making cuts, from closing camping sites to cutting back on seasonal and
backcountry rangers. Old and broken gear went unreplaced, including
Shenandoah's radios, which meant rangers often couldn't communicate
with one another. The dangers of that shortcoming became all too real
when a standoff with an armed man in the park resulted in gunfire. As
the first shot was fired, radios on the scene went silent. The remaining
rangers didn't know if the subject had shot himself or if a firefight had
broken out.

We're outmanned, outgunned, and desperately needing outside support,
one ranger told reporters shortly after. He said he and his colleagues were

forced to go to the Fraternal Order of Police to ask for help fundraising for new gear.

Nationwide studies by multiple independent organizations determined that national parks needed an additional twelve hundred rangers, including 615 law enforcement rangers, to adequately protect the resources and people there. The studies' authors called the assignment of rangers in parks "patently illogical and erratic." Those same studies also listed Shenandoah as one of the country's five most dangerous, in large part because of its awful radios and communication system. Ken Johnson was a lead investigator and law enforcement ranger at the time. "There really isn't time anymore to patrol the backcountry," he told a reporter who interviewed him about the report. "A ranger now isn't going to see the backcountry unless they are going back there to rescue somebody."

By spring of 1996, Shenandoah National Park was short a full five law enforcement rangers. Park administrators had also been forced to cut 80 percent of its interpretive ranger services—programs that helped visitors understand the park's history and ecology or just figure out where to get a meal or use the restroom. They'd furloughed trail maintenance crews responsible for removing downed trees and other hazards. Meanwhile, the private companies operating the resorts and lodges were struggling to staff concession positions. They ran ads in regional papers from Pittsburgh to Miami, promising big benefits and little experience required for busboys and dishwashers.

None of those factors had kept down visitor traffic, however. By May 1996, Shenandoah backcountry-use permits were at an all-time high, and the skeleton staff of rangers was struggling to keep tabs on the influx of backpackers. Finding two particular women presented a herculean challenge.

All backcountry campers are required to take out permits indicating their itinerary for each day they intend to be in the park. On Wednesday, May 22, Julie and Lollie had renewed theirs at the Thornton Gap entrance station, located at mile 31.5 on Skyline Drive. Barb Stewart, was the supervisory ranger there. That Wednesday had been cool and rainy, and Barb stopped in during the lunch hour to check on attendance numbers. Inside, Julie and Lollie had persuaded one of the entrance station attendants to let them wash their dirty camp dishes in a backroom sink. They'd made themselves at home, and Lollie had recognized a few Unity College friends in a collage of park employees photos hanging on the wall.

That Unity connection was what had first grabbed Stewart's attention: several of her favorite interns had been students at the college. The two women struck up an easy conversation as the station attendant filled out their new backcountry permits. Stewart could tell right away that Julie and Lollie both seemed like experienced hikers: they'd already memorized the backcountry regulations and were able to recite them even before the woman working the desk asked. The two backpackers told the staff at Thornton Gap that they intended to stay in the central district of the park—an area that extends from Skyland around mile 40 down to South River at mile 62. They asked Stewart about good water sources in that area. Lollie seemed particularly concerned about what to do with leftover food and gray water from their dishes. Stewart advised her to fling both in as wide an arc as possible to avoid inadvertently attracting bears.

While Lollie and Barb chatted, Julie finished filing their new backcountry permits. She told the attendant they planned to head out of the park the following Monday, May 27. Their permits reflected that date, along with their plans to leave Julie's Toyota 4Runner at the Stony Man Overlook parking area, located at mile 38.5 on Skyline Drive. On those same permits, Julie listed Taj as her primary method of travel. Lollie noted the dog in a column asking about pack and saddle stock.

In addition to their obvious humor and backcountry competence, what Stewart really remembered was the women's persuasiveness. One of the women—she couldn't remember if it had been Julie or Lollie—had admired a brightly illustrated poster advertising a wildflower weekend in the park the previous year. She'd asked if they could take it with them. Because it seemed like such a bold request, Barb considered it. *Why not*, she finally concluded. *We can probably get another one from the gift shop.* She and the attendant carefully peeled it off the wall and removed the Scotch tape from the back.

After Julie's father had reported the two women missing, one of the lead rangers in the Williams/Winans case contacted the supervisors at each of the park's four entrance stations and asked them to comb through all the permits submitted in the previous two weeks.

Barb Stewart's husband, Ken Johnson, was the senior investigative ranger for the park by then. When Barb received the request to search permits that Friday morning, she sent Ken an email detailing her interaction with the women at the entrance station on May 22. Meanwhile, rangers were also on the lookout for Julie's car. By 10:00 a.m. on Friday, May 31, a ranger had found it right where the permit had indicated it would be. The ranger left a note on Julie's windshield, asking her to check in at an entrance station as soon as she saw the note.

By 1:00 p.m. that afternoon, the two women still hadn't been located. Johnson assigned Tim Alley to head the case. By that point in his career, Alley had worked poaching stings, emergency evacuations, and hundreds if not thousands of searches—more than enough of them to know it was still too early to worry.

He called Tom Williams, looking for more information about the missing women. Williams assured him that they were both experienced, well-equipped backpackers who didn't knowingly take risks or deviate from their stated plans.

Alley and his team then began making additional calls—this time, to Derek and to Julie's other friends. *Most agreed that Julie might miss a few appointments in order to extend her trip*, Alley noted in the case log. *Her friends all agreed, however, that she would never intentionally miss a day of work.* Julie was about to start a new job at a Lake Champlain watershed nonprofit, so one of the rangers left a message there, too. Derek had told

Alley that Julie wasn't due for her first day of work until Monday, June 3. *They could return to their vehicle Sunday morning and still make it in time*, the law enforcement ranger added.

Alley made the decision to dispatch some of the backcountry rangers on a hasty search—a quick sweep of trails and other likely places where the overdue hikers might be. Rangers have another name for this level of investigation: a "bastard search"—as in, *Where is the bastard?* The majority of the time, they say, he's in a nearby motel or at his girlfriend's house or safely back home, kicking back with a drink and a ballgame. For this particular search, Alley restricted the area to parts of the park listed on the women's backcountry permits. Late that Friday afternoon, and armed with a description of Julie, along with a photo faxed over from Tom, two rangers ascended the Nicholson Hollow Trail, at mile marker 37.9 on Skyline and listed on the women's permits as their final destination before exiting the park. Two other rangers remained at the base of the trail, interviewing hikers. No one had seen the women or Taj.

By 8:30 p.m. that Friday, as twilight fell upon the park, Alley suspended the search for the night. He remained certain the women would show up the next morning.

Saturday, June 1, 1996
7:00 a.m.

Saturday—three days after Derek had expected Julie back—broke warm and bright. Barb Stewart drove up the mountain for her shift thinking, *The visitors are going to stream in. Oodles and oodles of them.* It would be a busy day for everyone on duty. Already, rangers on dawn patrol had come upon a car parked at Bacon Hollow Overlook, located at mile 69 on Skyline Drive, and found a man sleeping in the backseat. He told the rangers he had been camping nearby, at Hightop Mountain, just off the AT. During the night, he'd been spooked by a strange noise and decided to hike out of the area. The rangers ran his license, saw that it was suspended, and escorted him out of the park. A half hour later, they cited two other park visitors for smoking marijuana.

At 8:00 a.m., the on-duty law enforcement rangers convened to talk about the Williams/Winans search. Tim Alley had a scheduled day off—he was home with his son while his wife, also in law enforcement, auditioned to play an extra in a Hollywood movie being filmed nearby. The on-duty rangers reviewed Alley's logbook and agreed the search urgency remained low. If Lollie and Julie still hadn't turned up by evening, they'd initiate a full district-wide search the next day. In the meantime, they kept interviewing hikers and Skyland guests; they also began checking AT shelter registers to see if Lollie and Julie had signed in.

After lunch on Saturday, Shenandoah rangers finally reached someone from the Lake Champlain nonprofit. That person corroborated what Derek had said, that Julie wasn't due for her first day of work until Monday, June 3, still two days away.

Then, around 3:00 p.m., the managing supervisor of the Lake Champlain nonprofit called the park, asking to speak with the ranger in charge. *Julie wasn't due in on Monday*, Williams's supervisor corrected. *She was actually supposed to start work Sunday morning.* Ken Johnson confirmed that Julie's car was still at the Stony Man Overlook parking area; there was no way she'd make it to Vermont in time. He made the decision to escalate the search, dispatching seven rangers to sections of the AT, park trails around Stony Man, and the Nicholson Hollow Trails. He issued a BOLO, or "be on the lookout," this time also including employees of the Appalachian Trail Conservancy.

The approximately twenty-two hundred miles of the AT cross through national forests and parks, private land, and state parks. It's a complex jumble of jurisdictions and management systems, and the NPS allocates just one full-time ranger to the trail itself. As a result, the Appalachian Trail Conservancy, the private organization that manages the trail, also employs "ridge runners," paid employees who maintain and monitor sections of the trail from Georgia to Maine. That Saturday morning, Ken Johnson asked permission from the conservancy for the ridge runners to join rangers in interviewing hikers. Once that permission was granted, park administrators provided the ridge runners with a script of standardized questions.

Word of the ranger's and trail runners' inquiries began to circulate among hikers, particularly backpackers on the trail. As rumors spread, the tone among hikers became edgy and guarded. Backpackers would later say that it seemed clear from the nature of the questions that authorities suspected foul play.

At the Thornton Gap entrance station, employees were becoming visibly upset about the continued disappearance of Julie and Lollie. Something was clearly amiss. Barb Stewart tried to keep them focused and on task. *They didn't know anything yet*, she told them. *There was no reason to worry.* But even she no longer believed that.

Saturday, June 1, 1996
4:00 p.m.

As the dinnertime rush at Skyland neared, a retired Maryland couple set out on a paved trail from their room in Raven's Nest, a freestanding block of rooms on the north end of the resort. They were planning an early supper up at the lodge's main restaurant and were ambling down the path when the couple encountered a golden retriever mix with no collar. The dog, they later reported, was friendly but seemed lost and dazed, *like it was looking for its master*, they recalled. The couple spoke to a few members of the housekeeping staff who were just getting off work and waiting for a ride home. The staff agreed to keep an eye on the dog until their ride arrived, and they walked over to pet her in the meantime. Certain the dog was in good hands, the couple made their way to supper without a second thought.

An hour later, a pair of rangers pulled into the Limberlost parking area at mile 43 on Skyline Drive. There, they encountered a group of day hikers who said they'd also seen a yellow dog, this time at the junction of the Bridle Trail and the fire road. The dog had followed them up the fire road a bit before turning back and returning to the Bridle Trail. The rangers made a note but incorrectly recorded the hikers' addresses and phone numbers, so it was never possible to get back in touch with them.

Fifteen minutes later, a ranger on his way to the Skyland lodge was flagged down by a young couple near the Whiteoak Canyon parking area (mile 42.6). Once the ranger stopped, the couple pointed to a retriever mix that was nosing around the woods next to the parking lot. The couple said they had been hiking back up the Whiteoak Canyon Trail, about a mile or so from the parking area, when the dog had come running out of the woods to greet them. The dog wasn't wearing a collar, but she seemed friendly and glad to have the company. She followed them all the way back to the parking lot. The ranger whistled for the dog, who came right over. He motioned for the dog to hop into the truck, but the dog didn't budge. The ranger tried coaxing her, but that failed, too. He called the dog again, this time using the name he'd heard at the briefing earlier in the day. *Hop in, Taj.* The dog immediately complied. The ranger radioed Ken Johnson and said he was pretty sure he had found Julie and Lollie's dog.

At that same time, Barb Stewart was still at the Thornton Gap entrance station and heard the radio call. Her heart sank. She knew there was no way the women were still alive—not without their dog. She also knew she couldn't say anything to her staff. She kept thinking to herself, *I just have to get us through this day.* She tried to content herself by mentally listing all the ways the women might have died of nonviolent causes. Maybe one of them fell down a waterfall; the other slipped trying to help. Maybe they overdosed. Maybe they . . . *what?* Stewart didn't know. But she needed to believe someone hadn't deliberately harmed them. Not in her park. She and Ken had gotten married here. She'd lived the best moments of her life here.

Meanwhile, her husband, Ken, asked the reporting ranger to take Taj to the Stony Man Overlook, where Julie's car was parked. Someone had managed to find a leash, which they wrapped around the retriever's neck. The rangers then proceeded to walk the dog around the parked vehicles. She showed little interest in any of them until they got to the 4Runner. There, Taj stood up and put her paws on the passenger's-side window, looking inside as if to check to see if her humans were there. That was all the confirmation the rangers needed: they now felt certain they had the missing women's dog. One of them took Taj to an enclosed animal pen at the district ranger headquarters, located at Big Meadows, mile 51.2 on Skyline Drive. The others returned to Whiteoak Canyon. For the next two hours, they walked up and down the trail. Other rangers remained posted at the parking area, asking if anyone had seen the women or the dog. No one had.

Bridget Bohnet, the law enforcement ranger responsible for patrolling that section, had begun another hasty search of the area. She hiked down the Bridle Trail, calling out Julie's and Lollie's names. She passed within a hundred yards of their tent but didn't see it through the foliage. She detected no odor. She turned down the fire road and kept searching.

Ten miles south of Bohnet, a young boy lost his footing and tumbled down Dark Hollow Falls, a steep waterfall located next to a popular trail. A radio call went out, saying that someone was badly injured and in need of immediate medical assistance. For a brief moment, Barb Stewart hoped it was Julie or Lollie. Her heart sank when she learned it was not.

At least half the rangers looking for the two women were diverted to the waterfall rescue. It would take an hour before the medivac helicopter arrived. By then, it was after 6:00 p.m. The rangers who had rushed over to Dark Hollow Falls were back on their hasty search detail. Park radios were mostly silent, save for the occasional check-in. At Skyland, the Saturday dinner rush came and went. A single ranger stood near the main doors, showing visitors the faxed photos of Julie. *Had they seen this girl?* No one had. Families returned to their cabins and rooms. The ranger took the photos to Skyland staff members. A manager said he'd definitely seen Julie at some point, but he couldn't remember when.

Another ranger called in to say he'd just received reports that two female backpackers were spotted coming up the Whiteoak Canyon Trail, looking for a campsite. *Could they be Lollie and Julie?* Missing-person's reports in the park almost always ended this way. Johnson redirected search efforts yet again: "Shift tactics from containment to increase hasty search efforts of trail corridors near Whiteoak, since the observed women would likely be settled off trail at a campsite," he wrote in the case incident log.

The sun set in the nearby town of Luray at 8:33 p.m. that Saturday. Dusk had fallen in the Shenandoah woods even earlier. At 8:40 p.m., Ranger Bobby Fleming and his partner descended the Bridle Trail, again looking for any sign of the women. Ten minutes later and about a quarter mile down the path, one of them spied a blue-and-yellow tent nestled near the stream. They approached the site, announcing themselves as they neared.

The two rangers didn't have to get far to see that the scene around the tent was chaos. The tent's rear rainfly had been cut or torn open, leaving wide, angry gashes in the nylon. A leash and empty dog collar, both with cut marks, were lashed to a fallen limb abutting the rear of the tent. Just outside it, three hiking boots lay on their sides, their laces a tangle on the ground. Around them was a sea of detritus: a giant Ziploc bag of macaroni, half its contents spilled on the ground and looking water damaged. A roll of toilet paper, flattened and saturated with blood. Overturned dog dishes. A jar of Italian spices, also on its side.

According to the rangers' subsequent report, Fleming's partner approached the north end of the tent. Fleming circled around to the south, where two heavy backpacks sat stacked one upon the other. Fleming opened one of the packs, looking for identification. As he lifted the top flap of the pack, a pair of glasses tumbled to the ground. Before he could pick them up, he heard his partner's voice. *Something smells dead*, Fleming later recalled his partner saying, *it smells like a dead animal.* Fleming circled around to the other end of the tent, where the fly had been slashed or torn. Inside lay what appeared to be a human figure, cocooned in a blue sleeping bag and shrouded in a cloud of down feathers that had escaped a giant gash in the bag. Using Fleming's asp, a collapsible baton commonly carried by law enforcement, the rangers nudged the sleeping bag. No response. They poked the sleeping bag again, then lifted up a torn portion of the bag. There lay the undeniable shape of a human head, facedown, its hair matted with blood.

The two rangers later stated that with this discovery, they backed away from the tent. Fleming got on his radio. He called in to Ken Johnson and told him they had a "find." As Fleming was radioing in, his partner scanned the campsite. About sixty feet away and down the stream's short embankment he saw another body, also bundled in a sleeping bag.

Those same two rangers later stated that they then stepped farther away from the site, scanning the area for signs of movement. They saw none. They walked closer to the Bridle Trail, stopping so that each one could stand on lookout. One made sure to note in his log that they'd both touched the tent while examining it. *Their fingerprints would be all over the rain fly and entrance flap at least*, he wrote.

Meanwhile, Ken Johnson radioed Greg Stiles, the park's assistant superintendent, telling his supervisor to call the *boys in blue*. Stiles remembers that phrase distinctly: he was confused at first. He didn't know if Johnson was saying there was a hostage situation or what Johnson was saying he needed: More law enforcement rangers? The state police? A SWAT team? It took a minute or two before he realized Johnson was trying to avoid announcing the crime scene over the radio. The assistant superintendent jumped into his truck and sped to Skyland. While en route, he ordered all available rangers to establish a secure perimeter around the area. He next called Tim Alley and urged him to return to the park as fast as he could. In the meantime, Fleming began to brief the other rangers on what he had seen. At this point, the phrase "murder/suicide" began to emerge, and it remained the dominant phrase in the park investigation for the next forty-eight hours—as in, *It appears we are dealing with a murder/suicide.*

However, when first questioned by Stiles, Bobby Fleming said he assumed that both deceased individuals at the tent site had been the victims of a bear attack. If anyone questioned how a bear would neatly zip its victims into their respective sleeping bags so that only the crowns of their heads were showing, they gave no indication. Perhaps Fleming assumed both women crawled into their bags after being mauled and that they later bled to death there—a scenario only slightly less lacking in logic. Fleming also reported that it looked as if a good deal of Lollie's hair was missing as a result of severe decomposition. No one questioned that observation, either, despite the fact that the women had been reported missing just a few days earlier.

Saturday, June 1, 1996
9:20 p.m.

Tim Alley arrived at the Big Meadows ranger station. Taj was there, being cared for by some of the employees. The dog walked up to Alley and immediately began licking his hand. "No fear," Alley remembers. "All affection."

He and Clyde Yee, another law enforcement ranger, began surveying Williams's SUV. Like Alley, Yee had worked on the Colonial Parkway at the time of the 1986 murders of Cathy Thomas and Becky Dowski, the young couple who had been found with their throats slit. Now the two rangers found themselves inventorying yet another young woman's vehicle. In this case, the resulting list included Lollie's wallet and driver's license, along with a recent issue of *USA Today*. The wildflower poster the women had persuaded Barb Stewart to give them. A twenty-pound bag of Purina Dog Chow. Two sets of dog bowls and an oversize crate for Taj. An extra sleeping bag. Bottles of cooking fuel. Gallon jugs of water. A set of bongos. Camping dishes and a fork. Grocery bags still half-full of peanut butter, hummus, and pita bread. Dirty clothes and socks. It was clear the women had been using the car as a home base while in the park.

Once each item had been logged, the rangers sealed the SUV with evidence tape and waited for a local towing company, which transported the Toyota to a secure parking bay, where it wouldn't be disturbed.

While the rangers waited for the tow truck, Greg Stiles was on the phone with the FBI. When it comes to investigating major crime, most national parks are within the joint purview of the NPS and the FBI, but Stiles knew there was little question who was really in charge when a crime occurs.

Three years earlier, park police patrolling Virginia's Fort Marcy had discovered the body of Vince Foster, one of President Bill Clinton's senior lawyers. They delayed contacting the FBI for several hours while they began their own investigation. Later, the entire park service was called out for the delay by the Department of Justice and members of Congress. Stiles wasn't about to let that happen again. He phoned the FBI field office in Richmond and was advised it would be hours before agents could arrive.

According to Virginia State Police records, their bureau of criminal investigation, located in the nearby town of Culpepper, was not contacted by park authorities until 10:40 p.m.—almost exactly two hours after the bodies were found. Dispatch there told park rangers that state investigators wouldn't arrive at the park before midnight—at the earliest. The rangers also called the county coroner around that time but initially got no answer. Fifteen minutes later, the coroner called back and authorized rangers to begin processing the scene.

In the meantime, Karen Malmquist, a dispatcher for the park, was assigned the job of acting as runner. Later, she and Bobby Fleming would marry. But on that night, she was a twenty-three-year-old working an entry-level job in the park. One of the rangers at the murder scene first radioed and asked Malmquist to bring a shotgun down to the scene, presumably out of concern that the assailant might still be in the area. Later, they asked her to bring food and water.

And then they all continued to wait.

Sunday, June 2, 1996
12:18 a.m.

True to their word, the state police investigators arrived at Shenandoah National Park not long after midnight. They were joined at 2:00 a.m. by several FBI agents. Together, along with Tim Alley and another senior ranger, they began the dark walk to the crime scene. Alley remembers that the adjacent stream was raging that night—even in the dark, he could hear that the water had grown wide and deep. The resulting rapids were loud enough that it was difficult to have a conversation.

Using their flashlights, the investigators attempted to assess the scene. They pulled back the crown of both sleeping bags and observed that the women had been gagged. They made note of the fatal wounds on both necks. They then inventoried the backpacks, removing the contents as they jotted down each item. They took a few Polaroids and then made the decision not to process the rest of the crime scene until daylight: even with all the flashlights, it was just too dark to really see anything.

Alley appointed several rangers to secure the scene and stand watch for the night. The remaining investigators slowly made their way back up the trail. They'd all try to catch a few hours of sleep in a vacant ranger apartment located at Skyland and then return again at first light.

Alley hurried ahead of the rest of the crew to make the phone calls he'd been dreading. He first tried Lollie's mom, Laura, who was sound asleep at her estate in Grosse Pointe. *We have found the bodies of two deceased women in the park and believe that one of them may be your daughter,* Alley said. *I am very sorry.* Laura Winans received the news in such a state of shock he couldn't tell if she actually comprehended what he had told her. Next, the ranger called Tom Williams. There'd been no positive ID, of course, but it seemed pretty clear they'd finally found his daughter and that she was dead. Williams thanked him and said he'd be on the first flight to Virginia.

Sunday, June 2, 1996
3:30 a.m.

Back on the Bridle Trail, the state police investigators and remaining rangers couldn't help but speculate on the similarities between this crime and another recent murder in the area. Exactly three months prior, Alicia Showalter Reynolds, a pharmacology doctoral student at Johns Hopkins, had awoken early in her Baltimore apartment. She showered and dressed, then kissed her husband of two years goodbye and slipped into her white Mercury Tracer. Petite with shoulder-length hair and freckled cheeks, Showalter Reynolds looked far younger than her twenty-five years. That morning, she was on her way to rendezvous with her mother, Sadie, in their native Charlottesville, Virginia. Alicia's twin brother was about to be married, and the two women needed dresses for the ceremony.

The drive normally took about three hours. Alicia was always prompt. After waiting more than an hour for her daughter to arrive at the store, Sadie found a pay phone and called Alicia's husband, Mark. He confirmed that she'd left on time and should have arrived by then. They talked about what to do next. The most direct route would have taken Alicia south on I-95, around the DC Beltway, and then southwest on US Route 29. In 1996, that remote stretch of state highway cut mostly through woodlands and agricultural fields: if your car broke down there, you'd most likely wait a while before help arrived. Mark offered to call the state police. They told him a trooper would take a swing through that stretch and, in the meantime, they'd issue a BOLO for Alicia's car.

State troopers eventually found Showalter Reynolds's Tracer two miles west of the town of Culpeper and about twenty-five miles east of Shenandoah's Thornton Gap entrance station. The car was parked on the side of the road, a white take-out napkin tucked under a windshield wiper—a common indicator left by a driver to say, *Hey, my car broke down; I'm working on getting it towed.* The troopers noted several cigarette butts and a pair of black gloves lying next to the vehicle. They knocked on the doors of a few nearby houses. Several residents there said the same thing: the driver of the Tracer, a young-looking brunette, appeared to be having car trouble. A clean-cut man, probably in his midthirties, wearing a flannel shirt and jeans and driving a dark pickup truck, stopped to help her out. She climbed into his truck, and they both left the scene. Later that day, a local police officer found one of Showalter Reynolds's credit cards lying on the side of a road back in the town center of Culpeper. Two days later, a woman discovered Showalter Reynolds's size 2 jacket lying in the mud near a remote pond about ten miles away. There was still no sign of Alicia. State police escalated their missing-person's search.

As news of Showalter Reynolds's disappearance spread, women—twenty in all—started coming forward. Their stories were disturbingly similar: all about a clean-cut Caucasian man, thirty-five to forty years old, driving a dark pickup truck, who would pull up alongside them, frantically waving and motioning for the women to pull over. Those women who ignored him watched with increasing fear as he exploded in a tirade before eventually speeding off. Those who complied and pulled over met a polite good Samaritan. Most of the women said the same thing: the man now known as the Route 29 stalker was articulate, concerned. He always offered a gentle variation on the same theme—*I saw sparks flying underneath your car. If I were you, I'd have that looked at.* Never pushy. Just worried about their safety. If anything, he seemed maybe a little patronizing or parental. Three of the women accepted his offer of a ride to a nearby gas station. They later told police the man appeared to be about six feet tall, with reddish-brown hair parted on one side. He was clean shaven and wore a wedding ring. The interior of his truck was immaculate. He made pleasant conversation and waited until they had found a station attendant before driving away.

"He was so nice," one woman told the Associated Press (AP). "Unbelievably friendly."

As with the other vehicles, nothing discernably wrong could be found with Alicia Showalter Reynolds's SUV. Police suspected that the stalker had used a similar ruse to get her to pull over. Using information from the other women who came forward, FBI profilers began creating a composite of Showalter Reynolds's suspected abductor. At press conferences, they speculated that the man had spent that winter practicing his routine and getting up the nerve to commit a serious crime. Maybe those other three women he dropped off at gas stations didn't fit his profile of an ideal victim. Maybe they seemed like they'd put up too much of a struggle. The profilers theorized that as time went on, the stalker had become bolder and more persuasive.

These pronouncements intensified the growing fear in the Shenandoah region. Women began buying handguns and pepper spray. They told spouses and family members that they were afraid to drive alone. And still there was no sign of Alicia Showalter Reynolds.

Then, early in the morning on May 6, a logger was making his way to a cleared patch of woodlot in rural Lignum, an unincorporated village about twelve miles southeast of Culpeper. The woodlot itself was located on a barren gravel road and abutted the Rapidan River. As the logger picked his way through the bark and tangled limbs from the most recent cut, he noticed a committee of turkey vultures swooping overhead. The logger followed their path, walking down an incline and deeper into the razed detritus of the cut. Just shy of the river lay a partially buried body. It was too badly decayed for the logger to know if he was looking at a man or a woman. But whatever lay before him was undeniably human.

The same state police crime scene investigators walking up the Shenandoah Bridle Trail in the early morning hours of June 2, 1996, were also the first called to the Showalter Reynolds scene. The terrain where Showalter Reynolds's body had been found was so rugged that they'd requested—and received—assistance from park law enforcement rangers. For most of the rangers, Showalter Reynolds's case was the first violent crime they'd ever worked. Initially, the state of decomposition had made determining the cause of death difficult, but the state medical examiner eventually found evidence of asphyxiation and ruled her death a homicide.

The ruse to get Alicia Showalter Reynolds to pull over, the gloves near her vehicle, the way her personal effects had been deliberately scattered around the area all suggested that this was a meticulously executed crime. Investigators knew that alone was a rarity: nationwide, fewer than 10 percent of all murders are premeditated. Most, instead, erupt sloppily and from a quick, unplanned chain of events: a robbery goes bad; a bar fight escalates; a domestic abuser arrives home drunk and belligerent. Showalter Reynolds's assailant, by contrast, had clearly planned out what he was doing. He'd no doubt gotten away with crimes in his past, and all signs suggested he'd act again. Investigators told residents in the region to be on the lookout for someone who probably seemed like the guy next door. He was dependable, helpful to neighbors.

"It's very important to catch this guy," the lead detective had told reporters in mid-May. "Alicia is the first homicide he's committed, but if we don't catch him, he'll kill again. Once you do it—once you kill—it's no big deal the second time."

Two weeks later, walking up the dark and empty Bridle Trail, no one had to articulate what the officers were now thinking: it looked like they might now have a serial killer on their hands.

5

Sunday, June 2, 1996
6:15 a.m.

TIM ALLEY AND THE OTHER INVESTIGATORS returned to the murder scene. They began by laying the bodies of both women, still in their sleeping bags, atop a bright blue tarp. Then they unzipped the bags. The on-site state police crime lab technician recorded what appeared to be small contusions on the women's arms, chests, and faces. He made note of the two gags, both apparently fashioned from the women's long underwear. Duct tape was wound tightly around both women's wrists, binding their arms behind their backs. Lollie's ankles were also bound with what appeared to be a third piece of long underwear belonging to the women. The technician also observed no obvious sign of decomposition. Investigators took photos of the women lying prone, as they were found, then rolled them onto their backs and took additional pictures. They then rezipped the sleeping bags.

More local law enforcement officers began to arrive. Most just stood around, awaiting instruction and drinking coffee. Rangers came and went. One of them noticed a discarded duct tape roll on the trail, a few hundred yards up from where the women's bodies had been found.

Nine miles to their south, Ken Johnson and several members of the Virginia State Police Investigative Unit met with Greg Stiles, the assistant superintendent of the park. They told him the crime scene was complex. Preliminary evidence suggested a double homicide. Stiles thanked them. He sat down and penned a confidential memo outlining his thinking on the case, along with possible scenarios that would explain how two people had come to die in his park. Probably, he concluded, "one woman killed the other, then had committed suicide," he wrote. "This was considered the most likely scenario as they were apparently in a romantic relationship, and one of the women allegedly had previous drug and alcohol problems based on other information developed as a result of the search investigation." Aside from Lollie's occasional use of recreational drugs at school, there was no evidence either women had a regular drug habit, let alone a problem; nor was there any evidence either woman had any issue with alcohol. Nevertheless, Stiles concluded that any lingering danger to park-goers was unlikely. He wrote down his justification for this conclusion in a ten-point bullet list, which outlined factors including the rarity of stranger-on-stranger homicides and the low murder rates in national parks. He noted that previous murders in Shenandoah had been isolated incidents and that except for immediately after the killings, few visitors were endangered. He also noted the lack of reported crime or suspicious activity in the park over the previous two weeks. Finally, he stated that most homicides are committed by people who are not only known to their victims but who also are in some kind of domestic relationship with them. Without naming her, he stated that one of the women in this case had just ended her romantic relationship with a man and, as a result, was about to move out of the residence she shared with him. This final justification was, of course, also false: Julie and her roommate were not in a romantic relationship and had lived together platonically. Lollie, who had been briefly engaged two years earlier, hadn't lived with her former fiancé, Ken, in over eighteen months.

In his confidential memo, Stiles went on to speculate that once news of the women's deaths became public, park visitors would clamor for a heightened law enforcement presence. The park already had a ranger shortage. Those on staff were going to quickly tire with all the extra overtime and would need rest. Stiles theorized that AT thru-hikers had probably already heard rumors of the deaths and so would be policing themselves. He determined no further action was required there. After listing all these reasons, Stiles concluded the memo with his final determination:

Decision: wait until news organizations discovered the incident on their own before making any announcement.

Sunday, June 2, 1996
7:00 a.m.

The group of five friends woke early at a motel in nearby Luray and prepared to set out on a weeklong backpacking trip. Three of them, commonly called "the Annes" because they share a first name, had met in a physical therapy graduate program several years earlier and had become instant friends. On this particular trip, they were joined by a favorite couple of theirs, Chip and Laura. All five individuals were young, fit, and adventurous. They were also brand new to the world of backpacking, so they had planned their trip with what they admit was an overzealous amount of detail.

For years, the Annes had been talking about doing a section hike on the AT, but they worried it would be too dangerous for three women alone. They eventually settled on Shenandoah because they figured that as a national park, it would be the safest part of the trail. They mapped out each day's itinerary on three-by-five-inch notecards and did all the research they could on clothing, gear, water, and food. By their count, they made at least ten different trips to an outdoor store, making sure they had the right backpacks and boots and water purifiers. With each visit, their excitement built: the trip, they were certain, was going to be amazing.

When it came time to pack, they went heavy on luxury items, including cribbage boards, beach towels, and extra shoes. It would add a burdensome amount of extra weight, but they figured they could jettison what they didn't need along the way. Their planned itinerary was a seven-day traverse of the trail as it passed through Shenandoah National Park: 101 miles in total. They would begin near the park's north entrance and shuttle their two cars along the way, making it easy to drop off gear if need be.

On the morning of Saturday, June 1, the three Annes rendezvoused in Philadelphia, then drove the four hours to Shenandoah. There, they met up with Chip and Laura, went out for an early dinner, and then bunked in a couple of cheap motel rooms for the night.

Just after dawn, the fivesome arrived at Shenandoah's north entrance station, obtained their backcountry permits, and began their hike. They estimate they'd been under way for less than an hour—just a couple of miles, really—before they met their first thru-hiker. He was skinny, rugged looking, about thirty or forty. The Annes were thrilled: after all that time thinking about the trail, it felt like meeting a celebrity. One of them had a film camera in her pack; she asked if she could take the thru-hiker's picture. He agreed. As she was rummaging through her backpack, he seemed to grow nervous. He asked the group where they were heading and how long it would take them to get there. He also wanted to know if they were planning on going anywhere near Skyland. *Had they heard what happened there? It was crazy last night*, they remember him saying, *what with those two girls getting killed.*

It wasn't just the content of what this thru-hiker said that so bothered the group. There was also something about his demeanor—the way he seemed to be probing them for information. They also felt as if he really wanted them to know about his own itinerary: where, exactly, he'd been the previous few days, and that a friend was going to pick him up just outside the park and drive him farther north. Once he finished the AT, the hiker said, he planned to immediately hop a plane for California and the 2,650-mile Pacific Crest Trail.

Growing leery, the Annes told him they'd better start walking again if they were going to maintain their own itinerary. As soon as the hiker was out of earshot, the fivesome stopped to debrief. *What had just happened there? Was the thru-hiker a freak? Was he just messing with them? And how could he know what had happened forty miles south of them—easily a two-, or even three-day hike from where they had begun?*

The Annes didn't know that at the time the only people informed about the murder of Julie and Lollie were their respective families and the investigators involved. But what the hiker had said to them was enough for them to contemplate abandoning their trip altogether. They talked it over and eventually decided to keep hiking.

A few miles later, the trail emerged in a parking area. There, the Annes found a ranger sitting in his truck. They approached him to find out what was really going on—and if what the thru-hiker said was true.

We're not saying anything, the ranger told them. *There's crime everywhere. Just be careful.*

The Annes described to the ranger their planned itinerary, which would have them at Skyland in two days. They asked if they should change their plans. *Nope*, he assured them, *You're good.* Walking away, the group reconsidered their plans once again. In the end, they decided to keep going. *Maybe the thru-hiker was some kind of kook*, they concluded. *If we were walking right toward a violent crime scene, surely the rangers would have to tell us.*

Sunday, June 2, 1996
10:00 a.m.

Back up on the Bridle Trail, a park employee arrived at the crime scene around 10:00 a.m. bearing coffee for the investigators. Local sheriff's deputies helped themselves to Styrofoam cups and shifted their weight from foot to foot, hoping to pass the time. They'd been there for four hours, and it seemed like the only thing to be done was stand around. An hour later, two rangers arrived with several rolls of garbage bags. They set them on the ground and chatted with their coworkers, then left again. Everyone else continued to wait.

"I was very surprised," one of the deputies told the local paper. "I assumed we were going on a manhunt. But we ended up just sitting around doing nothing until about 2 o'clock in the afternoon."

By then, a state police officer driving a sports utility hearse had arrived at the park. Rangers met him at the eastern boundary, unlocked a series of gates, and directed him up the rutted fire road that connected with the base of the Bridle Trail.

The trooper unloaded a wheeled stokes basket—a metal litter akin to those used to transport injured skiers in mountain rescues. This basket was outfitted with a single fat tire, and the state police officer pushed it in front of him as he and the rangers climbed up the steep trail. At the campsite, investigators bundled Julie's remains into a double layer of body bags, then strapped her body onto the basket. It took nearly an hour to trundle her to the SUV, load her remains, and then return to the site for Lollie.

Once both bodies had been loaded, the trooper departed for a funeral home in Orange, Virginia, about forty miles away, with a plan to leave them there overnight and then transport the remains to the state medical examiner's office the following day.

At 2:00 p.m. on Sunday, members of the newly formed Richmond field office ERT arrived on the scene. Eighteen hours had passed since the discovery of the women's bodies. The ERT cleared a team of dog handlers to investigate the scene. Rangers began arriving with their own wheeled litters to transport evidence. Within the hour, they had filled several trash bags with items found at the campsite. They began a grid search, fanning out shoulder to shoulder in search of more evidence.

What remained to be seen was what to do with the evidence they found.

Tim Alley says he was adamant that the investigators use the park helicopter to fly the evidence bags directly to the FBI's crime lab in Washington. *It's not like we're in the wilds of Alaska,* he remembers telling them. *We're literally just fifteen minutes away by chopper.*

But the ERT refused. Much of the evidence was soaked with rainwater. It would have to be dried before it could be examined. They wanted to conduct a thorough inventory and analysis before the evidence was moved from the park. Alley and the FBI agents continued to debate the issue. Alley grew heated. He was tired and hadn't slept in over a day. And he'd seen backcountry cases like this one go wrong before.

The ERT agents pulled rank. They insisted that the evidence remain at the murder scene, where it could be inventoried and examined. Alley offered a compromise: they could load the bags into park vehicles and transport them to an empty ranger apartment located nine miles away at

the Big Meadows station. It would be secure there. The FBI agents reluctantly agreed.

The remaining rangers and law enforcement officers fanned out, collecting any item that looked relevant. In the stream, near where Julie's
body had been found, they bagged a knit cap and wad of used duct tape.
On the opposite bank, they found the shaft of a hunting arrow, along with
a game trail leading back to Skyline Drive. Based on the scat, it seemed
that the trail was frequented by both deer and bears—and poachers looking for both. About a hundred yards down the trail from Lollie and Julie's
campsite, they also found a small clearing, the only place on the trail from
which the tent was visible. There, they collected two Winston cigarette
butts and an empty Budweiser can.

Back at the campsite proper, investigators found a pair of black gloves,
size small, that didn't appear to belong to either Lollie or Julie. They found
Lollie's camera sitting in its case amid a jumbled pile of unopened maxi
pads, three cans of cooking fuel, a lidless Nalgene water bottle, a first-aid
kit and rain jacket, a jar of vitamin C, and second knit cap.

Atop the pile, perfectly centered on a black canvas bag, sat a white
cylindrical vibrator about five inches long. Officers agreed it seemed
deliberately placed. *Staged*, crime scene investigators call that sort of
thing: a calling card left by a murderer to make a statement or to confuse
investigators. Investigators weren't sure what kind of message they had
here, but they felt confident it hadn't been left by accident.

Inside the tent, where Lollie's body had lain, blood and down feathers
had pooled on much of the floor and covered the remaining contents.
Investigators found a badly stained paperback book, its cover ripped off
and lying on the tent floor. They found a notebook with pages written
in Lollie's handwriting. They also discovered a folded page of notebook
paper in Julie's handwriting, also torn and stained. "I am wondering what
the difference is between 'accepting' something—a word, an offering, a
reluctance, an engagement, a touch, an embrace, a release—and *accepting*
it," the passage reads before becoming indecipherable by blood. Next to
it lay an unblemished envelope addressed to Julie at her parents' home in

St. Cloud and postmarked June 12, 1995. Written on the back, also in her handwriting, was the rough draft of a poem:

> Water waves at me in every direction
> Rippling up and down
> As it sings the sinking
> Sun to sleep
> Seagulls strut &
> Come to see what
> We will eat.
> Lollie spreads out her gear
> And futzes with her stove
> Her favorite thing to do.
> She says she will remember
> This always and knows,
> Now, what MN is all
> About.

On the front, next to the canceled stamp, Julie had added a final verse:

> Falling
> Falling together
> Fall in love
> Falling apart family
> Drifting away.

Sunday, June 2, 1996
1:30 p.m.

Tom Williams was as staid and law abiding as you'd expect a Minnesotan funeral director to be. But accompanied by his brother, he'd caught the earliest flight possible out of Minneapolis that morning and then drove like a Formula 1 racer to get from the airport to Shenandoah early that Sunday afternoon.

As the brothers entered the park, they saw no evidence that anything was amiss. They parked their car at Skyland and let a ranger know they were there. The crime scene was still being processed, they were told, and they wouldn't be allowed to visit until the FBI's ERT had finished their work. In the meantime, the ranger promised to get word to Tim Alley that they had arrived. The two brothers sat on a park bench for what felt like hours, watching the Sunday crowds of park visitors grow around them. Sometime later, Tim Alley arrived. He shook both men's hands and apologized that they wouldn't yet be able to visit the campsite. Instead, he offered to take them to Julie's SUV, still secured in the maintenance vehicle bay. Williams wanted to see his daughter's things, yes. But he also had a very specific request: he wanted to know what music she'd last been listening to so that he would know what to play at her funeral.

At this request, Alley nodded but didn't say anything—the idea had choked him up enough that he couldn't speak. The three drove the short distance to the maintenance shed, and Alley unsealed the 4Runner.

Investigators hadn't yet begun bagging up the contents of the SUV. Tom was struck by how much of the casual detritus of his daughter's life it still contained: a scrunchy hair band; an empty soda cup from Taco Bell; a collection of rocks and feathers filling the center-console cupholder. He suspected many of the tapes and CDs were more Lollie's taste than Julie's: lots of Grateful Dead bootlegs, a few mixtapes featuring Jamaican dub poets and early ska. But he recognized a couple of Dave Matthews CDs along with a mix of some of Julie's favorite jazz standards, including Ella's Fitzgerald's "Russian Lullaby." That one seemed particularly apt to him.

With nothing else to do for the time being, the two Williams brothers checked themselves into a nearby motel and waited for news.

Sunday, June 2, 1996
5:00 p.m.

Word was spreading on the trail. No one knew anything for certain, but the combination of search interviews and rumors of crime scene tape and hordes of investigators had begun to morph together, and the implications were terrifying. The Annes, along with Chip and Laura, continued their slow walk southward. Earlier that afternoon, they'd met a couple visiting from Germany. The pair confessed they were concerned about bears and asked if they could all team up. The Annes related their own concerns. The seven backpackers talked it over. They decided there was strength in numbers. They'd set up their tents together and take turns standing watch so that everyone could get at least a few hours of rest. As it turned out, no one was able to sleep a minute that night. An instant friendship had been struck between the two parties, sure, but how could either be certain they hadn't just aligned their fate with violent killers?

6

THE VIRGINIA STATE medical examiner had begun her autopsies on Julie Williams and Lollie Winans. The doctor saw no obvious sign of sexual trauma; however, both women had what the examiner described as an "oily substance" in and around their genital areas and anuses. The residue was too thick to be a lubricant like K-Y jelly, noted the examiner, and she recommended samples be sent out for further testing.

She also noted the presence of multiple abrasions and contusions on the face, neck, chest, and back of both women. Julie had sustained the brunt of them: sharp blows that left narrow, well-defined wounds only a quarter of an inch in width and an inch in length. Their assailant had struck her on the forehead and the nose, as well as her lower lip and the side of her head, just below her left ear. Lollie had similar wounds, measuring an inch or so long and about a half inch wide on her right eyelid and cheek, along with her chin and forehead. Both women had long, deep gashes in their necks, enough to cleave their tracheas, carotid arteries, and jugular veins. Julie's wound was larger and deeper than Lollie's, but both were clearly the cause of their deaths.

Both women tested negative for alcohol and drugs, and no other foreign substances were noted in their blood. Lollie's stomach was empty. Julie's contained a yellowish liquid. Also noteworthy were the presence of fly eggs on Julie's gag and in some of her wounds. Both bodies also presented with signs of rigor mortis in their lower extremities; the medical examiner noted evidence of early decomposition on both women as well.

All three observations—noted insect activity, the presence of rigor mortis, the degree of decomposition—can be used to help determine time of death. In general, rigor mortis begins to set in the jaw and face about six to eight hours after death. After about twelve hours, the entire body has grown stiff and will remain so for another twelve hours. Rigor mortis exits the body the way it came, beginning with the face and smaller muscles and last leaving large leg muscles about thirty-six hours after the time of death. Cooler temperatures can delay the departure of rigor, as can deaths involving a violent hemorrhage. It can also linger longer in athletically built individuals. The presence of fly eggs but no active larva or maggot activity usually indicates that a person has been deceased for no more than a week. Decomposition most often begins with skin slippage and some hair loss, both of which begin to occur anywhere from the day of a person's death to five days later. During that same time period, a body will begin to show early signs of discoloration, with the extremities taking on a dark brown or black hue. Based on all these standards, it appeared that Lollie and Julie had been killed within the week.

The medical examiner also charted the level of potassium ions in eye fluid taken from both women. Unlike other forensic signs, potassium ion levels increase at an observable and steady rate after a person's death. Notably, this increase does not appear to be affected by temperature and humidity, nor by factors including the age or physical condition of victims or the manner of their death. As a result, vitreous humor potassium tests are widely considered the most reliable means of determining a time of death. However, they too are not precise. Lab contamination and errors in analysis can skew results, and even the most carefully garnered sample will still yield results with a variability rate of plus or minus five hours from any estimated time of death. As a result, analysis of vitreous humor potassium levels is best used to determine the *day*, rather than the *time*, of death.

With all this in mind, the medical examiner concluded her analysis and began to prepare her report. She phoned the FBI's Richmond field office with her findings. An agent there immediately sent an internal email to Washington headquarters:

VSME [Virginia state medical examiner] telephonically reported results from vitreous humor potassium tests regarding eye fluid from both victims indicates results of each victim are consistent with each other, indicating time of death at approximately 130 hours prior to autopsy performed at 8:00 a.m. on June 3, 1996. This would place approximate time of death at 10:00 p.m., May 28, 1996. **Time of death should not be made public.**

Monday, 3 June 1996
3:00 p.m.

Someone had leaked news of the murders to the press.

It was never clear who or how or why, but by early afternoon that Monday, word had gotten out, and multiple news crews were now on their way to the park. Assistant Superintendent Greg Stiles and his staff scrambled to plan an impromptu press conference. Meanwhile, Tom Williams and his brother, still hoping to visit the place where Julie spent her last moments, had returned to their bench at Skyland. They watched as the satellite vans and sedans emblazoned with newspaper mastheads began to arrive and maintenance workers installed a lone awkward lectern. Around it, the various news outlets jockeyed for position, never once guessing that the two men sitting near them had anything to do with the case.

At park headquarters, senior administrators were stalling. They'd been told to delay the presser until they had an official FBI statement regarding the crimes, but it still had not arrived. At 4:30 p.m., the Richmond office faxed over one. The document was riddled with factual errors. Stiles determined it had too many inaccuracies to use, and he and other officials began drafting their own version. Just after 5:00 p.m., they departed to meet the press. At least forty-four hours had elapsed since the bodies were first discovered.

The climate of the press conference was tense. Journalists present were incredulous that nearly two days had passed since women had been found murdered less than a half mile from the park's most popular resorts. When asked about the delay, the park's spokesperson replied, "We weren't sure a crime had been committed." The reporters pressed for clarification. He listed some of the previous theories: natural causes, an animal attack, murder-suicide.

Stiles interjected. He told the reporters that park authorities were certain the crime was an isolated incident. The journalists asked if he had evidence that the women had been specifically targeted. Stiles said he could not comment on any specifics of the case. One member of the media asked what the authorities were doing to keep park visitors safe. Stiles assured them that additional rangers were being dispatched immediately to all major trails in the park. They would alert backpackers to the situation and maintain extra patrols. It was a well-intended reassurance. But there hadn't been any additional rangers since the budget cuts back in January. And not a single hiker ever recalled receiving this notification.

In Washington, major media outlets prepared to go live with the story. A reporter at the *Washington Post* contacted a national spokesperson for the park service, looking for corroboration of some facts. The spokesperson said it appeared as if the women had been dead for only twelve to fifteen hours before their bodies were discovered. The reporter quoted him in their story, further fueling the fire that the park service was deliberately obfuscating the risk posed to park-goers. That same NPS spokesperson told the AP it appeared that the women were the victims of a homicide. The AP ran that information in its story. But back in the park, authorities were still saying they had reason to believe that the event was a murder-suicide.

When contacted by a Florida newspaper, Lollie's father, John Winans, didn't try to hide his disgust. "This is ridiculous," he said. "It is almost as if there was a public relations ploy to calm everyone down."

THE ANNES, ALONG with their little band of fellow hikers, had made it as far as Elkwallow Wayside, a resupply store and gas station at mile 24.1 on Skyline Drive. They stopped inside to grab some snacks and phone their families. One of the Annes called her brother back in Minnesota. He told her the story was already on the news and that national channels were calling it a double suicide. Anne felt horrible for the women and their families, but she also felt safer with that news. By then, it was getting late. The seven hikers pooled their money and splurged on a forty-dollar rental fee for a rustic cabin operated by the Appalachian Trail Conservancy. It was a cramped, dark place, with creaking metal bunk beds and well-worn mattresses. But it also had a door with a lock, and that made everyone feel better. They got their first real sleep of the trip that night.

7

BY THE AFTERNOON OF TUESDAY, JUNE 4, the Annes had been on the trail for almost three full days. It felt like longer. As they passed the Panorama resort complex at mile 31.5, they decided to stop. They'd order lunch—maybe a burger and fries—and get an update on any news about the deaths. They exited the AT and lugged their packs up the steep set of stone steps connecting the resort's parking lots and buildings.

Just outside the main lodge, the group was stopped by a reporter from *USA Today*, asking for an interview. *Why?* the Annes wanted to know. He told them two women had been murdered in the park a few days earlier. The Annes were confused—incredulous, even.

No, no, it was suicide, they said. *Our families saw it on the news.*

The reporter apologized—and disagreed. He said he'd been to the crime scene and watched the investigators working. There was no doubt about it: this was definitely homicide. The Annes were shocked and angry and terrified all at once. The reporter sat with them on a bench outside the lodge. He was kind, they say: he didn't push to get a quote for his story, and it seemed like he was more interested in making sure the group was okay.

Eventually, the reporter left to phone in his piece. The Annes remained on the bench, dumbfounded.

Holy crap, one of them finally said. *What do we do now?* It was what they all had been thinking.

For starters, they all agreed they'd lost their appetites. Instead, they spent their time at Panorama strategizing. The group's two cars were miles away—one back near the park's north entrance; the other a two-day hike south—at least. They thought about booking rooms at the lodge, but it had no vacancy. They decided to take a chance and return to the trail, where they could spend the night at one of the conservancy's three-sided shelters. At least, they figured, they'd be amid other hikers. The group arrived at the shelter midafternoon, only to discover that it was already packed with hikers looking for similar cover. The fivesome reluctantly set up their tents nearby, where they joined a handful of thru-hikers and a couple of dads who had been camping with their kids. As folks milled around the shelter, setting up tents and preparing early dinners, everyone seemed to be eyeing one another with an air of suspicion.

As the afternoon and evening wore on, hikers began to share stories they'd heard on the trail. One thru-hiker said he'd been told the women were stabbed to death for their gear and that they were definitely on the AT when it happened. He told the Annes to be on the lookout for someone carrying a pack that looked like it didn't fit. *What does that mean?* the Annes wanted to know. *And how would we possibly be able to tell whether or not a pack fit?* The hiker just shrugged. The Annes returned to their tents. One of them began walking ever-widening circles around their site. When another hiker asked what she was doing, she told him she was trying to memorize every sound. That way, if someone approached her tent in the night, she'd at least know how close he was—and how much time she had left.

BY WEDNESDAY MORNING, paper notices began appearing around the park, reminding hikers always to hike in groups and to be wary of strangers. They urged hikers to refrain from telling anyone other than close family members their itineraries and also to always avoid camping near roads or developed areas. What they didn't say was why these warnings suddenly seemed relevant.

Meanwhile, newspaper wire services across the country had picked up the story of Julie and Lollie's death, making it national news. So too was the delay in notifying park visitors. At the now-daily press briefing, journalists focused again on why news of the homicide had been so late in coming. The park's spokesperson repeated what he had said before: "It took us a while to figure out exactly what we had. It is not all that uncommon to find deceased people in the park," he said. "It's taken us quite a while to determine the deaths were homicides, rather than suicides or accidents." Reporters grilled him about what had led park authorities to the eventual conclusion that a crime had occurred. He declined to comment but stressed again that there was no danger to other visitors. The *Washington Post* covered the presser and reported it this way: "Spokesperson Paul Pfenninger refused to explain why officials think other visitors were not in danger, other than to say that 'something investigators found at the site led them to believe it was an isolated incident.' He would not say what that was." Off the record, rangers on hand told reporters they weren't sure what Pfenninger was referring to either. Another reporter asked when the women were murdered. "We can't pin down the time of death," replied an FBI spokesperson standing at the lectern.

After the press conference, AP journalists scoured the park for visitors who had been notified of the murders, but they could find none. Two female backpackers, identified only by their ages (twenty-three and twenty-seven), told one reporter they were "shocked" to hear about the crime. When asked if they'd been approached by rangers providing information about the crime, they said no. "No one has said anything," one told the journalist. "I'd much rather know." Another hiker told a reporter she'd always been cautious on the trail, but spotty news of this crime had created a real terror for her. She said she and her companion had decided to forego camping on the AT and instead were trying to reserve a cabin at one of the park resorts. "We'll feel safer behind locked doors," she explained. Another said she had grown so frustrated trying to determine if she was safe that she'd decided to leave the park altogether. "They won't tell us anything," she said. "We don't know the whole picture."

The Annes had reached a similar conclusion. When they arrived at Skyland, yellow crime scene tape still littered the area. Dozens of reporters and camera crews were competing for footage and hunting for hikers willing to be interviewed. It was chaos. The Annes decided they had had enough. They vowed that as soon as they could get to their car, they would leave the park. They'd go whitewater rafting, find a beach rental, something. Anything that got them out of Shenandoah.

8

ON A COOL AUGUST EVENING in 2018, two of the Annes sat down with me
to talk about the Shenandoah murders and their own time in the park.
I found their names in a nationally syndicated news story that had been
written the week after the murder, and I wanted to hear their perspective
firsthand. Now in their midfifties and residing in the Upper Midwest, they
are smart, funny, and affable. That evening, as we talked, they repeatedly
called each other by their longstanding nicknames, Kozzie and Mags, and
made friendly conversation in Kozzie's pumpkin-colored dining room
that looked out onto a terraced patio and backyard. So much about the
scene was warm and cozy and familiar to me. But there was also a palpable heaviness as the two women talked about the continued impact of the
1996 killings. Kozzie's large dining-room table was covered with dozens of
newspaper clippings about the crime, along with scrapbooks from their
trip and articles they had preserved about Julie and Lollie, all labeled with
the date and publication name written in blue ink by a tidy hand.

"This is just a snapshot of all the information we kept," Kozzie told me.
"Our experience in Shenandoah truly changed my life."

Mags nodded in agreement. "We were so excited to be hiking and
meeting thru-hikers and learning about their backstory. That evaporated
almost as soon as we set foot on the trail. The whole scene there turned
into paranoia and anxiety. All the hikers were looking at one another and
thinking, 'Is that the guy?' You could tell: even the thru-hikers were completely freaked out. For all any of us knew, we were hiking straight toward
a murderer."

They say that, even today, they remember every noise they heard out-side their tents at the AT shelter, from the sound of rain on the fly to someone turning over in their sleeping bags. They've never forgotten that sensation or the real fear they experienced. Mags admitted that she hasn't camped since and that she worries each time her nieces head out into the woods.

Kozzie says she's been back out on the trail but only with her brother or a couple of male friends. "If it were just us girls doing it, I don't think I could go," she admitted. "Even hiking in state parks with my husband, I'm still like, 'I don't know if I can do this.' I always think about those two women, and it brings me back to that terrible week."

They asked what I had learned about the case. I told them about my long conversations with Tim Alley and the stacks of paperwork relating to the case that I had requested from the NPS, which included the inci-dent command logs from the preliminary investigation. Reading the files, I could see both the chaos and the urgency of those first days and weeks. In no time at all, the rangers had amassed a truly disturbing list of potential suspects, all of whom were in the park around the time of the murders. That list included a felon who had escaped a New York mental institution, where he had been serving time for stabbing his mother. During his months at the facility, he'd secreted away a stash of cash and hatched a plan to disap-pear on the trail. He'd made it from Harpers Ferry to Shenandoah when hikers in the park reported him after he harassed them, demanding food and gear. Another hiker was arrested just outside the park after confront-ing multiple women on the trail with a large survival knife. A Knoxville, Tennessee, police officer phoned to say that two male thru-hikers stopped at a cafe just outside the Great Smoky Mountain National Park, where they had threatened to rape and kill a female hiker. Meanwhile, a hiker arrived at a motel in Harpers Ferry with scratches on his face and arms. The next morning, a maintenance worker found a large knife stashed in the woods behind the motel. A restaurant owner in a Pennsylvania trail town told authorities there that another hiker had been acting disruptively and had bragged that he killed two women on the trail in Virginia.

I admitted to the Annes that while I still believed the overwhelming majority of hikers are good people, reading report after report of these individuals left me feeling overwhelmed and exposed. So too did the reports of the number of convicted sex offenders, pedophiles, and wanted criminals who were in the park the week Julie and Lollie were killed, which made me wonder just how many dangerous sadists hung out in national parks and whether the rest of us ought to avoid public lands entirely.

That feeling only intensified when I found the reports concerning Shenandoah employees. Within a week or so, reports of violent individuals and potential evidence bubbled up throughout the park. I tried to summarize them for the Annes in the least distressing way possible. But the sum total of stories was still overwhelming and disturbing. Multiple resort employees had a history of brutal behavior toward women, and their offenses ranged from domestic abuse to attempted murder. Coworkers came forward with reports of harassment, of drug deals gone bad between employees, of stashes of bloody sheets and uniforms and all kinds of weapons. When I had first visited Shenandoah, one of the rangers quipped that the best hiring day at the park's lodges was Thursday, when the nearby prison released inmates. I'd assumed that the joke was just cynical law enforcement humor, but now I had begun to see the park through their eyes: rangers weren't just policing visitors; they were also policing their own staff—and sometimes for good reason.

Early on in the investigation, all these individuals—the wanted criminals who were visiting the park, the suspicious and harassing hikers, the offenders working in and around Skyland—had been suspects in the murder of Julie Williams and Lollie Winans. The Annes wanted to know if the bizarre thru-hiker they'd encountered was on the list. As far as I could tell, he never had been.

"Why?" asked Kozzie. "What made them so sure he was irrelevant when they didn't even take the time to hear about our experience?"

The Annes say they spent months trying to get the attention of the FBI, once they realized the time line of the crime. There was, they say, no reasonable explanation for how and why that man could have known about the murders. They wrote letters and made phone calls explaining that they had his photo, along with their own detailed journals about the events, but they say it seemed like none of the authorities cared.

"It felt like they wrote us off before they even heard what we had to say," said Mags.

It was a sentiment I'd already heard from other people associated with the case, particularly within the AT community, where insiders felt like no one in the investigation was advocating for hikers that summer or concerned about their safety on the trail. When I read the internal memo justifying the decision to withhold information about the murders from the media and park-goers, I began to understand why they felt that way. Despite everything they said at the time, park administrators had no reason to believe the killer had deliberately targeted Lollie and Julie, nor did they have any proof the murderer was no longer in Shenandoah, nor was there any reason to believe that the thousands of other visitors streaming in each day were safe from another violent attack.

During our conversation that August night, I read the confidential park memo to the two Annes. In a way, I didn't really have to hear their response: the sense of hurt and betrayal showed all over their faces. It took several minutes before either one of them spoke. And when they did, it was with the halting, fragmented disbelief that comes with processing something big and upsetting.

"They had a responsibility to take care of us," began Kozzie.

"Especially since we were so vulnerable," agreed Mags. "We were miles from our cars, from civilization. We were stuck in the wilderness with no ability to just say, 'We're done, we quit.'"

They said that what bothered them the most was that park officials felt no duty to warn hikers so that they could make their own decision about whether to stay or go—that hikers could have been in real danger without even knowing it or having the opportunity to prepare. Not doing so, they said, seemed more than irresponsible: it felt to them like a deliberate cover-up that could have cost them their lives. Who was telling *that* story, they wondered.

I BECAME A reporter because I believe in the sanctity of the fourth estate: that it is the responsibility of journalists to require powerful institutions and organizations to show their work and to be held accountable when they do not. I have also come to believe that telling other people's stories is one of the most important ways to build empathy and connection in a world that can often feel divisive and factioned. That includes the narratives of the lives not fully lived or those at risk of being forgotten altogether. If I can write those stories in a way that makes readers care, then I feel like I have done a job worth doing. After having spoken with Tim Alley and some of the other investigators and lab scientists involved in the Shenandoah case, I knew there was a book to be written about the unsolved investigation and the significance not only of the two extraordinary women who lost their lives but also of our country's first federal capital hate crime case and what it meant for contemporary questions about social justice. After speaking with the Annes, I came to realize just how little of this narrative I really understood. As far as they were concerned, the real story was about what *hadn't* happened in the investigation—and all the hard work that still remained to be done in the Shenandoah case.

The problem was, I didn't want to write that book. I had just finished two years of research and reporting on Gerry Largay, a sixty-six-year-old grandmother and retired nurse who had vanished without a trace while completing a flip-flop hike on the AT. It took more than two years before authorities were able to retrace her final days and discover her body. In the intervening months, I had become consumed by the case, staying up late into the night poring over police records and eyewitness accounts, scrolling through discussion boards, and hiking the section of trail where Gerry had been last seen. Along the way, I'd learned a lot about the importance of empathy and victims' rights and how backcountry investigations unfolded, as well as the seductive allure of believing you can find answers in a case that has otherwise stumped experts. But I'd also found the dark side to that kind of work as well. I have never been someone adept at compartmentalizing my feelings or differentiating which of those feelings are mine and which belong to other people. When the Maine State Police accidentally sent me photos of Largay's decomposed body, I was unable to sleep for several days afterward. Instead, I sat at my computer, fixated, obsessively scrolling through the images and trying to make sense of what I saw there. In the weeks that followed, I spoke and visited with the Largay family often. As lovely as they all were, and as admirably willing as they were to share intimate aspects of their love and their grief, I soon discovered that I was unable to prevent myself from absorbing that anguish and dragging it wherever I went, an invisible weight.

Unpacking the murders of Lollie and Julie, I knew, would be far worse. I worried I didn't have the emotional strength and resolve to not let it eat me alive. I'd seen what had happened to other writers who had undertaken similar projects: the growing reliance on sedatives, the breakdowns, the failed marriages and emptied retirement accounts. But I, like a lot of other people in this country, had also been raging against a culture of intolerance and misogyny that was allowing violence to continue, seemingly unpunished. I'd watched along with everyone else when the #MeToo movement gave voice to so many and also endured its own backlash, even among women. One afternoon, I sat with an elderly family member in her living room as a story about the movement sprawled across her television. *They should just learn to be quiet and take it*, she complained. *That's what I had to do.*

It took her assertion to make me think about just how dangerous it can be to remain quiet. At the time, I had also just published an editorial about my own experience with sexual assault—the first time I had ever made any public mention of it. That decision had strained some of my closest family relationships, but it had also prompted dozens of women to write me and share their own previously untold stories. It had always been clear to me that the Shenandoah case was a complex one, but hearing firsthand from the Annes about the trauma they still carry and the ways in which they felt abandoned by the people sworn to protect them was the first real moment I understood how much of this story still needed to be told. By this point, I'd spent hours interviewing former rangers and nursing pints of beer with some of Julie's and Lollie's closest friends. They all had their own anecdotal grievances and theories about why the case had never been closed and how they felt underserved by the process. Now I was beginning to feel underserved as well. For years, the Annes had quietly questioned how the narrative of the Shenandoah murders had been constructed. They doubted whether everything had truly been done to solve the case—and to keep people like them safe in the meantime. Like a lot of Americans who had followed the story, it had never occurred to me to ask those questions. But once I heard the conviction with which the Annes posed them, I knew I would never rest until I tried to find the answers myself.

BACK AT HOME, I sat down and handwrote a letter to Julie's surviving family, explaining why Julie's story had resonated with me for so long. I told them about the experience of visiting her campsite with the investigators and the raw emotion those individuals clearly still carried. I told the Williams family I wanted to understand who we are in the backcountry and why women continue to be targeted there. And I explained that I wanted their permission before I proceeded. Tom Williams emailed me the same day he received my letter, saying that his initial reaction was that he would be pleased to help but that he first wanted to review some of my published work and talk over the matter with his family. I sent the stories I had written about Gerry Largay and waited to hear back.

After receiving my clippings, Tom wrote back and asked if we could schedule a conference call with him and one of Julie's siblings. It was the first day of Christine Blasey Ford's testimony before Congress regarding her accusations of sexual assault against Supreme Court nominee Brett Kavanaugh, and I was holed up in a Colorado hotel after a speaking engagement the night before. Our call began shortly after the Republican-appointed prosecutor had begun her examination of Ford, and I couldn't breathe as I sat on the edge of the hotel bed, watching this proxy interrogate and critique every aspect of Ford's memory.

Julie had been a sexual assault survivor, a victim of high school date rape, Tom told me. In a lot of ways, hers mirrored my own experience of high school sexual assault. For my part, it had taken several weeks for the physical injuries to heal; the emotional ones lingered far longer. That September morning, as the prosecutor sought to poke holes in Ford's recollections, invalidating her account because of the few details Ford couldn't remember, I was catapulted back to my own imperfect memories. Had we been in his bed or on a sheet he'd lain on the floor? I could no longer say for sure. I wondered how my own story would be critiqued by pundits and how many women were making the choice to remain silent after asking the same questions of their own stories. I thought about both Julie's and Lollie's individual struggles to make sense of their experiences with sexual assault and what the congressional inquiry would mean for narratives like theirs. As we spoke, Tom and his surviving daughter were emphatic that they didn't want Julie's life politicized. I agreed. I told them one of the conditions Tim Alley had made before committing to be a part of the book was that I dedicate a portion of any proceeds to an outdoor organization that would honor the memories of the women. The Williamses agreed that that seemed like the right thing to do.

A week later, I received an email from Julie's mom. She wrote about the advocacy work she has done since Julie's death, particularly surrounding gender and safety on trails. "I would be happy to answer any questions you may have about Julie and to tell you a lot of stories about my spunky girl."

More than anything, I wanted to hear them.

9

THE VIRGINIA OFFICE of the Chief Medical Examiner had released the bodies of Julie and Lollie. Tom Williams couldn't bear the idea of his daughter in the cargo hold of a commercial plane, lying there in the cold and the dark with mail and luggage and whatever else. He chartered a small jet so that he could stay close. He contacted Laura Winans to see if he could deliver Lollie to her as well, but she didn't seem to understand what he was offering; she sounded so far away.

Back in St. Cloud, Tom Williams accompanied Julie's body back to his own funeral home. He and Patsy picked out the casket they thought their daughter would like the best. The whole time, all they could think about was the fact that even after a lifetime career in the funeral industry, they had no idea how to do so much of what was required of them. And while Tom Williams didn't realize it at the time, for the rest of his career he'd stumble each time he entered the showroom of sample caskets, always thinking to himself, *That one is Julie's.*

As the Williams family finalized their funeral arrangements, FBI agents began fanning out up and down the Eastern Seaboard. Joined by park rangers and AT ridge runners, they collected the logs from all the shelters along the trail, leaving the remaining hikers with no way of communicating with one another. The agents posted checkpoints at popular trailheads and road crossings, where they interviewed every backpacker who passed by, ticking through a preset list of questions:

Were you in the Shenandoah area from the nineteenth of May through the first of June?

Did you see two white females and a golden retriever?
Did you talk with them?
What were they wearing?
Where were they?
Were they with anyone?
Did you see anything unusual?

But getting usable information proved nearly impossible. Most hikers knew one another only by their trail names, and those were constantly changing. You might start the trek and give yourself a cute moniker like Amtrak, but after a few nights of leaving your gear all over the shelters, your fellow thru-hikers will rename you Trainwreck or Yard Sale. Sundial can become Sundown halfway up the trail. Some hikers get off the trail for a month and hop back on with a whole new nickname. The ridge runners who tried explaining this to the agents felt like they were illuminating an entirely foreign universe.

NPS and FBI agents also traveled to Vermont and Unity, looking for information and additional suspects. They combed through Lollie's apartment and storage unit. There, they boxed up six cartons of potential evidence: journals and letters, computer disks, photo albums, and bank records. They appeared at the college's administrative offices with subpoenas for her academic files and all medical records, including her meetings with the campus mental health counselor.

While there, they requested yearbooks, copies of the campus newspaper, and class rosters, along with a list of her friends and coworkers. One Unity College student told the agents she had seen Lollie and a male classmate exchanging numbers at the end of the semester. That classmate was added to the growing list of possible suspects. A former faculty member lived in the Shenandoah Valley and sometimes gave rides to students on breaks. He went on the list as well. Lollie's roommate and classmates were shown student directories and asked to mark the names of her closest friends. Those individuals were added to the Rapid Lead file, too.

Eventually, the agents began drilling down on Andrea and Emily, two of a handful of other Unity college students who'd been in Shenandoah at the same time as Lollie and Julie (no evidence has ever linked these two women to the murders; therefore, and although their full identities appear in court and FBI documents, I am only using their first names). According to mutual friends, Lollie and Andrea had had a brief fling shortly after Lollie had moved to Unity. Would that be enough to set off Andrea now that Lollie was in love with someone else? Andrea said no way. But the agents kept at her. They had her backcountry permit: at times, she and Emily had been just a mile or so away from the same route Lollie and Julie had recorded.

Agents tracked down Andrea at her boyfriend's home in Connecticut. In their subsequent report, they noted that Andrea seemed distrustful of law enforcement. That deepened their suspicion. They observed that she did not want to be fingerprinted or photographed. They also recorded the presence of her nose ring, though of what significance they thought that accessory merited, they did not say.

Agents interrogated mutual friends of Lollie and Andrea's for hours, often arriving at the parks and camps and gear stores where those survivors worked. That summer, several of Lollie's friends were raft guides in Maine's western mountains. There, the agents separated the Unity students and interviewed each individually in the backroom of one of the guide companies. Once reunited, the friends all agreed the agents were pitting them against one another, hoping someone would make an accusation. But the real focus of the agents' inquiries, they also agreed, was clearly Andrea. As far as the student guides could glean, the agents thought Andrea had killed the women because she felt rejected by Lollie and jealous of Julie. Even longtime friends began to wonder about her guilt: *I mean, the agents wouldn't have told us they thought it was her if they weren't sure, right?* Factions formed: those who believed the agents; those who trusted Andrea. Tensions rose. Bitter arguments erupted. Even then, the friends knew those rifts would never heal.

In Vermont, FBI agents and Shenandoah law enforcement rangers were focused on Julie's roommate, Derek, and Lollie's onetime fiancé, Ken. They still assumed Julie must have had a sexual relationship with the former—*why else would the two of them be living together?* They also assumed that relationship must have ended badly—*why else would she be moving out?* Mutual friends said, yes, there'd been an argument that spring. Agents began surveilling Derek's home and his movements around town.

But the real focus of the Vermont inquiry was Lollie's former fiancé, Ken. Greg Stiles was right: most women murdered in America are killed by someone known, often someone close, to them. Surely, the agents concluded, that was the case here. And so, with the documents removed from Lollie's storage unit, along with the interviews conducted thus far, they began to piece together a backstory that might prove them right.

SOON AFTER GRADUATING from Sterling College, Lollie met Ken, another alum. He was a decade older and worked as a mason. Everyone thought he was at least as cool as Lollie. He knew where to find the best weed, how to get the best Grateful Dead bootlegs. The two fell hard for each other and soon began sharing a small apartment. In time, he proposed. She said yes. But the relationship was tricky. Lollie confided that she had been repeatedly sexually assaulted and had barely begun to unpack the trauma it had caused, so any kind of sexual intimacy was a struggle. She suffered from endometriosis, which left her anemic and just wanting to stay in bed. That made keeping a job hard, too: she'd last just a few days cleaning hotel rooms at a resort on Lake Champlain, a few weeks pulling weeds on an organic farm, before she was too depleted to continue. By then, Ken was working for Vermont's Department for Children and Families, operating a kind of foster home for kids looking to become independent. The couple agreed to take in a teenage boy, an abuse survivor who'd been in the system for molesting his younger sister. In hindsight, everyone agreed it was a terrible idea. The kid couldn't be left unattended, and he had an explosive temper. Life in the tiny apartment became fraught. Everyone's emotions flared. There wasn't enough space to contain it all.

Ken and Lollie began dividing their time supervising the boy into shifts. Each adult would have a full day off to run errands, take a class, or whatever else they needed to stay on track. Lollie spent part of hers with a therapist. It was her first real foray into counseling; she told Ken and her closest friends that the process terrified her. Together, though, she and her therapist began unpacking her sexual abuse. Lollie was hopeful that the therapy was working, but it was clearly not going fast enough to keep up with all the memories now surging to the surface. She began canceling dates with friends and picking fights with Ken. She told him she couldn't be alone with their charge. When Ken would try to leave for an appointment, Lollie would run outside and park herself in the driver's seat of his car, knowing he'd never break state protocols and leave the boy alone. She'd say later that she knew she was being unreasonable and destructive. She just couldn't stop herself.

Her community of friends worried. They began calling one another, fretting about what to do. One of them worked at the Burlington animal shelter. A litter of ridiculously fluffy Labrador and golden retriever mixes had just been dropped off there, and the friend brought Lollie to see them. As the two women approached the kennel, all the puppies leaped forward, standing up on their tiny paws and begging for attention. All but one—the smallest female. She hung back warily. And that, Lollie said, was how she knew the puppy was her dog.

Lollie agonized over what to name the retriever mix. She and Ken would drive around, listening to the radio, debating names. It all clicked when Taj Mahal came on the public access station. Lollie didn't care that everyone would assume her puppy was a boy. The blues singer had soul. The puppy had soul. It was a perfect fit. And thank God, that puppy had nine lives. Lollie and Ken came home one day and found the dog nearly suffocated, an oatmeal container lodged on her head. Once, Taj was run over by a car; miraculously, the tire missed every major organ. She ate rat poison. After that incident, the vet sent Ken and Lollie home and told them to keep Taj sedated and rotate her every hour so she wouldn't aspirate. Thirty-six hours later, the dog pulled through. Later, the vet told them Taj had had less than a 2 percent chance of making it.

But even with all that new puppy love, Lollie's depression deepened. She called her friend Lyrica, another Sterling alum, one day and told her she was in trouble. Lyrica rushed over. Together, they sat on Lollie's bedroom floor for seven, maybe eight, hours. Lollie told her entire life story in what felt like a single breath. It was the first time she'd ever shared the whole thing like that. *It felt good to get it out*, she said. She and Ken began the difficult process of examining their future. They both agreed they needed some space. Lollie wanted to finish college. She'd been thinking a lot about what she was gaining in therapy. She'd never stopped loving her time in the backcountry and had found a kind of salvation there. Maybe other abuse survivors could, too.

Once she settled on Unity College, Lollie loaded up Taj and her bongos and the few other things she owned. She found a roommate and a place to live. She and Ken had kind of broken up, kind of not. There was a lot of uncertainty that next fall. But somehow, Lollie thrived. Once again, she found her people: jamming with faculty and students at end-of-semester dance parties in the Tavern, completing grueling ten-day wilderness trips in the mountains. Back then, Unity College was a big, messy hippie culture, complete with a 1990s version of free love. No one paid much attention to sexual orientation or norms or anything else. It was a snuggly milieu with friendly stakes and plenty of space to figure out things for yourself. That first fall semester, Lollie and Ken decided they were better friends than lovers, but they still visited and wrote to each other. In one letter, Lollie described her first hookup with a woman. Ken wrote back that he was sincerely glad she'd found a way to make sex feel fun and freeing.

When the FBI agents arrived at his door, Ken told them all of this. The agents were immediately suspicious of his story. For the next several weeks, they surreptitiously shot photos of him entering and exiting vehicles and local stores; they took pictures of his friends and labeled them as "known associates." They knocked on doors around Ken's farmhouse and found and interviewed acquaintances from decades earlier. It was clear to Ken from early on that they were making a case against him. The weekend of May 25, he'd been working on his farm in northern Vermont, planting his enormous vegetable garden. He didn't have much of a confirmable alibi other than visiting his sister for dinner one night. The FBI subpoenaed his phone records, saw that he'd only made one phone call—to a weather hotline. *How did they know he wasn't checking the weather in Shenandoah?* agents challenged.

The FBI asked him to come to Burlington to take a polygraph test. He agreed. And passed it. They asked for hair and saliva samples. He provided those, too. Nothing linked Ken to the crime, but agents kept at him. They said they'd heard he lost his temper and shouted at a friend when a political discussion had gotten heated. *Of course I did*, Ken replied. *The guy was spewing neo-con nonsense.* They said a neighbor saw him at the hardware store with a scratch on his arm. *She's right*, he said. *I spent the weekend pulling brush on my farm.* The agents remained skeptical. And Ken remained one of their top suspects.

Meanwhile, mutual friends learned that Taj was still in Virginia. They called a Unity classmate of Lollie's, who was spending the summer not far from the park. He picked up Taj and drove the dog up to Vermont. When the classmate pulled down the long gravel road leading to Ken's farmhouse, Taj jumped out of his car and walked with cautious, measured steps toward Ken. Once she reached him, she stuck her snout between his legs and stood there for an eternity, just shaking.

"If Taj could have talked, she would have told me everything that had happened to Lollie," says Ken today. "Everything."

PART II

10

SOUTH OF DOWNTOWN MINNEAPOLIS, and not far from the Mall of America, sits a small two-story bungalow decorated in red awnings and faux white stucco. A row of overgrown lilac bushes flowers against one side of the building; a crumbling wooden slat fence protects the other. In between rests a low detached garage and oversize parking area. The surrounding neighborhood blocks contain tidy homes, a brick-faced barber shop, and an old-timey hardware store built a century earlier and still advertising tackle and live bait. Were it not for the exhaust from municipal buses and the constant din of planes flying in and out of the Minneapolis–St. Paul International Airport, you'd think you were in any other corn-fed midwestern town. Today, that red-bedecked bungalow houses a State Farm insurance agency. For nearly two decades, it was the heart of a revolution in the outdoor industry, headquarters for an organization called Woodswomen, Inc.

Woodswomen was founded in 1980 as a place where women could find their own way in the wilderness. Theirs wasn't the only organization to lead women on backcountry trips, but it was one of the first to buck the longstanding masculine model for getting women outside. The paradigm they sought to dismantle was centuries old. Take the history of hiking. In England, the pastime was first known as "pedestrianism," a term coined by the great Romantic walker William Wordsworth, who famously strolled, on average, twenty miles a day and wrote often of the splendor to be had roving past "endless woods / Blue pomp of lakes, high cliffs, and falling floods."

By the dawn of the nineteenth century, he and countless other men of means had converted the simple act of walking into a recreational pursuit deemed worthy of the emerging middle class. These pastoral pedestrians considered themselves "travelers": individuals who made their own way through the world, often off road and over difficult terrain, so as to better suck out the essence of an experience. In that regard, they distinguished themselves from mere "tourists," who were content to be plunked down at a site and offered an organized, distanced experience.

A similar phenomenon was occurring in America. Four years after Thoreau left his cabin at Walden Pond, he spoke before the Concord Lyceum about the virtues and benefits of wilderness rambles. The lecture was published posthumously in 1862 by the *Atlantic* as his now-iconic essay "Walking." In it, he advocates for "absolute freedom and wildness" gained when we see ourselves as a part of nature. For Thoreau, this lived truth was best achieved by a willingness to "saunter," a word he erroneously ascribes to both "a *Sainte Terrer* (one who walks to the holy land) or *Sans Terre* (without a home)." Neither is correct etymologically (according to the authors of the *Oxford English Dictionary*, the word is of "uncertain origin despite many absurd speculations"). But it is true that both of Thoreau's erroneous suppositions make for great metaphor: in the case of the former, the idea is that a woodland saunter, even in one's own backyard, could achieve the same kind of spiritual significance as a religious pilgrimage; in the latter, that the best hikes are those where we proceed as if we have no home or, perhaps more exactly, that we shuffle through the world like a snail or a turtle, with our homes on our backs. This idea comes with an appealing kind of simplicity: that thrift and austerity, even if it is temporary and artificial, can grant us peace and liberty. Sauntering, we are free to walk for days, stopping when and where we choose for a snack or a nap or to set up camp for the night.

Early American devotees referred to this practice as "tramping." The word "hike" didn't appear until the nineteenth century and originally was a colloquialism meaning to make people scarce (as in, *Go take a hike!*). It didn't become a fun verb (as in, *She hiked the trail*) until the twentieth century. As the American tramping craze continued to grow, so too did organizations of like-minded people looking to get outside. Most were white, educated, upper-middle-class men either on the East Coast or in California. The exclusionary nature of this pastime was something Thoreau only briefly acknowledged, lamenting in his essay "Walking": "How womankind, who are confined to the house still more than men, stand it I do not know; but I have grounds to suspect that most of them do not *stand* it at all."

Few wilderness organizations have been as influential as the Appalachian Mountain Club. Founded in 1876 by a group of professors and scientists from Harvard and MIT, the club was headed by Edward Pickering, a noted astronomer and physicist. By the tony standards of Cambridge, he was also revolutionary in his gender egalitarianism: his Harvard observatory was peopled by women skilled in computation and data collection (not unlike NASA's famous "hidden figures"—though it's worth noting that the females in Pickering's observatory were widely known as "Pickering's Harem," a sobriquet he purportedly enjoyed a great deal). To Pickering's credit, the Appalachian Mountain Club did admit some women from its inception. But that allowance tells only part of the story. Of the 217 members that first year, only forty-four were women (and nearly half of those were enrolled as the wives of male members). The female members included in these early years played next to no role in the governance or administration of the organization, nor were many of them present on most of the club's rugged outings.

In 1884, Edward H. Clarke, a physician and one of Pickering's Harvard colleagues, published *Sex and Education*. In this book, Clarke maintained that both physical and educational exertion came with a heavy price for women, including, but not limited to, uterine disease, hysteria, chorea (an involuntary movement disorder), increased menstrual cramps and hemorrhaging, along with "a dropping out of maternal instincts, and an appearance of Amazonian coarseness and force." For that reason alone, Clarke contended that women should be kept inside.

His reasoning was twofold. First, from a physiological perspective, Clarke—whose medical specialty was in hearing disorders and the physiology of the ear—argued that women have wider pelvises, which when mounted with the weight of the body cause their thighs to splay out, making standing and walking more difficult (and thus more taxing) than it is for men. Second, he maintained that the development of a woman's ovaries and uterus, particularly during her teens and twenties, was such an exhausting physical feat unto itself that the body could not tolerate any additional stress, particularly when it came to exercise and "outdoor pursuits." As a result, Clarke advocated fewer physical and intellectual demands for women overall and total bed rest during the weeks of their periods. A failure to do so, he concluded, would undoubtedly cause a woman to lose "her feminine attractions, and probably also her chief feminine functions."

It's tempting to turn Clarke into a caricature or intellectual straw man: an easy grab in an attempt to show the ridiculous sexism inherent in Victorian ideology. Nevertheless, his theories became pervasive in American thought and defined expectations about access to wilderness for generations. Multiple outdoor organizations prohibited female membership, for example, including the influential hiking group the White Mountain Club. The club's founder, John M. Gould, was a bank clerk and amateur Civil War historian. In his *How to Camp Out*, first published in 1877, Gould advised young men to view their expeditions as regimental exercises: hikes were best considered "marches"; male camping pals were instructed to form "companies" with clear duties and timetables. Most marches, he warned, would be too difficult for ladies, particularly if routes included loose rocks or tangles of low-growing trees. And because women ought not stray far from home, sites where they might camp must be chosen accordingly. Any overnight locations should be such that stoves could be delivered to make women more comfortable, along with discarded doors that women could stand upon while dressing. Sleeping outside was out of the question during any kind of precipitation; instead, schoolhouses or sawmills should be located as shelter.

By the dawn of the twentieth century, in both Britain and America, wilderness education had become based almost solely on this military training model. Take the founding of the Boy Scouts. Upon returning from the

Boer War, Colonel Robert Baden-Powell was dismayed to find what he saw as a "lack of virility" among Britain's youth. In his proposal for the Scouts, Baden-Powell suggested a program harkening back to Europe's chivalric knights and the ancient Samurai. He studied the Boys Brigade, a youth group that used military training to teach muscular Christianity, along with the Sons of Daniel Boone, an American-based group that encouraged boys to wear buckskin and always carry guns (on which they would notch their achievements toward what one contemporary social critic called "nativism and masculinity").

James West, the Boy Scouts' first chief executive, was emphatic that the Scouts and their camps remain the exclusive domain of males—a place for the kind of rugged masculinity Teddy Roosevelt espoused. And while West acknowledged that girls' camps were also beginning to burgeon, he insisted that they remain wholly separate from male organizations. (While serving as the head of a national organization of camp directors, he also famously insisted that any director of a girl's camp, regardless of that director's gender, not be allowed admittance into his professional organization.)

The discourse and metaphors surrounding outdoor recreation followed suit. Military-inspired language like "attacking" the trail, "conquering" a mountain, and "hitting" a section of rapids became commonplace. After World War II, members of the army's elite Tenth Mountain Division returned home with synthetic fibers, freeze-dried foods, and professional skills in pursuits ranging from rappelling and ice climbing to downhill skiing and slack packing. With their expertise and advocacy, outdoor recreation exploded. So too did organizations like the National Outdoor Leadership School, founded by Tenth Mountain veteran Paul Petzoldt. Shortly thereafter, fellow veteran Earl Shaffer became the first person to thru-hike the entire twenty-two-hundred-mile AT, claiming he did so to "walk the war out of my system." Thousands of Americans would follow him, along with the likes of David Brower, who founded the Sierra Club and published the widely read *Manual of Ski Mountaineering*, based on his service in the Tenth. In England, Outward Bound was founded by

German foreign affairs veteran Kurt Hahn to train young British seamen in survival skills and the stiff upper lip that comes with challenges to one's personal safety. Its model soon became the gold standard for all outdoor recreation programs.

In 1965, Outward Bound first experimented with allowing women into its courses. And even then, the decision was not without great internal controversy: "There was a strong feeling at the time among those valuing and cultivating Outward Bound's machismo image that the success of women in similar experiences would diminish that image," wrote Bob Pieh, founder of the Voyageur Outward Bound School, which hosted the first female class. Specifically, recalls Pieh, the concern within the organization was that Outward Bound would become defined by what he called "Amazon syndrome": namely, that Outward Bound would begin attracting stereotypically butch staff and female participants.

Despite these misplaced and reductive concerns, early female participants in the Outward Bound programs excelled, and individuals identifying across a wide spectrum of femininity participated. However, it is also true that many of these participants found the pedagogical approach of the program problematic. The Outward Bound model has long been based on a curriculum of increased risk: over the course of a session, which can span anywhere from hours to weeks, participants found themselves in activities that cause more and more stress (like advancing from trust falls to rappelling, for instance). The idea was that as participants' perception of risk and stress increases, so too would their sense of accomplishment. As those psychological states increased, participants were expected to practice emotional stoicism and the same conquering attitudes present in the early military-based programs.

Along with this almost-authoritarian approach, women interested in wilderness pursuits also faced a proliferation of sexually charged names for climbing and paddling routes, such as the ones encountered by my students at Unity (Throbbing Labias, Gang Bang, One Last Bitch), as well as continued and pervasive instances of sexual harassment. This resulted in a culture that proved, at best, exclusionary for individuals identifying as female, nonbinary, or queer, not to mention people of color who also often experience additional barriers to their well-being in the wilderness.

Woodswomen was founded as a corrective to that experience. The program's mission was one of fostering relationships and individual growth for women and girls by valuing holistic wellness, safety, and personal choice. Trips had leaders, but decisions were made collectively. Group process was paramount—whether it meant deciding who chops onions and washes dishes at camp or whether or not to portage a tricky rapid. For a lot of participants, a Woodswomen expedition was their first time camping in the wilderness. Ensuring it was a safe, positive, and affirming experience was a major priority.

Woodswomen is also where Julie and Lollie first met.

Denise Mitten was one of Woodswomen's founders and also served as the longtime director of the organization. She has since become one of the world's leaders in education and scholarship dedicated to gender and outdoor leadership. In the weeks before my first visit to the surviving family and friends of Julie and Lollie, I contacted Mitten. I wanted to know what Lollie and Julie had been taught about wilderness practices during their time at Woodswomen and, of course, more about who they were and how they fell in love. I also wanted to understand the impact of their deaths on the outdoor industry. Mitten and I talked on the phone for multiple hours over the course of several days. She spoke at length about the pressures and harassment encountered by women, gay, and nonbinary people in the field of outdoor recreation during the 1970s and 1980s.

"On mainstream wilderness trips, there was this pervasive sense of entitlement among guides that it was their right to sleep with some female clients and harass or belittle others. A lot of participants signed up looking for reparative experiences, and theirs were anything but," Mitten told me. "Woodswomen wanted to change the whole idea that we're out there to conquer and prove something. Instead, we just wanted clients to be in nature in the most positive sense. So many women are taught that if you could just change this or clean up that, you'll fit in. We wanted them to believe they were fine the way they were."

After our first marathon phone call, Mitten sent me on a guided tour of former Woodswomen expedition sites. They included Bde Maka Ska (formerly Lake Calhoun), a four-hundred-acre lake in the middle of Minneapolis, where Woodswomen hosted fishing events for women and kids, and county parks where they taught female correctional inmates to camp. The photos she also sent along, mostly from the 1980s, showed barefoot girls of many races and ethnicities netting minnows and being hoisted onto trip leaders' shoulders so that they could erect tent poles. Even after all these years, I felt a pang of envy looking at those images. As a child of that era, I had longed for those kinds of opportunities. For many of us, they were few and far between.

And for no small number of people, they still are. Continued scholarly research reveals just how many women, queer or nonbinary individuals, and people of color perceive very real barriers to their participation in wilderness activities. Recent survey participants list a variety of reasons for these barriers, including outdoor recreation's continued emphasis on physical strength and technical expertise, sexist and exclusionary programming, and a fear for one's personal safety while in the wilderness. A recent study of advertisements in outdoor magazines found that while women were present in 46 percent of ads, the majority of them appeared in passive roles, such as sitting around a fire with friends or holding outdoor gear rather than using it. Only the smallest percentage of these women were depicted alone and actively engaged in any kind of athletic pursuit while in the wilderness. Of all the women in the ads, a full 91 percent were white. No known trans or nonbinary models were used.

After we first spoke, Mitten also sent a large Priority Mail box filled with newsletters published by Woodswomen during the 1990s. By the spring of 1995, the place was clearly humming. Show up on any given day and you'd find clotheslines drooping with orange life jackets and wet gear draped from canoes and half-gorged trailers in the parking area. The front desk was staffed with recent college grads, cheerfully answering questions about accommodating dietary restrictions and sending welcoming letters to women who wanted more information about their first big adventure.

In the back kitchen, trip leaders would be stuffing bags with oatmeal and lentils.

The trips themselves were grueling by any standard, whether participants were climbing Denali or paddling the Boundary Waters. But they were also supposed to be nurturing—to show participants they didn't need to prove anything; that they truly were already great just the way they were. And that was no platitude. Instead, it was born out of experience, from cooking pancakes and chicken enchiladas in a collective backcountry camp kitchen, to setting up tents and planning the day's route with topographical maps and compasses. Along the way, participants would take moments to debrief about the day's highs and lows and what those moments sparked emotionally and psychologically.

The women who signed up for these trips were evangelical grandmothers and tattooed astrologers, rising executives and stay-at-home moms. Former guides estimate that a quarter of the clients, maybe as many as half, were gay. But even at Woodswomen, people treaded carefully around issues of sexuality. This was the Midwest in the 1990s, after all. "The outdoor world was still so much in the closet," one former trip leader told me. "It was hard to be open even at Woodswomen. We were on the cutting edge at the time, but the cutting edge was not all that progressive."

JULIE WILLIAMS FIRST arrived at Woodswomen in early May 1995, having registered for a canoe skills course. After a lifetime paddling with her dad, she was already proficient in a boat. Now twenty-three years old, she wanted to become an expert. She wanted to see if she had it in her to be an outdoor leader, too. A year earlier, she had graduated from Carleton with a degree in geology. After commencement, she drove cross-country, swung through California, and spent time with Derek and some other friends in Washington State. Eventually, she landed at Big Bend National Park in southwestern Texas. One of our nation's most remote national parks, Big Bend's own website, created by the NPS, describes the place as "splendid isolation," "at the end of the end of the road," and "weather-beaten desert"—and that's all in the one paragraph intended to lure visitors.

Despite the austerity, Julie loved it. While at Big Bend, she worked as a Student Conservation Association intern, mostly issuing backcountry permits, selecting rock samples for interpretive displays, and answering the same questions from guests over and over again. Her supervisors called her competent and quiet. They appreciated her interest in the park, the way she was always trying to learn everything about it.

Interns tend to get the worst of national park housing. At Big Bend, that meant ramshackle, mouse-infested doublewide trailers that probably should have been condemned years earlier. Julie shared hers with two roommates. She was convinced her room was haunted: she claimed an old chest cooler someone had left there was always moving around on its own. She tried smudging the place with burning sage to chase away unwelcome spirits. She lined makeshift shelves with her CD collection— all Tracy Chapman and Ani DiFranco and old, old folk singers like the Weavers and Kingston Trio. At night, she'd pull out her guitar and *Rise Up Singing* songbook. She and her roommates would belt out "Puff the Magic Dragon" and "This Land Is Your Land" without a hint of irony. When someone forgot to clean the kitchen sponge, she'd leave a funny poem reminding them. Some weekends, they'd all hike the remotest trails in the park. But Julie also relished her solitude. She'd take off on her own, spending a day at the local church or handing out food to homeless people or camping alone deep in the desert. That worried her roommates. They thought she could be too trusting, too quick to find goodness in people.

While Julie was at Big Bend, she began dating another park employee. Her roommates never really knew anything about him—he didn't come around, and Julie admitted that she felt conflicted about the whole relationship anyway. It always seemed like she would rather hang out with her roommates, visiting ghost towns or driving into Terlingua to hear cowboy music. At night, they'd venture out into the big, expansive desert, where it looked like a gazillion stars were about to rain down. They'd open up all the doors on her 4Runner and blast the car's lousy stereo. The Indigo Girls' "Galileo" was their favorite.

Her last night working at Big Bend, on her way out of the park, Julie stopped and played the song one last time. She was so busy singing, she forgot she'd left open the back hatch of the SUV. And so, as she drove out of the park, she left a plume of flying CDs and sheet music in her wake. By the time she realized what had happened, she was well on her way back to Minnesota. And all she could do was laugh at the image of massive RVs driving over and smashing her most beloved music.

At Woodswomen, Julie's trip guides fell in love with her at once. She was just so beautiful, with a personality to match. She wore ridiculous floppy hats that tied underneath her chin, along with old-lady pants and four layers of fleece pullovers, and she couldn't care less what she looked like. Although initially quite shy, as soon as Julie felt comfortable she opened up with an effervescent cheerfulness and lovably corny sense of humor. She was also clearly brilliant. At the end of the canoe skills trip, Julie confided to one of her group leaders that she wanted to come back and train as a guide. That surprised the veteran leader—Julie had been so quiet the entire trip. *God,* thought the guide. *This girl is going to have to learn how to talk.* But Julie's skills were undeniably stellar, and she just seemed to appeal to everyone. Mitten and her staff invited Julie back for a leadership course later that month.

In the meantime, Julie began hanging out with some of the Woodswomen employees. They'd meet up periodically at the few lesbian bars in Minneapolis, and Julie brought a girlfriend once or twice. The Woodswomen didn't care for this new addition—she seemed so urban, so into the club scene. They never said as much, but Julie came to agree. By the time she returned for the leadership course, she was once again single.

The course itself was unexpectedly traumatic. One of the participants, a registered nurse, broke her water filter on the first day. Rather than tell anyone, she instead made the decision to stop drinking water. By the third day, the nurse had gone into hypovolemic shock, a life-threatening condition that causes excessive vomiting and diarrhea and can also lead to organ failure. Julie and the lead guide tended to the failing nurse in her tent. Every half hour, they forced her to drink salt water or sugar water in a frantic attempt to keep her alive.

"It was the worst night of my life," recalls the guide now. "At least, it was the worst night until the night I learned that Julie and Lollie had died."

But, adds the guide, that first trip was also galvanizing. By the time they returned to Minneapolis, she and Julie had become friends for life. "You couldn't help but meet Julie and instantly bond with her on some spiritual level. She just embodied that."

Julie's calm head and paddling acumen on that trip earned her a role as an assistant guide back at Woodswomen. She spent the late spring of 1995 apprenticed to senior leaders on wilderness trips and helping with program logistics.

As soon as the school year ended, Lollie arrived to complete an internship as part of her academic requirements at Unity College. To the junior staff, Lollie, who was then twenty-five years old, appeared a rogue enigma: she smoked; she swore like a sailor; she just seemed so hard and tough. To the senior staff, she was immediately reliable: hardworking and so incredibly dedicated. She wanted to help everyone, and clients just naturally opened up to her, in part because she was so preternaturally tuned into whatever they seemed to need. After a year at Unity, Lollie also now had outdoor skills in spades. And the worse the conditions were outside, the more she seemed to come alive. If anyone could embrace the suck, it was Lollie.

Shortly after starting at Woodswomen, Lollie joined a seven-day advanced canoeing course on the Boundary Waters. Julie was working the trip as a support guide. They both returned glowing. A few weeks later, Lollie cornered a fellow employee named Kristin in the basement of Woodswomen. The two were the same age, but Kristin was a head guide. Julie was slated to support her as an assistant on an upcoming Northern Lakes canoe trip. *I just want to talk to you about Julie*, Lollie said in the basement that day. Kristin smiled, assuming that she was about to be let in on a secret: by that point, it was so clear to the younger staff that Lollie and Julie were enamored with each other. But Lollie had a very different objective in mind. She demanded to know Kristin's intentions and wanted assurances that Kristin wasn't going to try anything in a tent with Julie. It was all Kristin could do not to laugh. *I mean, here was Lollie in her long hair and pinstripe conductor's hat, acting like a 1950s biker guy laying claim to his woman*, she says now.

But that, everyone now agrees, was just how freaked out Lollie was by the fierce feelings she had for Julie. They'd both fallen so hard, so fast. And everyone could see it, the way the two of them beamed at each other and the secret language they already seemed to share. Over the next few weeks, Lollie mellowed out and seemed more comfortable with these new emotions. She wrote letters to her friends back at Unity, reporting that she was in love. For her part, Julie seemed to float around the bungalow, clearly enthralled. And everyone at Woodswomen couldn't help but think they were watching two people who'd really found each other.

"You just knew you were watching true love unfold," one guide told me. "Like, these were two people who had just found the loves of their lives. And they knew it."

Woodswomen was the perfect environment for big love. Everyone was super fit, super active. The women would depart for expeditions in places as far flung as the Galápagos and Ireland and return exhausted and starving and on a constant outdoor high that magnified every feeling, whether they were repairing gear in the yard or saying goodbye to clients. They'd lead trips for incarcerated women and come back gushing about hope and redemption. The collective Woodswomen community remained a tight one: long after trips had debriefed, participants would return to say hi. They'd post activity personals in the Woodswomen newsletter, creating social circles for female climbers or hikers or cyclists back in their hometowns. It was, by all accounts, the best kind of community.

"You look awesome, you feel awesome, and so does everyone around you," one guide told me. "You're having the time of your life and so is everyone else. Even being madly in love gets magnified out in the field."

As the summer of 1995 drew to a close, Julie and Lollie began to confront the reality of life outside Woodswomen. Would they continue their relationship? And who were they to each other, anyway? A committed couple? Two young women who hooked up for a summer? They wanted to believe they were the real thing. But they had no idea how to be together beyond the safety of those summer trips. Nevertheless, they committed to making it work.

On the last night of the season, Lollie and Julie joined some of the younger guides for one last barbecue. The party ran late into the night, and the pair was among the last to leave. As they hung out with Kristin over one last beer, Lollie told her they were planning a backpacking trip on the AT the next summer. She and Julie wanted Kristin to come along. *She'd always wanted to go*, Kristin told them. But she'd also been afraid. A female friend of hers had tried to become a ranger and very quickly decided national parks weren't a good place to be a gay woman. Maybe the trail wasn't either. *No way*, said Lollie. *It's exactly where we should be.*

11

Wednesday, June 5, 1996
5:00 p.m.

THE IMPACT OF Julie and Lollie's murder on the Woodswomen community was as immediate as it was profound. Liz was one of the senior leaders then. She and a group of clients had just wrapped up a ten-day trip on the Boundary Waters the day news of the murders broke nationwide. Still in a media blackout, the trip participants had loaded up their van and canoe trailers and were making the long drive back to Minneapolis. About an hour outside the city, Liz pulled into a rest stop to check in with Woodswomen headquarters and report on her ETA. Denise Mitten answered the phone.

I need to tell you something awful, the director said, *before your group sees it in the newspapers.*

After Liz hung up the phone, she walked back to the van as slowly as she could, trying to figure out how to tell the nine women inside what had happened. None of the participants had met Julie and Lollie, but they were still horrified. If you were part of Woodswomen, you were family, and any loss to that family was a tragic one. The trip participants spent the remainder of the drive reflecting on that. *It just as easily could have been us*, one of the participants observed out loud. The others agreed.

Back at the bungalow, the phones hadn't stopped ringing. News crews were stationed around the block. As word of the double homicide spread, so too did speculation about the true nature of Lollie and Julie's relationship.

Denise Mitten instructed her staff to funnel all media inquiries to her directly.

"I very quickly decided their personal lives didn't matter," she says now. "There were weeks and months to address the nature of their relationship. What mattered then and there was grieving these two remarkable people."

No matter what was asked by the media, Denise stuck to the basics: Yes, Lollie and Julie had been employed at Woodswomen the previous season. She extolled their skills as leaders, their proficiency in the backcountry, their utter competence and grace. No matter the query, she refused to deviate from that script. Internally, the staff agreed: *It was not their place to out them. Not theirs or anyone else's.* They never wavered. Instead, they hung black bunting outside the headquarters and worked on contacting the remaining guides out in the field. They cried a lot, sometimes collapsing into one another's arms.

The women also had long, impassioned discussions about what to do with the trips still scheduled to depart. By then, Kristin had left Woodswomen and was living with her partner in New Mexico. Denise phoned her there, asking if the guide would pinch-hit on an upcoming trip to the Boundary Waters.

"I ran from it. I kept saying no," says Kristin now. "I would literally have nightmares and be crippled at the thought of going back to the places we had shared together. It's impossible to describe how shaken you are when that kind of violence happens to people close to you—especially when it happens doing what you love."

NEARLY SEVEN HUNDRED miles from the Woodswomen headquarters, Laura Winans was making preparations to bury her daughter at the Ford family plot in Grosse Pointe, Michigan. By then, Wilson Hess had left his position as dean at Sterling College and become the president at Unity. He phoned Laura Winans personally to see what she needed. She asked if he could help retrieve Lollie's car from Julie's Vermont apartment. She also invited him to attend the funeral.

Hess and a caravan of Unity students left the campus first thing on Thursday, June 6. Wilson was driving one of the college's large fifteen-person vans, and it was filled with grieving students. A few cars packed with more of Lollie's friends streamed behind. They drove the six-teen hours to Grosse Pointe straight through: *We shotgunned it*, Hess says now. When they pulled up to the Wingford estate, says Hess, the students were like, *Holy Jesus. We had no idea.*

"They were fabulous in a way only Unity students can be," he says now. "They'd worn their cleanest flannel shirts. Some had even tucked them in." Laura, he says, wrapped her arms around all of them. "They were something of Lollie's she could hold. That meant an awful lot to Laura. And that meant a lot to the students as well."

Lollie's Vermont friends weren't so moved by their experience at Grosse Pointe. They objected to the formal funeral mass at the fancy Episcopal church; they hated that Lollie had been cremated and interred in the fam-ily plot, her tiny tombstone shadowed by the massive Ford crypt. *That was the last thing she would have wanted*, they all agree now. *This was no way to say goodbye to her.* At the reception following the internment, they began strategizing a proper wake—one with a funky band and a bonfire and dancing in a field and a potluck supper with lots of microbrews. They left Wingford, still making plans for the party. And no one—not the Winans family, not her friends from Vermont, not the Unity contingent—knew it at the time, but the FBI was carefully recording each license plate, shoot-ing photos of everyone entering and exiting Lollie's funeral, looking for the person who had killed her.

AGENTS WERE ALSO surveilling the multiple memorials for Julie in St. Cloud, where more than nine hundred people packed into St. Paul's Catholic Church for the service that Friday, June 7. Tom and Patsy had planned every detail themselves. The tombstone proved particularly pain-ful. What do you do when you don't even know when your loved one died? Instead of a date, they settled on an etching of a forested mountain scene and a passage by the fin de siècle Presbyterian clergyman, Henry van Dyke:

Be glad of life because it gives you the chance to love and to work and to play and to look up at the stars; to be satisfied with your possessions but not content with yourself until you have made the best of them; to despise nothing in the world except falsehood and meanness, and to fear nothing except cowardice; to be governed by your admirations rather than by your disgusts; to covet nothing that is your neighbor's except his kindness of heart and gentleness of manners; to think seldom of your enemies, often of your friends, and every day of Christ; and to spend as much time as you can, with body and spirit in God's out-of-doors. These are little guide paths to peace.

The Williamses had invited family members and some of Julie's closest friends for a private reception to be held in the hours leading up to the funeral. They were just wrapping up when Tom's brother appeared with the morning's newspaper. According to that day's top news story, Rebecca Strader, a Presbyterian pastor in Burlington, Vermont, had contacted the National Gay and Lesbian Task Force. She said she had reason to believe Julie was killed for her sexuality and that Lollie and Julie had been targeted because they were a lesbian couple. In response, the task force had penned a formal letter to Attorney General Janet Reno, demanding that she treat this double murder as a hate crime. They'd also sent the letter to multiple media outlets. It seemed like every major newspaper had picked up the story: "We are asking for your help to ensure that the FBI and the National Park Service are diligent in investigating all aspects of the crime, including the possibility that the murders were motivated by anti-lesbian bias," Melinda Paras, director of the task force, had written in her letter. That quote, along with several from Strader, had been reprinted in the wire service stories that outed Julie and Lollie that morning.

Tom's brother pulled Tom and Patsy aside and showed them the article.

"We didn't know what to think," Tom told me when we first met in person. "It wasn't that we cared whether or not Julie was gay; we just didn't

want her personal life made public—especially on the day we were bury-
ing our beautiful girl."

The three of us were sitting in the conference room of a Holiday
Inn at the Minneapolis–St. Paul International Airport on Mother's Day
weekend, 2018. After multiple phone conversations over six months, we
agreed we should meet in person. Patsy suggested it might be easier to
do so in a neutral space. The Holiday Inn conference room seemed like
the most convenient option for all of us. When we arrived, the hotel was
packed, and we seemed to be the only three people there not associated
with a regional youth hockey tournament. Tom and I recognized each
other as we waited in line at a lobby coffee kiosk. Two decades had passed
since he'd been photographed at press conferences and memorials, but
he still had the same dimpled chin and round cheeks he and Julie had
always shared. Later, as we sorted out our seats at a massive conference
table, the Williamses apologized, explaining their marriage had been in
trouble before Julie was killed. They separated not long afterward and
eventually divorced. Since then, they hadn't spent much time sitting at
the same table.

Patsy was soft spoken and petite, her hair now gray and her eyes damp
behind thick glasses. She had brought with her Julie's baby books and
photo albums, along with tributes sent to her after Julie's death. We flipped
through each of them, stopping to sigh and coo at Julie's baby pictures or
to laugh at Halloween costumes and awkward holiday photos. Julie and I
were just two years apart and had grown up in remarkably similar midwestern communities. In so many ways, flipping through those books was
like looking at my own childhood: First Communions, backyard fish fries,
snowy Easter egg hunts.

Patsy talked proudly of Julie's inner life and fierceness of spirit: about
how, when Julie felt strongly about something, she never backed down.
"Also," said Patsy, "she could be so, so funny."

Tom spoke about the experience of flying down to Shenandoah in the
days after his daughter's body was found.

"I wanted to see the place where she spent her final moments," he said. "That was important to me."

He also talked about the unexpected awkwardness of first walking down the trail with the ranger who patrolled that area of the park at the time. They were both so emotional, Tom recollected, and neither knew what to say or how to comfort one another.

"But I could immediately see the beauty of that spot," Tom told me. "I got right away why Julie wanted to be there."

With his brother's help, Williams spent that afternoon collecting rhododendron blossoms and mountain laurel for the wreath they would place atop Julie's casket. They sat near the place where her body was found, hoping for some sense of her presence. After a while, he clambered down the bank, cupped his hands, and drank from the stream.

"I wanted something tangible about her spirit to take with me," he explained to me, fighting back tears.

He also recalled that later that same day at the park, Peter Groh, the lead FBI agent on the case, briefed Tom on what the agency knew so far. Williams remembers Groh's saying, *If we don't catch this guy running down the street tomorrow, you're going to need to settle in for a long haul.* At the time, Tom was too stunned to really think about what that might mean for him and his family.

The real shock, he and Patsy agreed, was the national fervor surrounding Julie's relationship with Lollie. Both said they had a pretty good idea Julie and Lollie were more than friends: halfway through the summer of 1995, Julie had moved into the condo Laura Winans had bought for Lollie. And Julie talked about Lollie constantly and was always inviting her up to the family summer place. That season, Lollie and Tom were the only ones at the Williamses summer cabin who smoked, so they spent a fair amount of time together on the back deck, making idle conversation in between drags. But, said Patsy at our conference table, even though they may have suspected a relationship, she also knew her daughter was intensely private and would tell her family if and when she was ready. And that, her parents agreed, was absolutely fine with them.

Both the timing and the ubiquity of the news story outing the women as a couple was deeply upsetting to the family, the Williamses told me. "We were literally walking into her funeral when Julie's romantic and sexual life became front-page news," said Tom. After the funeral mass, they called a family meeting and asked her closest friends to join. The gathering was uncomfortable for everyone. A few friends knew about Julie's relationship and that she and Lollie were in love. They never imagined that this was how her family would find out.

"Julie's friends indicated it was something they knew we were unaware of," Tom told me in the conference room. "She had been telling and testing others. We learned we would probably be the last to learn."

"We just can't comprehend that we would have felt any differently about her," added Patsy. "What difference would her orientation have made to us?"

Julie was born on September 11. To commemorate the first birthday after her death, the Williams family planned to visit her campsite at Shenandoah and to hold a press conference. By then, investigators had ruled out all good leads, and the three-month-old case was threatening to grow cold. The NPS was also under increased scrutiny for its handling of the murder. After a bill to amend the National Park Foundation Act appeared before the US Senate Committee on Energy and Natural Resources that same season, multiple high-ranking congresspeople used Shenandoah's handling of the crime as an opportunity to call out the NPS for its missteps in the case.

"Can you tell us why the public could not have been informed more quickly?" asked Senator Frank Murkowski, chair of the Subcommittee on Parks, Historic Preservation, and Recreation at a subsequent hearing. "My concern is obvious. We do not want to scare people, but it seems to me if you have people hiking and camping in the area, they should be told as soon as possible that there is a potential danger lurking." Roger Kennedy, the NPS director, pushed back. "Obviously, neither you nor I want to say anything that would impede or make difficult an investigation," he began. "This is not a nonviolent society. Terrible things happen, but you are safe in the parks and that is not getting worse."

Murkowski was joined in his anger by other senators who demanded that the Department of the Interior take immediate action to improve confidence in the park service. But for both the Williamses and the rangers still investigating the murder, the congressional machinations felt too much like grand political posturing, which did nothing to soothe their grief or help close their case. Besides, there were more pressing problems. The already cash-strapped park had depleted its budget working on the case, having spent nearly five hundred thousand dollars on overtime hours alone. Administrators made a rushed application for emergency law-and-order funding and openly fretted about how they would fund the investigation in the meantime. Most of the reassigned staff from other parks had returned to their regular duties. Meanwhile, Shenandoah law enforcement rangers had just received word that Randall Smith, who had pled guilty to the 1981 AT murders of Robert Mountford Jr. and Laura Susan Ramsay in Virginia's Washington and Jefferson National Forest, was about to be released from prison. "It's safe to assume that Mr. Smith will not be returning to the Appalachian Trail," one corrections official promised the media. Few of the rangers up at Shenandoah believed him. And with just that one dedicated NPS ranger for the entire twenty-two-hundred-mile footpath, law enforcement officers at the park knew policing Smith, should that be required, could fall squarely on them.

Around that same time, James Snyder, a twenty-seven-year-old navy veteran and foreign service officer with a top-secret clearance, had gone missing from the parking lot at the Skyland lodge and hadn't been seen for days. Already frayed nerves crumbled further. Seasonal rangers were diverted to mount searches for the missing man. Snyder, they soon learned, had been in the process of applying for a position at the CIA.

During a requisite polygraph test with the FBI, he was asked if he had ever divulged classified information while working overseas. He said no. The polygraph indicated he was lying. His family worried he had taken his own life as a result.

Rangers were in their second full week of searching for Snyder when Hurricane Fran barreled down on the region. The storm, a category 3 when it made landfall near Cape Fear, North Carolina, quickly moved inland, bringing with it driving wind, storm surge, and rain. Over a foot of rain fell on Shenandoah, washing out Skyline Drive. It knocked down thousands of trees throughout the park, clogging streams and trails with debris. By the time Fran marched northward, now downgraded to a tropical storm, damage in the park was extensive. Senior administrators made the decision to close Shenandoah entirely. That also meant postponing the small memorial Tom and Patsy Williams had planned for Julie's birthday. In anticipation of the originally scheduled event, the FBI had installed video surveillance around Skyland and the Bridle Trail, with the hopes that whoever had murdered the women might also return. The storm took out much of that equipment. As maintenance crews struggled to clear Skyline Drive and several of the park's most popular trails after the storm, Richmond FBI agents returned as well, ready to record anyone who walked down the Bridle Path. Anyone who did would have seen a radically different patch of land. Downed oaks, still heavy with autumn foliage, barricaded entire sections of trail. The small open area where Lollie and Julie had pitched their tent was a tangle of fallen limbs and saplings. It was almost unrecognizable. But there, near the stream, the Williamses found the circle of stones left by one of Julie's friends—one for each of the dozens of places she'd visited in her short life. Tom and Patsy sat next to the circle of stones for a long time.

At the press conference they'd rescheduled for the week after Julie's birthday, Tom and Patsy told reporters they were glad they had returned.

"We want to continue to feel her presence in some way, to gain some sense of what she may have been thinking and feeling," Patsy told reporters.

"We know that she died in a place where she was enjoying herself, doing what she loved the most."

They stood behind a lectern, flanked on either side by posterboard collages decorated with photos of Julie—at the family cabin, portaging a canoe, studying for exams. Tom choked back tears and said the only birthday gift he could still give his daughter would be to find the person who murdered her and Lollie.

"Finding their killer can provide us and all those who mourn their deaths some sense of peace and help with our grief," he said that day. "Finding their killer also will help return to the woods some semblance of safety and tranquility for everyone who enjoys the beauty of the outdoors."

Park administrators and FBI officials were also on hand to answer questions. Reporters asked them to concede that they had deliberately withheld information about the murders in the days immediately after they found the campsite. The park employees grew defensive. Assistant superintendent Stiles kept to his original story, which was that investigators had initially been certain they were dealing with a suicide. The *Washington Blade* reported on the subsequent exchange: "One [reporter] asked Stiles incredulously, 'You weren't sure it was a homicide . . . with their wrists bound?' 'And their throats slashed?' chimed in another reporter. 'That is correct,' said Stiles. 'That baffles the mind,' observed a third reporter."

Stiles assured the media that in the months since the crime the NPS and Richmond FBI field office had exhausted every lead and ruled out every suspect. They had also worked with the FBI's Behavioral Science Unit to construct a profile of the killer. The subsequent report concluded that the murder of Julie Williams and Lollie Winans was a sexually motived crime perpetrated by one offender, acting alone. That offender, the report's authors surmised, had previously demonstrated behavior consistent with sexual offenders. Most likely, the assailant saw the attack on Lollie and Julie as an opportunity to act out a personal fantasy that linked physical aggression with sexuality. The report also stated that based on the crime scene and evidence collected so far, the offender had preselected Julie and Lollie as his victims. He'd conducted scrupulous planning to ensure that the crime unfolded based on his fantasy and with minimal risk of being discovered. Probably, the report concluded, he'd been traveling with a murder kit for some time, mostly likely in his vehicle. He was probably a prolific consumer of violent pornography. He liked to keep tokens from his crimes—personal items like underwear, jewelry, or wallets—to enhance his sexual fantasies after the crime. He also probably retained records of the crime, including his written plans, photographs or drawings, and newspaper clippings, which he would keep hidden and stored in a way that provided both security and ready access.

12

TOO SMALL TO BE CONSIDERED A TOWN, Lignum, Virginia, is designated as an unincorporated community on state records and federal census reports. In 1996, its approximately four hundred residents lived mostly on farms and sprawling rural acreage about thirty miles from Shenandoah National Park and ten miles from neighboring Culpeper. With little infrastructure of its own, Lignum residents gathered together either at one of the community's two churches or at the small gray post office, the only secular public building in the area. Thelma Scroggins, seventy-four, was the village's longtime mail carrier. She was also the Baptist church's only organist. On the morning of July 14, 1996, Scroggins failed to show up for Sunday service. Her fellow parishioners knew that Thelma never missed a worship engagement. After the service, several of them walked across the street to Scroggins's farmhouse. There, they found her lying in the front doorway, shot four times in the head. A subsequent autopsy revealed abrasions on her back, shoulders, hands, and feet. She also had contusions on her right shoulder and eyelids. Her purse and pickup truck were missing, which led police to theorize she'd been robbed for both. A month later, her truck was found in a wooded area, fifteen miles away. No one knew where it had been in the meantime. Local newspaper coverage at the time made repeated note of the fact that Scroggins's house was just a few miles from the remote logging site where Alicia Showalter Reynolds's body had been found.

On September 9, two days before what would have been Julie Williams's twenty-fifth birthday, Sofia Silva disappeared from the front porch of her

Spotsylvania home, about sixty miles east of Shenandoah. A sixteen-year-old junior at Cortland High School, Silva dreamed of becoming a cosmetologist one day. She wore her long black hair in the style of the time: big and curled. Her fingernails were manicure perfect—red one day, bubble-gum pink the next. She loved sparkly accessories—butterfly pendants set with crystals, snaking gold twisted into her initials, costume engagement rings—along with dancing and sports and Sunday school. On the day she went missing, Silva had just returned home from school. She was dressed in denim cutoff shorts and a light white sweater and had gone out to the porch to work on her homework. Her older sister and the family dog were both inside. Neither heard a thing. But by the time Sofia's parents returned home from work, it was clear she was gone without a trace. They found only her backpack, homework, and a can of soda. They had no reason to believe she'd run away. State police mounted a search. They found nothing. Her parents appeared on *America's Most Wanted*. That yielded a handful of calls but no leads.

Not long after, Anne Carolyn McDaniel also went missing. McDaniel, twenty, had short brown hair and glasses. Born with cerebral palsy, she struggled to have the typical young adult experience she'd so desperately wanted. After graduating from high school, she moved into an assisted living center for people with special needs—kind of a group home for residents looking to be independent—located in Orange, Virginia, about halfway between Spotsylvania and Shenandoah. There, McDaniel found a part-time job. She also told friends she'd recently started dating someone but was mysterious about the details. No one is quite sure when she disappeared, but the manager of the assisted living center reported McDaniel missing on September 20. Several of her friends said she'd told them she had a date that evening.

The following Sunday morning, September 22, two hunters were working their dogs in a forested spot of land off a gravel road in Lignum, about seven miles from the location of Alicia Showalter Reynolds's makeshift grave and four miles from the home of Thelma Scroggins. As the men and dogs approached an abandoned hunting camp, they found a body, badly burned and partially buried by branches and leaves. Investigators on the scene determined that the body was that of a young woman's. Her head and neck were encircled with duct tape, which also covered her mouth and nose. Her wrists and arms were bound with the same tape. Investigators also observed decomposition, including insect activity, on her body, which had been disturbed by animals as well.

It didn't take long to identify the body as that of Anne Carolyn McDaniel. The state medical examiner ruled her cause of death as asphyxiation and estimated she had been killed around September 20. A trace amount of DNA belonging to someone other than McDaniel was also obtained at the crime scene. As with the previous murders, local newspapers reported this story extensively. "You'd really have to know the area to even know where that camp was located. This has to be someone familiar with the place," the hunters who found McDaniel's body told reporters on the scene. "It's starting to look a whole lot like a serial killer is at work here, what with all these bodies turning up in the same area," Anne's father told those same reporters.

McDaniel's family hung a wreath on the road not far from where her body had been located. Another wreath hung on Thelma Scroggins's door. A third, faded by now, still fluttered alongside Route 29, where Alicia Showalter Reynolds had been last seen. Posters asking for information about all three women—which included a composite sketch of the so-called Route 29 stalker—were still tacked in between these three sites. Residents had a lot of theories and fears but no answers.

Weeks dragged on. Sofia Silva still had not been found. And then, on the afternoon of Monday, October 14, employees of Dominion Growers, a commercial tulip farm just outside Fredericksburg and about thirty miles from Spotsylvania, were working to remove a beaver dam that had been flooding their fields. It was late in the workday—nearly 5:30 p.m.—when one of the workers reached a stretch of creek engorged by the dam. There, mostly submerged, was a bundled form, swathed in a blue moving company blanket and bound with a long length of rope that had been tied into dozens of intricate knots. The blanket had slipped in places, revealing a single hand, its long fingernails painted magenta, its fingers bedazzled by gold-and-crystal rings. The body was badly decayed, but police immediately suspected they had found sixteen-year-old Sofia Silva.

Forensic records would soon prove them correct. The state medical examiner determined that Silva had been strangled to death. She was wearing the same shorts and sweater her sister had last seen her in, but her bra and panties were missing. Investigators wouldn't say whether or not the same was true for McDaniel and Scroggins, but in a way it didn't matter to local residents, who were now fearing for their own lives.

"The glaring factor here is the location," the Virginia state police spokesperson told the *Washington Post*. "Investigators can't ignore that it's unusual to have multiple unsolved homicide cases in this small a radius." From 1974 to 1994, this rural swath of central Virginia had seen fewer than ten murders. Now, in just six months, five women, including Lollie and Julie, had been killed there. That number did not include Silva, who had been found in nearby Stafford County. Some investigators began to speculate that all six women might share a common killer.

"Offenders like this are rare," retired FBI profiler Gregg McCrary told the press. "It's highly unusual to have two serial killers operating in the same geographic area at the same time." Robert Ressler, one of the founding members of the FBI's Behavioral Science Unit and the author of *Sexual Homicide*, agreed. "The likelihood of all these being separate cases is rare," he told a reporter. "When you have female bodies showing up in close proximity in a short period of time, it's an unusual circumstance." Ressler pointed to other disturbing similarities. Other than Scroggins, all victims were under the age of twenty-six. Other than Scroggins, all bodies were found in secluded wooded spots. Three were wrapped in blankets or sleeping bags. The other two were buried. "If it is more than one killer, this part of Virginia has some real problems," Ressler concluded.

EACH YEAR, THOUSANDS of scholars and practitioners attend the annual international conference of the Association for Experiential Education (AEE). And each year, a hundred or so attendees who work as professors and who identify as female break out for their own conference lunch. The fall 1996 AEE meeting took place in Spokane, Washington. That month, the cover story for the leading industry publication was a deep dive that examined issues of safety for women in the outdoors. The story made repeated mention of Claudia Brenner, the author of *Eight Bullets* who had lost her partner and had braved the brutal trek out of the woods while nursing her own gunshot wounds. It also focused on Julie and Lollie and included interviews with dozens of women, who said these crimes had led them to cancel hiking plans or even avoid wooded areas entirely. As the group of female adventure educators sat around tables in their hotel ballroom, they could talk about little else.

Nina Roberts was one of the women in attendance. A Fulbright scholar and professor who specializes in equal access to wilderness and the cultural barriers that prevent it, she was already well aware of the impact these crimes were having on anyone who identified as a minority and wanted to be outdoors. She told her peers about the hundreds of women who'd written to her about how the deaths had affected their own outdoor recreation—how they no longer hiked or camped or back-packed, even though those pursuits had once been a major part of their lives.

Roberts had also once served as a guide at Woodswomen. She knew Denise Mitten; she also knew Julie and Lollie were up-and-coming outdoor leaders. Although Roberts hadn't known the two women per-sonally, their deaths had hit her hard. Other people at the lunch agreed—they'd had a similarly powerful emotional reaction. And they hated hearing that women had stopped doing something they really loved. Lunch-goers began brainstorming. What could they do in response? No one remembers who first mentioned Take Back the Night, the global campaign to end violence against women. Begun in the early 1970s as marches at a few college campuses, the movement had blossomed into annual events around the world. Couldn't it serve as a model for what they had in mind?

By the end of the conference, they'd settled on their own initiative. They'd call it Take Back the Trails and host hikes and other conscious-ness-raising events the following May to mark the one-year anniver-sary of the Shenandoah murders. They created a small board of national coordinators and devised a logo and publicity campaign. The Winanses never responded to their calls or letters. When event organizers notified the Williamses, Patsy made a donation at once and asked if she could be involved. With her blessing, they began planning specific events around the country. Nina Roberts was living in Maryland at the time; she offered to organize one for Shenandoah National Park. Roberts quickly rallied about twenty other women, including Patsy and Julie's aunt, to commit to a hike, followed by a press conference at Skyland resort.

Park authorities were less than enthused. They wrote to Roberts and said they weren't sure they could grant a permit for something that seemed so inherently political. Roberts was angry.

"Actually, I was really pissed," she says now. "It's like they were pan-icked that a group of lesbians were about to start protesting in the park and generating bad press."

Roberts wrote back and tried to explain the mission of the project—that this was about promoting safety and stewardship. The park administrators remained, at best, hesitant. Dissension began growing in other circles as well. Staff members of the Appalachian Trail Conservancy objected to the plan. They thought the initiative was incorrectly implying that Lollie and Julie had been murdered on the trail. They worried that focusing on Lollie and Julie's gender excluded the men who had been killed on the trail. They pointed to the fact that more than seventy-seven million people had safely hiked the trail, so what exactly needed taking back?

When it came to the AT proper, they did have a point. By 1996, and not counting Julie and Lollie, official tallies stood at four women and three men who had been attacked and killed on the trail since its founding in 1925. Three of the victims were hiking with their heterosexual partners at the time; one was homosexual. *What's the pattern here?* wrote a senior staff member at the Appalachian Trail Conservancy. *How can we single out gender (or sexual preference) as the prevailing factor? Why not couples as prey? Or social workers?*

But it was also true that both Molly LaRue and Laura Susan Ramsay appeared to be the primary target in their attacks—and both appeared to have been sexually assaulted. And then there were those cases of assault on trails and in the wilderness outside the Appalachian Mountains. So many of them, it seemed, had a lot to do with gender. Take, retorted Roberts, the San Francisco "trail side murders," in which four women were killed while hiking between 1979 and 1980. Or the dozens of other women who had been killed hiking on federal and state lands. And then there was that 1995 report that had found that over half of all women working in outdoor industries had been sexually assaulted or harassed while in the field. *What about them?* Roberts wanted to know.

She and the other national organizers for Take Back the Trails refused to back down. They scheduled events across the country that spring. In Unity, Maine, the college awarded Lollie a posthumous degree and unveiled the stone fireplace in the college's new welcome center, which was dedicated in her honor. The stones for the fireplace had been reclaimed from centuries-old cobblestone streets in Portland's historic Old Port—a fact, say her friends, that Lollie would have adored. At St. Cloud State University in Minnesota, Tom Williams served as the honorary chair for a hike that brought over a hundred people together, including a young father carrying his baby daughter in a backpack. That man told reporters it was his hope that someday his young daughter could hike on trails without worrying for her own safety.

At Shenandoah National Park, Roberts rendezvoused with Patsy Williams and several dozen other women. They were joined by friends of Rebecca Wight and Claudia Brenner, who had driven from Blacksburg,

Virginia, and Ithaca, New York, for the event. Faded reward posters still hung at the park's entrance. After the hike, Patsy agreed to participate in a small press conference. She told reporters that despite the continued grief over losing her daughter, she didn't want Julie's death to keep people from spending time in the woods. But some of the participants also said the lack of leads in the case couldn't help but make them feel wary. "The fact that the murders are unsolved preys on everyone's mind," one woman who lived in the Shenandoah Valley and took part in the hike told reporters. "Violence against women is extremely prevalent, but for it to follow you all the way into the woods, where you expect to be safe, is enraging."

ON MAY 1, 1997, two sisters—Kristin Lisk, fifteen, and Kati Lisk, age twelve, were abducted from their home in Spotsylvania, not far from where the Silva family still lived. In the intervening months since Sofia's death, another Spotsylvania resident had been indicted for Silva's murder and was awaiting trial. The man's landlord had reported him to police shortly after Sofia's disappearance: according to the landlord, the individual had grown mercurial, was suddenly prone to violent outbursts, and had begun binge drinking. A search of his criminal record turned up a history of indecent exposure, assault and battery, and drug abuse. Police obtained a warrant to search his home and van and found fibers that looked like those found on Silva. The state lab confirmed these findings. But months after the suspect was arrested, additional lab tests called those results into question, and the state was now preparing to drop the charges against him. The disappearance of the Lisk sisters in broad daylight and at their own house seemed only to strengthen the possibility that the state had the wrong man.

Five days after they went missing, the bodies of the Lisk sisters were found in the Santa Anna River, about forty miles from their house. Both were partially clothed, and Kristin was missing her bra. Authorities would not reveal her—or Kati's—cause of death. "The details are known only to us and the assailant," said the Sheriff Department's spokesperson. The autopsy report, which was never released to the public, found evidence of multiple nonlethal injuries on both girls. Kati had narrow red abrasions and contusions on her face, arms, and back similar to those observed on Lollie and Julie: a three-eighth-inch mark below her red eye, a half-inch bruise on her left lid; a quarter-inch laceration on her left brow. Her wrists and ankles showed clear signs of being bound. She also had a large contusion on the back of her head—about two by two inches—believed to have been the cause of her death. Kristin had similar abrasions to Kati's on her arms, wrists, and ankles, along with a deep scalp hemorrhage on the lower part of her skull. Autopsy records reveal that the medical examiner determined that she most likely died of asphyxiation.

That same autopsy report noted a head hair on Kati's sock and one on Kristin's clothing, both of which were believed to belong to their assailant. State crime investigators immediately began comparing those hairs to evidence from the Silva case. At no point did they request permission to compare those hairs to ones found at the Shenandoah crime scene. Instead, investigators focused on the age of these three victims, certain that they were dealing with a pedophile. It didn't seem to matter that both Sofia Silva and Kristin Lisk were physically mature, nor that it appeared Kristin, rather than Kati, was the true target of their joint attack. The FBI also began echoing the notion that Silva and the Lisks were most likely killed by a pedophile. In their initial report of these three murders, FBI behavioralists could only add, "It is the opinion of our experts that the guilty person may have experienced some stressful event in his personal life." They suggested investigators look for someone who had skipped school or missed work recently and who had escalated his use of drugs, alcohol, or cigarettes. Beyond that, they didn't have much to offer.

At a press conference shortly after the bodies of the Lisk sisters were found, those same FBI agents were asked for an update in the Williams/

Winans case. "There have been no new developments in quite some time," said an FBI spokesperson. "Most of the leads have been run down, but a few are being reviewed again." The number of agents and rangers investigating them, he said, had been "scaled back to just a handful."

WEDNESDAY, JULY 9, 1997, dawned cool and dewy at Shenandoah National Park, but temperatures soon rose into the nineties. Two friends parked their car and set out for a day of cycling. One (who would prefer not to be named) was the stronger athlete, and so the two had established a routine: he'd pull ahead, then wait for her at a designated lunch or break site. The other cyclist was Yvonne Malbasha, a thirty-five-year-old newly minted paramedic from Ottawa, Canada. As the sun beat down on Skyline Drive that morning, Malbasha made her way through the park's central district. Around noon, she had reached mile marker 57, just shy of the access road to Lewis Mountain cabins and campground, when a light blue pickup truck passed her. She watched as the driver turned around and passed her going the other direction. A few minutes later, the truck passed again, this time perilously close. As it did, Malbasha felt a hard thump on her back and looked back to see a can of soda on the ground. At that point, she says, the driver of the truck—Darrell David Rice—shouted multiple obscenities, including something along the lines of *Show me your titties*. Certain she was about to be attacked, Malbasha turned onto the Lewis Mountain access road, hoping to find help. She says that Rice followed her there and used his truck to force her off the road. According to Malbasha, he then got out of his truck, saying, *I'm going to get you*. She panicked and hurled her water bottle at him. When he continued to approach her, she tried using her bike as a shield and began to scream. At that point, she reported, Rice returned to his truck and sped away. It was then she noticed that the truck had no license plates.

As soon as Rice left, Malbasha managed to flag down a couple staying at the nearby campground. The woman ran to the campground store and told the manager what had happened. He tried to phone park dispatch, but the communication center phones were down that day. The woman left the store and tried to use a yellow emergency phone at the campground, but it was out, too. Finally, she and her husband located a ranger, who radioed in the incident. His supervisor, in turn, immediately issued a BOLO for Rice's untagged truck.

Sometime after that, it appears that Rice changed out of the green T-shirt he'd been wearing when he accosted Malbasha and into a white one with the logo from the Rolling Stones *Sticky Fingers* album. He reattached the license plates to his aging Ford truck and then continued to drive south, making it as far as mile 65 on Skyline Drive, where he got caught behind a slow-moving tour bus and was soon stopped by rangers. When first questioned, Rice denied ever encountering Malbasha. The rangers told Rice she had identified him as her attacker. He then admitted that he had been "rude and threatening." He said he'd thought about "going after her body" but checked himself before he did. He also said he had been up all night, had smoked marijuana, and was having trouble at work. Rangers searched Rice's truck. It was clear it had not been cleaned in a long time. Among the fast-food wrappers and other detritus, they found a package of plastic zip ties and a screwdriver. They concluded that Rice intended to use the former as restraints and the latter as a murder weapon.

The rangers arrested Rice, handcuffed him, and drove him back to Lewis Mountain, where Yvonne Malbasha was waiting. As the rangers drove by, Malbasha identified Rice as the man who attacked her. The rangers decided they needed a second identification, so they then parked their vehicle and walked Rice over to where Malbasha was standing. As Rice approached, he appeared concerned and apologized to Malbasha, asking her if she was hurt. The rangers would say later his concern for her appeared genuine.

Thunderstorms had been building throughout the day and now threatened to swamp the park. The rangers impounded Rice's truck and then drove him to the Big Meadows station for further questioning.

Along the way, Rice volunteered that his father lived in nearby Culpeper and that he was a frequent visitor to the park. He said that he was an avid cyclist and had recently seen a bear during one of his rides. He admitted that his life had hit a rough patch in recent months. And then he asked if they had ever caught the person who killed the two women the previous year.

At that point, the rangers had already decided that Rice was a strong new suspect in the 1996 murder case. They radioed dispatch and requested that Tim Alley and Ken Johnson meet them at the Big Meadows ranger station as soon as possible. The two senior officers arrived shortly before 3:00 p.m. They read Rice his *Miranda* rights, and he agreed to answer questions. During the subsequent interrogation, Rice admitted to throwing a rock at the windshield of a car, which had been parked at Little Stony Man earlier that season. He said that the day before attacking Malbasha, he had been so angry at work that he slashed someone's car tire. Johnson and Alley asked him about his assault on the cyclist: *Did he think she was attractive? Was he hoping to have sex with her?* No, said Rice. Mostly, he said, he was trying "to nerve-wrack her" and ruin her day. "I wanted to violate her privacy," he told Johnson and Alley. "I was just trying to aggravate her, and I just got too close. After I reached out my hand, I kind of caught myself."

Rice admitted that he removed the license plates from his truck. He also admitted that he'd once yelled obscenities at a woman jogging in Annapolis and that, in another instance, he had spit on a woman's shoes. He said he was hearing voices—that doctors thought he was bipolar, maybe schizophrenic. The investigators asked if he was in the park when Julie and Lollie were killed. Initially, he said he was not. When they asked again, he admitted that he had been and that he'd visited with two friends around the time the bodies were found. Johnson and Alley decided they had enough to hold Rice. Alley drove him to the FBI office in Charlottesville. There, he and FBI agent Peter Groh continued to interrogate Rice late into the night. Just after midnight, they transferred Rice to the Albemarle-Charlottesville regional jail, where Rice was booked for his assault on Malbasha. And then the investigators began making their case that Rice had also murdered Julie Williams and Lollie Winans.

Top: Lollie Winans (left) and Julie Williams together in early 1996.

Bottom left: Julie Williams, photographed by Lollie in Shenandoah National Park.

Bottom right: Lollie Winans, believed to be atop Hawksbill Mountain in Shenandoah National Park.

Above: Julie Williams collecting cooking water in Shenandoah National Park's White Oak Canyon.

Right: Julie's apartment in Richmond, Vermont. The two women departed from here on either May 18 or May 19, 1996.

Left: Julie and Lollie, just after arriving at Shenandoah National Park late in the afternoon on Sunday, May 19, 1996.

Below: Taj, Lollie's beloved dog, hunkered down in the shade near White Oak Canyon, not far from where Taj would eventually be found.

Bottom: Skyland Resort, located across Skyline Drive from the head of the Bridle Trail.

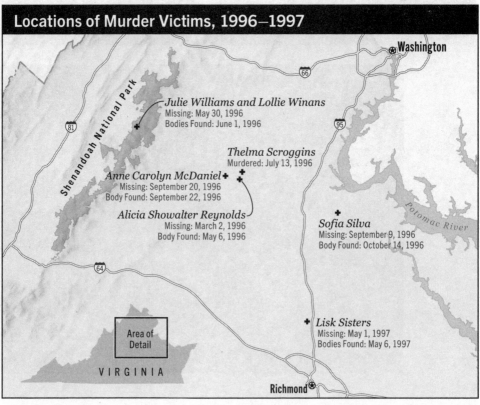

Locations of Murder Victims, 1996–1997

Washington

Shenandoah National Park

Julie Williams and Lollie Winans
Missing: May 30, 1996
Bodies Found: June 1, 1996

Thelma Scroggins
Murdered: July 13, 1996

Anne Carolyn McDaniel
Missing: September 20, 1996
Body Found: September 22, 1996

Alicia Showalter Reynolds
Missing: March 2, 1996
Body Found: May 6, 1996

Sofia Silva
Missing: September 9, 1996
Body Found: October 14, 1996

Potomac River

Lisk Sisters
Missing: May 1, 1997
Bodies Found: May 6, 1997

Area of Detail

VIRGINIA

Richmond

Top: The view from Hawksbill Mountain, which the women hiked the afternoon of May 24, 1996.

Bottom: The locations of women murdered in the general area of Shenandoah National Park.

UNIT LOG	1. INCIDENT NAME Bridal Trail	2. DATE PREPARED	3. TIME PREPARED
4. UNIT NAME/DESIGNATORS. Command	5. UNIT LEADER (NAME AND POSITION) C. Jordan IC	6. OPERATIONAL PERIOD 5/31/96 (Friday)	

7. PERSONNEL ROSTER ASSIGNED

NAME	ICS POSITION	HOME BASE
Tim Alley	Investigator	
Tim Woosley	Hasty Search	
Jonathon Holter	Hasty Search	

8. ACTIVITY LOG (CONTINUE ON REVERSE)

TIME	MAJOR EVENTS
@ 1300	Briefed by dispatch about overdue backpackers. Vehicle found by Pauley in AM @ Stoney Man OL. Two BC permits located by dispatch in AM. Second permit 5/22-5/27. I interviewed Mr. Williams by phone. All indications are that the women are experienced, well equipped backpackers. Strategy to concentrate on investigation to help determine search urgency.
@ 1400	Alley assigned to investigations. Over the rest of the afternoon he interviews a number of folks (friends, employers, relatives). Most agreed that though Julie missed a couple of commitments it was quite reasonable to believe that they were

Above left: The case log maintained by Shenandoah National Park rangers during the initial search for Julie and Lollie.

Above right: Tim Alley, visiting the murder scene with the author in 2017.

Bottom: The rear of the women's tent, which investigators believe was slashed with a knife by their killer, and a close-up of the detritus presumably left by the killer while rummaging through the women's belongings.

Bureau of Criminal Investigation
Culpeper, Virginia

PHYSICAL EVIDENCE RECOVERY

Date	Type of Crime	VSP Case No.
6-2-96	HOMICIDE	96-82-00-033B

Victim: 1. LAURA WINANS   2. JULIANNE WILLIAMS
Scene Location: SHENANDOAH NATIONAL PARK - CAMPSITE OFF SKYLAND - BIG MEADOWS HORSE TRAIL
Evidence Collector: SA's STAN GREGG / JEFF PARSONS.

Item #	Evidence Description	Recovery Location	Packaging Container
1	GREEN/PURPLE/BLACK BACK PACK (SEE ATTACHED)	SOUTH SIDE OF TENT	PLASTIC BAG
2	BLACK/BLUE BACK PACK (See ATTACHED)	SOUTH SIDE OF TENT	PLASTIC BAG
3	PLASTIC BAG w/ ASSORTED ITEMS (See ATTACHED)	SOUTH SIDE OF TENT	PLASTIC BAG
4	CANNON 35 MM CAMERA	SOUTH SIDE OF TENT	PAPER BAG
5	PURPLE BANDANA	INSIDE ITEM # 2	PLASTIC BAG
6	PLASTIC BAG w/ ASSORTED ITEMS (SEE ATTACHED)	NORTH SIDE OF TENT	PLASTIC BAG
7	ROLL OF TOILET PAPER (RED STRINGED)	NORTH SIDE OF TENT	PLASTIC BAG
8	PLASTIC BAG w/ ASSORTED ITEMS (SEE ATTACHED)	INTERIOR OF TENT	PLASTIC BAG
9	NOTE BOOK	INTERIOR OF TENT	PLASTIC BAG
10	BLOOD SAMPLES (3 EA)	BOTTOM OF SLEEPING BAG	PLASTIC BAG
10A	CONTROL FOR ITEM 10	BOTTOM OF SLEEPING BAG	PLASTIC BAG
11	NOTE PAD w/ WRITING (SEE ATTACHED)	INTERIOR OF TENT	PLASTIC BAG
12	PLASTIC BAG w/ ASSORTED ITEMS	INTERIOR OF TENT	PLASTIC BAG
13	PIECE OF GRAY DUCT TAPE	CREEK	PLASTIC BAG
14	KNIT CAP	CREEK	PLASTIC BAG
15	SLEEPING PAD	CREEK	TRASH BAG
16	PIECE OF WRAPPER	AREA BETWEEN TRAIL & TENT	PLASTIC BAG
17	TAPE ROLL (EMPTY)	TRAIL - NORTH OF SITE	PLASTIC BAG
18	CIGARETTE BUTT (WINSTON)	TRAIL - SOUTH OF SITE	PLASTIC BAG

Page 2 of 3

Reporting Technician SA STAN GREGG

Rev. 1192WTS

SM-005879

Above right: A partial inventory of items recovered from the crime scene.

Above: A cylindrical, battery-operated vibrator believed to have been staged at the crime scene by the murderer.

Right: Glove obtained at the scene and believed to have been worn by the women's killer.

Left and bottom: Deirdre Enright, founding director of the Innocence Project at the University of Virginia School of Law, and just some of the dozens of boxes of evidence at UVA.

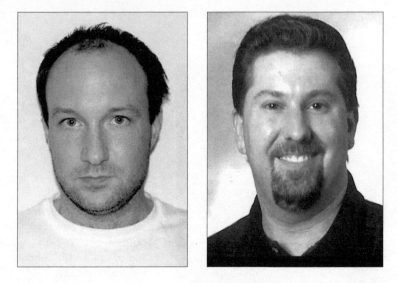

Above left: Darrell David Rice. Photo taken by authorities after he was apprehended in Shenandoah National Park in July 1997.

Above right: Richard Marc Evonitz, photo origin and date unknown.

Bottom: FBI posters issued in June 2016, the 20th anniversary of the murders.

SEEKING INFORMATION
JULIANNE "JULIE" WILLIAMS

Shen

Julianne Williams, 1996 photo

Age: 24 years old (At time of death)
Height: 5'9"
Build: Slim
Race: White

Julianne was commonly known by her nickname "Ju

The Richmond Division of the FBI and the National
with identifying and convicting the person(s) respo
1996, the bodies of both women were found at the
been hiking with a golden retriever named "Taj" an
Whiteoak Canyon Trail.
**If you have any information concerning this p
Consulate.**

Field Office: Richmond

SEEKING INFORMATION
LAURA "LOLLIE" WINANS

Murder Victim
Shenandoah National Park, Virginia
May 24, 1996

Laura Winans, 1996 photo

DESCRIPTION

Age: 26 years old (At time of death)	**Height:** 5'8"
Weight: 160 pounds	**Build:** Medium
Sex: Female	**Race:** White

REMARKS

Laura was commonly known by her nickname "Lollie."

DETAILS

The Richmond Division of the FBI and the National Park Service are requesting information from the public that would assist law enforcement with identifying and convicting the person(s) responsible for the double homicides of Laura Winans and Julianne Williams. On Saturday, June 1, 1996, the bodies of both women were found at their campsite near Skyland Resort in Shenandoah National Park in Virginia. The women had been hiking with a golden retriever named "Taj" and were last seen on May 24, 1996. The dog was located and turned over to rangers near Whiteoak Canyon Trail.

If you have any information concerning this person, please contact your local FBI office or the nearest American Embassy or Consulate.

Field Office: Richmond

13

"**YOU HAVE TO REMEMBER:** we literally had no good leads," Tim Alley explained to me in the breakfast area of yet another chain motel. It was a sparkling afternoon in October 2018, and I'd returned to Shenandoah. By then, Tim and I had spoken about the case by phone more times than either one of us could count. On this particular trip, I brought with me Brenda Blonigen, a career sheriff's deputy who specialized in crimes against women and children and who had grown up on a homestead that sat in the shadow of the park. I'd known Blonigen socially for several years at that point. Shortly after meeting with the Williamses, I had invited her to lunch. I wanted to know how she managed to dedicate her professional life to investigating unimaginable violence while still retaining an enviable lightness and joy about her. Instead, we ended up mostly talking about the details of the Shenandoah case. I hadn't known she and her siblings had grown up so close to the crime scene. And I didn't know how familiar she already was with the specifics of the crime. She told me she'd been meaning to visit her family and asked if I wanted some company on my trip. Of course I did.

So there we were, the three of us, now wedged into a vinyl booth in an otherwise vacant breakfast area. Around us, several widescreen TVs were cycling through daytime programming, shifting from the applause of game show contestants to a celebrity chef's enthusiastic instructions for making caramel apples. Tim Alley fidgeted, first with an empty cinnamon roll wrapper and then with my pen.

"Sorry," he said, after realizing I wasn't able to take any notes without it. "I'm usually on the other side of the table."

After the three of us made polite chitchat, I asked Tim to walk me through the case once again. Rice, I knew, had been arrested and convicted for the 1997 assault on Malbasha. But before that trial had even begun, investigators were building a case against Rice for the 1996 murders. Over the next five years, they went to extraordinary lengths, not just relying on forensic analysis and physical evidence but also employing extensive psychological profiling, exhaustive interviews, and an undercover FBI agent whom they embedded in Rice's cell. In the end, the evidence they had implicating Rice was, by Tim's own admission, only circumstantial. Cameras at the park entrance stations recorded Rice entering Shenandoah several times in the days surrounding the murders. Two jailhouse informants claimed that Rice had confessed to them that he had committed the crimes (at least one of them agreed to wear a wire in an attempt to record Rice reiterating any such confession; however, once wired, he failed to persuade Rice to confess or claim any responsibility). Prior to assaulting Malbasha, Rice had thrown that rock and shattered the windshield of a car that was parked at Little Stony Man, the same area where Julie's car had been found a year earlier.

The strongest piece of evidence against Rice was a one-minute call he made on Tuesday, May 28, 1996. Around 10:30 a.m. that morning, Rice dialed the direct extension of Janie Spahr, the director of the Spectrum LGBT Center, located in San Francisco. In November 1995, Julie had recorded in her journal Spahr's name, along with an anthology she had edited, *Called Out: The Voices and Gifts of Lesbian, Gay, Bisexual, and Transgender Presbyterians*. Spahr's was one of several books, all selected by her church book club, that Julie included in that journal entry.

Investigators theorized that Julie then met Spahr at a conference or lecture in the spring of 1996. Although Spahr's business card did not include her direct extension (and, in fact, Spahr said she did not give out that particular number), they speculated that Julie somehow had recorded that direct number and included it in the notebook she carried with her in Shenandoah. Their theory was that Rice had taken the journal with him as a souvenir. Once at home, he had become curious about the telephone number and dialed it but then hung up just after hearing Spahr's voice mail greeting.

"Super cool lady, by the way," said Tim at the breakfast booth. "I traveled to New York to hear Janie speak. She even signed a book for me."

Although Spahr said she did not recall ever meeting Julie, and investigators were unable to establish that Julie ever attended any of Spahr's talks, they continued to view this call as the keystone of their investigation. Alley and Peter Groh, Tim's FBI counterpart, repeatedly pressed Rice about that call, including at a marathon interrogation in December 1999. To prepare, the FBI had reserved a block of rooms at a hotel near FCI Cumberland, the prison where Rice was being housed. They outfitted one room with cameras and microphones and set up recording and monitoring stations in the others, which were staffed by additional FBI agents. In the interview room, they displayed evidence collected from the campsite, including Julie's sleeping pad and some of the women's gear. Then, just after 8:00 a.m., they collected Rice from the prison.

As the interview progressed, Groh and Alley showed Rice a photo of Williams and asked if he thought she was attractive. He said she was. They showed him photos of the crime scene. They laid out pictures demonstrating that his father's car was in the park on May 25 and May 26, 1996. They told him surveillance aircraft had recorded the identities of everyone who had walked down the Bridle Trail that week (to which Rice replied, *That's great, right? It means you should have footage and photos of the guy who did this*). They asked Rice what he knew about the Spectrum Center. Rice said he had seen a few Grateful Dead shows there, apparently conflating the LGBT organization with the Philadelphia sports arena that shared the same name. They showed Rice his phone records, which proved that he had dialed the number. He said he didn't remember calling, but it looked like he had maybe mixed up a couple of numbers.

Groh explained that he was retiring, that he needed to close this case. He told Rice that confessing would be the best Christmas gift he could give Lollie and Julie's families. He told Rice they already had enough evidence to take him to court—that the only thing he could do was make it easier on himself.

"We brought all those bags of evidence," said Tim. "We displayed Julie's sleeping pad, a sleeping bag, everything."

"And what did Rice do?" I asked. "Did he have a reaction?"

"None," said Tim. "He must have known we didn't have the smoking gun. But he also never denied doing it. I think he was toying with us."

In the end, investigators never turned up any physical evidence linking Rice to the crime. Nevertheless, by the summer of 2001, Tom Bondurant, the lead prosecutor in the case, felt he had enough for an indictment against Rice. Early in the morning on September 11 that year—"*the* September 11," Tim stressed to me and Brenda—he and Bondurant hiked down to the murder scene one last time. It was Julie's twenty-ninth birthday, and Tim recalled Bondurant's saying that he was hoping for just one more bit of anything to strengthen their case.

"Most US attorneys never would have attempted to prosecute that case with what we had. He's a more aggressive guy who isn't afraid to take a chance," Tim told me and Brenda.

Alley recalled that on the morning of September 11, 2001, he and Bondurant spent hours at the scene walking through every detail—where they'd found the tent and the women, the leash and collar, the chaos of the gear, and that vibrator, sitting so front and center.

"Bondurant is a real Daniel Boone type," Tim told us. "He has this big booming voice and wears scuffed up boots that never match his suit. It always plays really well with juries." But that morning, Tim recalled, the attorney seemed hesitant. Their case against Rice was thin. Was there anything they'd missed? Anything at all that would put him at this secluded scene?

Tim Alley can't remember how long they stayed down there, but he felt like it was a long time. Eventually, the two men hiked up the incline and back to their cars in the busy parking lot. By the time they returned, everything about the world had changed. And while neither could have imagined it that sunny September day, seven months later they would be

standing next to Attorney General John Ashcroft as he made his high-profile announcement.

What I still didn't understand was why Rice had become a suspect in
the first place. *What*, I wondered, *made the investigators shift their focus so
entirely to Rice after the Malbasha assault?*

"We were desperate," Tim said. "Normally you can narrow in on a few
leads. But by the summer of 1997, we had nothing."

"But why Rice?" I asked again.

"He attacked another woman in the park. He threw a rock at a car
where Julie's car had been parked. He was bizarre as shit and dressed like
a pervert for starters," Tim responded.

"Dressed like a pervert?"

Tim laughed incredulously. "Short shorts and a T-shirt that says 'Sticky
Fingers'? I'd say so."

I asked Tim if he was a Rolling Stones fan. He gave me a blank look.

"And Rice was schizophrenic?" I asked.

"I don't remember if we ever got an actual diagnosis," said Tim. "But
it certainly seemed that way. He was talking about hearing voices and the
government being out to get him." Alley then began outlining the case
again. "We always assumed the girls were killed the evening of May 24.
One of our dispatchers had dropped them off at that parking lot where we
met when you first visited. The theory was that Rice followed them down
to the campsite and waited for them to set up camp."

I told Tim I didn't understand how Rice could have committed the
crime without leaving any trace that he had been there.

"If I had a golden ticket to go back and change something, it'd be the
way the crime scene was processed," Tim told me and Brenda. "No doubt
about it. Everyone was busting their ass, and we were leaning on the people with the most experience and training, but we should have slowed
down and made sure we got it right."

As Brenda and I listened, Tim described again his frustration with the
FBI's decision to process the evidence at the park. By the time investigators arrived, all the gear had been saturated with rain, so the first thing the

ERT did was hang it up to dry in the Big Meadows ranger apartment. Tim shook his head at the memory. "We got so little back from the lab. You'd think we would have found plenty given the intimacy of the crime. Who knows what might have fallen out and been lost forever on the apartment floor." Brenda looked as frustrated as Tim. He continued listing his objections. "Take the vibrator. You've got numerous places to find fingerprints. And then you've got the batteries inside, which should also have fingerprints. They overdid the supergluing and destroyed any opportunity to get prints."

I interrupted. *Supergluing?*

Brenda translated. Known in the field as cyanoacrylate fuming, supergluing is a common technique in evidence analysis. Lab technicians place an object containing fingerprints into an airtight chamber, along with warmed superglue. The fumes from the superglue adhere to the oils comprising the fingerprints, permanently preserving the prints without damaging them. "Done right, it's a very accurate technique," Brenda told me. Tim snorted. "They used a coffee mug warmer and put it under a garbage bag. They were trying to do this shit on a picnic table." Brenda looked dismayed. Even I knew enough to think it sounded like a terrible idea.

"They totally overdid it," continued Tim. "Literally by the time we got stuff to the lab, we were hearing we'd get no results back. It was crazy."

Tim said that the rangers and ERT had bagged over two hundred pieces of evidence. After it was all processed, the investigation was left with a total of twenty-one latent fingerprints and palm prints on various objects around the campsite, including eight latent fingerprints on a Wal-Mart bag and bottle of Mountain Dew found at the scene that did not appear to belong to Julie or Lollie. It also included an oily handprint on Julie's sleeping pad, which investigators were able to photograph and measure. They of course had the duct tape that had been used to bind and gag the women, as well as the balled-up pieces in the stream and the empty roll that had been found on the trail itself.

Adhesive experts working for the FBI were able to determine that the tape had been cut with a serrated edge and that it was removed from the roll in a different order than it had been applied to the women. This fact, those same experts speculated, meant the killer had taken his time—that perhaps he'd cut the strips of duct tape and hung them from the side of the tent before applying them, one by one, to the women's wrists. On the wadded duct tape found in the stream, they found two "forcibly removed" head hairs belonging to Julie, which had led investigators to conclude that the women's assailant had first gagged them with tape before binding them with the long underwear. In the tape used to bind the women's wrists, they also found two light brown Caucasian fringe hairs, which are hairs that grow in places other than the head or pubic area—places like a person's arms, legs, back, or neck. They also found additional fibers in the tape—separate blue, red, and white cotton fibers, along with orange synthetic fibers, none of which appeared to match clothes or gear carried by Lollie and Julie, as well as several knuckle hairs found in the pair of black gloves at the scene.

"And that was pretty much it," Tim said with a brittle laugh. "If I ever have another homicide outside, I'm going to bring the lab to the woods. None of that shit is leaving until it's packaged individually and taken straight to the lab."

IF ANYTHING WAS becoming clear in my conversation with Tim Alley that day, it was that investigators had exploited every possible avenue to tie Darrell Rice to the crime. They examined his truck with luminol, looking for blood splatters. They vacuumed it for hair and fibers. They obtained a warrant and did the same for his father's car and house. "The place hadn't been cleaned for eons," said Tim. "There were wine bottles and dirty dishes everywhere." But nothing agents found could link anyone in the Rice family to the murders. They compared Rice's fingerprints to those taken at the scene. They ran his DNA against the hair. All negative. Investigators redoubled their efforts. There are rare moments of humor here and there—like when agents arrived at the home of a woman Rice had once dated to take hair samples from the woman's golden retriever, Jed. In their subsequent report, agents wryly noted, "Jed did not respond to questioning, however, did permit hair samples to be taken from various areas of his body."

But most of the investigative work was grim. In the spring of 1998, Tim Alley traveled to British Columbia with the long underwear that had been used to bind the women. Once there, he met with a Royal Canadian Mounted Police officer who was also an internationally recognized knot expert. "One of the reassigned rangers had said he thought the knots were the kind used to hobble horses. We thought if we could identify them as a particular type, we'd learn something about the suspect's background," Tim told me and Brenda. He said he and the evidence had flown on a commercial plane to Vancouver. After a tense interaction with the K9 unit patrolling the airport about what his luggage contained and why, Alley and the knot expert spent two days together painstakingly examining the long underwear and the knots used to tie them.

"Granny knots," Tim told us. "Just ordinary overhand knots like you'd use to tie your shoes." The knots did yield two additional hairs, but he didn't know if the FBI ever had them tested.

"But as we prepared for trial, we still thought we had Rice with the untested DNA on the gags," said Tim. "We sent it out for a hail Mary pass, and it bit us in the ass."

A DNA sample taken from at least one gag was sent to an independent lab, where it was tested using the more sophisticated Y-STR analysis, which had by then begun to replace mtDNA testing (Y-STR examines short tandem repeats on the Y chromosome). Results from this test confirmed that the DNA did not belong to Rice. Nevertheless, the prosecution still felt they had a case. According to Tim, Bondurant was planning on calling an expert witness to explain away the presence of the hairs found in the duct tape and the black gloves. Employed as a scientist at the FBI lab, that expert witness was prepared to state under oath that the hairs might have belonged to a friend of Lollie's or Julie's roommate and had been unknowingly carried to Shenandoah in the women's clothing or gear. But then, just one day before jury selection was set to begin, the expert witness changed her testimony and said she believed the hairs most likely belonged to the perpetrator.

"I was literally sick to my stomach," said Tim. "I had to go outside when I got the news. I was sure I was going to throw up."

I asked him if he thought this case could ever be solved.

"I think we did solve it," he said. "But solving it and winning a court case are two different things."

What, I also wondered, *did he think about the decision to try the case as the first capital hate crime?*

"Political theater," said Tim, without missing a beat. "That sentencing rule was so new none of us down here had even heard about it. And I don't think any of us ever thought that's what this murder was really about."

He referenced the attack on Claudia Brenner and Rebecca Wight and the fact that their assailant had never attempted to hide his disdain for their relationship.

"I never got a taste that Rice had any problems with gays," Tim said. "His roommate was gay. Some of his friends were gay."

Brenda raised her eyebrows at this. "Then the hate crime angle doesn't make a lot of sense," she offered.

By then, it was nearly 5:30 p.m. Tim needed to get home and make dinner for his son. He offered to return later that evening if we thought of anything else or to chat on the phone the next day. As we got up to leave, he hesitated for a moment, shaking his head.

"That crime scene was so precise," he said. "We know Rice had started to fall apart well before May of 1996 and that he had serious mental issues. The dilemma in my mind is, How does this guy who's so mentally unstable pull this crime off? That is something I'll go to my grave never understanding."

THAT NIGHT, BRENDA and I met up with her family at a nearby Mexican restaurant. Her eleven-year-old niece had just come from dance class, and she taught me some clogging steps in the parking lot before we went inside. Our party filled up a large table, and I was seated across from Brenda's two older sisters. Both had lived their entire lives just outside the park—a place they still refer to as "up the mountain," as do most people who come from this area. When the park was conceived in the early

1930s, the federal government began evicting homesteading families in order to claim land through eminent domain. President Franklin Delano Roosevelt opened the park with a grand speech on July 4, 1936, dedicating Shenandoah "to this and succeeding generations of Americans." It was a platitude that came across as cruel irony to the more than one hundred families who had already received eviction notices. By the time the park was completed, more than five hundred families had been displaced, just some of the untold numbers of people, many of whom were Native American, forcibly removed from their homes during the establishment of our national parks. Countless others had also lost hunting and foraging privileges as well (national parks prohibit both activities). For some of the descendants of those who lost their homes in the Shenandoah Valley, the injury is still very real.

Brenda and her sisters were circumspect about the ethics behind the creation of the park, although they did joke with a knowing wink that their father's beloved hunting dogs sometimes tended to wander off and "get lost" inside park boundaries. But the women grew serious at mention of the 1996 murders. Both of Brenda's sisters said they'd followed news of the crime closely, along with coverage of the other killings that year. It had affected the tenor of their community considerably, they agreed.

"Why do you want to go up there and get involved in that kind of thing?" one of them asked me. "Are you crazy?"

Maybe, I told her. Brenda just laughed.

The two of us left not long after finishing dinner. Our plan was to get up early and return to the crime scene. We woke up before dawn and packed up our shared hotel room. As we were walking out of the room, Brenda pointed at the two double beds. Even though we'd only been there one night, multiple head hairs were clearly visible on both sets of pillows and sheets.

"There should have been so many," she said. I agreed.

Up at the park, she and I drove past the head of the Bridle Trail several times without finding it. I finally relented, texted Tim Alley, and asked him to send me a pin. As Brenda and I walked down the trail, I kept looking over my shoulder. It was one thing to visit with a platoon of rangers and FBI agents. Just two people felt a lot more threatening, even if one of those people was a newly retired police officer. I asked Brenda what her preliminary thoughts were, having spent the previous day listening to Tim.

"I keep going back to Rice's mental state and what a mess even his truck was," she told me. "How could he have pulled off such a bold, organized crime?"

In the world of law enforcement, "organized" has a particular meaning. Criminologists use the term to distinguish between it and "disorganized" crime, which is often marked by a notable absence of logic or rationality. Disorganized criminals are spontaneous, impetuous, and driven by an immediate reality we can't see or know—often because they suffer from psychosis or another significant mental illness. It rarely, if ever, occurs to a disorganized offender to plan a crime in advance or to make any attempt to hide evidence. Like their homes and vehicles, the crime scenes of disorganized criminals are sloppy. They tend to kill in what criminologists call a blitz attack—a sudden shower of violence that often leaves their victims ravaged far beyond the fatal wound. Outside the crime scene, disorganized criminals have difficulty maintaining relationships and work, mostly because they are regularly disruptive and have a hard time understanding social cues and norms.

Organized criminals, on the other hand, are driven by logic and planning. They're like Hollywood's depiction of the classic serial killer, often motivated by years of fantasy and the rush they get mentally rehearsing each step of their crime. They target their victims based on criteria like age or appearance or lifestyle. They practice surveillance of both victims and potential crime scenes. They bring with them rape or murder kits, the contents of which have been refined through experience and assessment. They know not to leave evidence and to avoid detection or anything that may link them to the crime. Another reason they are hard to catch is that no one suspects them: organized criminals are great at maintaining the illusion of a normal, well-adjusted life. They're often married or even have children; they hold down regular jobs. Take Cary Stayner, who killed four women in and around California's Yosemite National Park in 1999. Stayner grew up a celebrity by association. His younger brother, Steven, was kidnapped at age seven by a known pedophile named Kenneth Parnell. It was only after Stayner hit puberty and Parnell sought out a new, younger victim, that Steven escaped, famously telling police, "I know my name is Steven." His reunion with his family was televised nationally. He and his parents appeared on morning shows; their lives became the plot of lightly fictionalized films.

Through it all, Cary Stayner appeared the all-American teen. Underneath, however, he was already suffering in ways no one could imagine. He was first molested by an uncle at age eleven, who also introduced him to child pornography. At that same time, Cary's father had begun sexually assaulting his own daughters—Cary's sisters. Stayner began suffering from bouts of anxiety, pulling out his own hair. He began peeping on his sisters and other young girls, surreptitiously recording them and taking photographs. He quickly advanced to molestation offenses of his own. He stole his uncle's collection of pornography and began masturbating to it. Meanwhile, he began constructing his own detailed fantasy: a sexual encounter in which he would be in complete control. He wanted to watch two young girls submit to his demands and then feel what it was like to strangle the life out of them. He told investigators that once he settled on his plan, he spent every waking moment looking for his first victim. By this point, he'd begun traveling with a murder kit: at first, just a tire iron he figured he could use to knock someone unconscious. Later, he realized he'd need more to be safe. He started carrying a backpack containing a gun and knife, along with a roll of duct tape and a camera. He studied the methods of other serial killers, watching true crime shows to figure out how not to get caught and how best to throw investigators off the trail. He even knew to get rid of trace evidence.

Stayner was calculating in his choice of victims. He thought he had found them when he began dating a woman with two young daughters, ages eight and eleven, who fit his profile. He fantasized often about killing the mother so that he could rape and molest the daughters—maybe even persuading them to have sex with each other. And on multiple occasions, he arrived at their house prepared to enact this plan, but something always got in the way: an unannounced visitor, newly installed floodlights, or one of the girls away on a sleepover. Foiled, Stayner began stalking teenagers at the lodge where he worked, which was located just outside Yosemite. He eventually settled on Carole Lund, her fifteen-year-old daughter, and a sixteen-year-old family friend, all of whom were staying in a nearly vacant section of the lodge early in 1999. After the three women settled in for the night, Stayner knocked on the door and announced himself as a lodge handyman. He said the guests above them had called about a water pipe leak and that he'd have to access it from their bathroom. Lund initially resisted—she said they'd already turned in for the night and that they didn't want to be disturbed. Stayner told her that was fine but that the lodge would have to move them to another room. By then, Carole and the girls were tired. The prospect of packing up and stepping out into the cold seemed inconvenient. So Lund unlocked the door and allowed Stayner to enter. Once inside, he pulled a gun and told the women he intended to rob them. He ordered the two teenagers into the bathroom, bound and gagged them both with duct tape, then shut the door behind him. Next he strangled Carole Lund and placed her body in the trunk of her rented Pontiac. Back in the hotel room, Stayner tried to force the two teenagers to have sex with each other. The girls were too terrified to do anything other than cry. He dragged one into the bedroom, then strangled the other in the bathtub and placed her body in the trunk of the car as well. Stayner's fantasy had been wrecked—the girls were supposed to please each other and then him. But he convinced himself that he could still have an encounter with the surviving girl. That night in the hotel room, he attempted to rape her several times. When Stayner was unable to maintain an erection, he removed her gag and forced her to perform oral sex. Afterward, he moved her to an adjoining room and gathered all the evidence from the original room, including sheets and bedding, which he piled into the Pontiac's trunk. Stayner then staged a morning scene, leaving wet towels in the bathroom so it would look like all three of the women had showered and left of their own accord. He also shaved all his own body hair, thinking it would make it impossible to obtain an evidence sample if he was eventually caught. Then he wrapped the surviving teen in a bedspread and led her to the car. He drove her to a nearby wilderness area and carried her down a remote trail. As Stayner would later recount in his confession, he laid her down on a wooded hillside, told her he loved her, and then slit her throat. Then he returned to the car, drove it a hundred miles, and parked it on a disused logging road at the other end of Yosemite. There, he lit the car on fire, but not before first removing Carole's wallet. Later that day, he scattered her identification and credit cards in a town several miles away. In the weeks that followed, he sent law enforcement fake clues implicating other people.

That is the behavior of an organized killer.

Brenda and I paced out the area surrounding the Shenandoah crime scene, trying to reconstruct a scenario in which a single individual with no known criminal history could subdue two women.

"He must have had a gun," speculated Brenda. "Did Rice?"

"Not that anyone knew of," I told her.

"It just doesn't make sense," she concluded.

We talked about the location of the campsite. The duct tape roll was found on the trail heading back toward Skyland. Had the killer really been so brash as to walk back to the lodge after murdering two women? Wouldn't he be afraid he'd be noticed?

"And wouldn't he have been . . . bloody?" I asked.

"Not if he brought a change of clothes," Brenda replied.

"And how did he ever find the women here," I asked. "That's what I keep coming back to."

As an experiment, Brenda walked back to the trail. Before she'd reached it, she'd disappeared into the foliage and was invisible. I waved. She waved. Neither of us could see the other. I joined her. We walked farther down the trail, to the place where investigators had found the beer can and cigarettes. It was the one place with a clear line of sight to the campsite. We could see even the backpack I'd left on the ground as a placeholder. Once I'd retrieved it, we continued down the trail to the fire road. From that intersection, there were multiple ways to leave the park.

"That's how I'd do it," Brenda said. "And if I was really clever, I'd leave the duct tape roll going the opposite way to throw off the cops."

We stood and thought about that for a few minutes. From everything we knew, it just didn't seem like the same person who was so sloppy in his assault on Malbasha could have been so sophisticated just a year earlier. As we were mulling it over, two women about my age came hiking by. I stopped and asked them if they knew about the 1996 murder. Both did and said they'd grown up in this area.

"Do you ever worry about your safety hiking here now?" I asked.

"Definitely not," one of the women replied. "They caught the guy years ago."

ON OUR WAY back to the airport, I phoned Tim Alley. I told him about our visit to Skyland and the Bridle Trail and the surrounding area. I mentioned that both Brenda and I remained hung up on what a sophisticated crime Julie and Lollie's murders had been and how that just didn't square with everything he had told us about Darrell Rice. I asked Tim what he would say to a person who said it seemed so unlikely that whoever had perpetrated such a sloppy attack on Yvonne Malbasha could have succeeded in such a calculated crime the year before.

"I'd tell that person that Rice was smoking pot the morning he attacked Malbasha," he said. "That he knew he had to hurry because he was on Skyline Drive and it was broad daylight. And then you go back to all of the things we know that he did do: attacking her, throwing the rock at that car, slashing tires."

As far as Tim was concerned, Rice's legal team had managed to destroy a legitimate case against a guilty person. He was especially angry with Deirdre Enright, a well-known capital defender who had worked doggedly on Rice's team, systematically calling into question each aspect of the prosecution's case and befriending Rice along the way.

After Bondurant announced that he was suspending his murder case against Rice, state and federal officials pursued Rice for the Route 29 stalking cases. Enright represented Rice there as well, and she was unapologetically aggressive in her attempts to vindicate him. After Rice was released from prison in 2007, having served his prison term for the assault on Malbasha, he returned to eastern Maryland. There, community members raged and fretted about his appearance, certain that a murderer was in their midst. Deirdre Enright, along with several other members of Rice's defense team, had written a letter to the editor at the local newspaper. In it, they reiterated their belief that Rice posed no threat and that they counted him as a good and trusted friend. Tim believed this was an overstep, professionally speaking. A few years later, Alley showed up at the park early one morning to find Darrell Rice just outside the entrance, sleeping in his car. That struck the ranger as wantonly brazen behavior.

"And Rice is still out there, acting strangely," Tim told me over the phone. "Every once in a while, we get wind of a report where some officer somewhere has stopped him for some random shit. He's driving someone's car and says enough random stuff that the police leave with their heads spinning. My biggest fear is that we're going to get one of those calls one day, and they tell me they found a body in the trunk."

I asked the question that had been plaguing me since I began this project. "Do I need to be worried about Rice?"

"I don't know what he'll do when he finds out you're writing a book," Tim replied.

"Do you know where he is?"

"I don't, but I can guarantee you Deirdre Enright does. I know for certain that they are in regular touch."

"Should I contact her?"

The line went silent for a few beats. "My fear for you is, if Deirdre is still in touch with Darrell, the minute you call her, he's going to be the next call she makes. And who knows what she would say."

I laughed nervously at that. Tim did not. "I'm serious about this," he said. "She would have no problem giving up your name and your address and your phone number and who knows what else."

When I returned home, I sent a request for all the court documents that had been generated in Rice's case and now lay in a federal archive outside Philadelphia. I needed to know what had made Bondurant and the FBI so certain about Rice and his motives for committing the crime. I next called Tim with a few follow-up questions about the crime scene and the presence of the vibrator there. He said he'd send me a PowerPoint presentation he'd given at some law enforcement conferences about the case. The presentation had a photo or two of the vibrator in it, Tim thought.

"I don't know that there's anything useful there, and I'm sure you've seen everything, but just in case," Tim added.

It was just before 7:00 p.m., and I was about to meet my partner, Ray, and the Blonigens at a neighborhood restaurant to thank Brenda for her time. But as soon as Tim and I hung up, a message from the ranger popped up in my email. Without thinking, I opened the slide presentation. One of the first images was a close-up of Lollie's bound arms, still duct-taped behind her back. It was the first photograph I'd seen of either woman at the crime scene. Lollie's fingers were slender and pale, with just the slightest dark discoloration under the nails. She still wore her sports watch. However, it was the streaks of blood that had trickled down through the downy hair on her forearms that knocked the wind out of me. I sat in my dark office, staring at the image for a long time and studying the way the dried blood had pooled around each tiny follicle and pore, magnifying the texture of Lollie's skin. Minutes ticked by as I fought back tears, still unable to look away from the computer screen. Suddenly everything about the case felt so real and so very tender. And there I was, paralyzed with grief for a woman at once a stranger and now so very familiar. Twenty minutes later, I arrived at the restaurant late and still shaken. I ordered two strong cocktails, even knowing they'd make me sloppy and sleepless.

Later that night, I awoke sometime around 2:00 a.m. with an icy start. Someone was in the house, I was sure of it. I lay motionless, wondering if the intruder had already made his way into our room. It was hours before I fell back asleep. The same dream woke me up the next night. And the one after that. During the intervening days, I was neurotically edgy. When a washing machine repair man tried to let himself in the back door, I panicked and ran upstairs, shut myself in our bedroom, and called Ray, a full-time military officer. When he didn't pick up, I left a mostly unintelligible message as I hid behind our window blinds, peeking out at the driveway and the unmarked repair van. Ray called back right away from the base and offered to drive home. Embarrassed, I tried to assure us both I was okay.

The psychological distress I so feared would accompany this project had clearly set in. And I already felt held hostage by it. Up until this point, I had held my own fears at bay only barely, and mostly by just practicing an unhealthy brand of avoidance. That strategy had now become impossible in the face of the gruesomeness of the evidence in this case and the mere idea, however unlikely, that the killer might try to find me. I knew I didn't want to live a life in fear and that neither Ray nor I would survive in a house where I barricaded myself upstairs with each knock on the door. The next night, when again I couldn't sleep, I got up and began scrolling through the internet. A self-defense class, I decided, would do little to protect me against someone capable of murdering two strong women (in fact, Julie graduated from such a program while living in Washington State). I had always found the idea of owning a handgun disturbing and dangerous; however, in that moment I decided that doing so might be enough to make me feel safe. Just before dawn, I enrolled in a weekend course at a professional firearms academy. And while I'm not entirely comfortable admitting it, I immediately felt more at ease.

Early the following Saturday, ten of us arrived for our first weapons training session. Two were young police officers. Another man was working toward a concealed carry permit in Massachusetts. Our instructor, a retired state police officer, began the class by asking us to go around the room and explain why we were there. Outside, the sound of automatic rifles ricocheted off one of the shooting ranges. "Advanced SWAT," our instructor offered, as if this somehow explained everything. The older couple sitting next to me told the rest of us that they'd had a revolver in their bedside table for years but had never really learned to shoot it. A young man said he wanted to protect his liberties. When my turn came I decided to tell the truth. *I'm researching a book about two women who were murdered in a national park, and I don't feel safe anymore.* We spent the next half hour unpacking the details of the case as I knew them. During breaks, and while we learned to disassemble, clean, and reassemble our pistols, my classmates and instructor offered their own theories of the crime.

After lunch, we fumbled with our bulky ear muffs and safety goggles, then lined up in a cold indoor shooting range. We loaded our magazines with bullets and waited for the command to shoot. When the classmate on either side of me began to fire, the heat and flash of light made me yelp. I flinched each time I pulled the trigger to my own pistol. But by the end of the weekend, my final paper target, which was printed with a cartoonish man wearing a sleeveless flannel shirt and gangster sneer, had multiple bullet holes in his forehead and chest. I took him, along with my course completion certificate, home. The latter got tossed into a drawer. I hung the former on my office wall, next to my map of Shenandoah. It was an absurd gesture, I know. But it somehow made me feel better.

14

BY JUNE 21, 1996, Attorney General Janet Reno had responded to increasing pressure from LGBT groups wanting action on the murder of Julie and Lollie. She issued a formal statement insisting that the sexual orientation of the two women had "been part of the investigation from the outset." Reno did not make a statement about whether or not the Department of Justice would treat their case as a formal hate crime. By all accounts, the subsequent pronouncement made by her successor, John Ashcroft, at his April 2002 press conference, had come as a surprise to everyone involved. Both Tim Alley and the Williams family tell the story the same way: they, along with Lollie's parents, were in Charlottesville, Virginia, that week, working with Tom Bondurant to prepare the public announcement of the indictment against Rice. The day before that press conference was to take place, they received a phone call from the Office of the Attorney General: Ashcroft would be handling the announcement personally, and he would be applying new federal hate crime statutes in order to seek the death penalty.

"We didn't see it coming," Tim Alley told me. "We literally had to jump in a caravan of cars and hightail it to Washington."

There, Ashcroft met privately with the families and then read his formal statement at the well-attended press conference. Darrell David Rice, he said, had sought out Julie and Lollie because of their sexual orientation. Rice had admitted that he enjoyed assaulting women and there was strong evidence to demonstrate he hated homosexuals. Moreover, said Ashcroft, Rice had made statements that Julie and Lollie deserved to die because of their sexuality. Consequently, the Department of Justice would be seeking enhanced penalties against Rice. "Today's murder indictment makes clear our commitment to seek every prosecutorial advantage and to use every available statute to secure justice," Ashcroft concluded.

Reporters present at the press conference asked why Rice was in the park, how he could have known about Lollie and Julie's sexuality, if and where he was being held. Ashcroft answered none of the questions. They asked the attorney general if he would support legislation to include gay and lesbian people more formally in hate crime legislation. "The pending hate crime legislation in Congress is under review in the Justice Department at this time," Ashcroft responded. "We're inclined to prosecute hate crimes like this one."

The truth was that any sweeping hate crime legislation had been slow in coming. In 1993, the US Supreme Court heard the case of *Wisconsin v. Mitchell*. Todd Mitchell had been part of a group of young Black men who, after watching *Mississippi Burning*, had decided to seek retribution against white oppression. They targeted a white fourteen-year-old boy and beat him until he was unconscious. At trial, the presiding judge doubled the penalty received by Mitchell and his accomplices, stating that the crime was racially motivated. Mitchell appealed the case to the Supreme Court, arguing that his enhanced sentence was unconstitutional and a breach of his rights because the sentence attempted to police his thoughts and beliefs, both of which he maintained are protected under the First Amendment. The Supreme Court disagreed and upheld Mitchell's sentence by a 5–2 ruling. This decision was the first real test of hate crime legislation in this country, and the decision by the Supreme Court that hate crime provisions punish actions, not thoughts, led to additional state provisions and tests across the country. By the following year, at least twenty-eight jurisdictions had introduced protocols to allow for enhanced hate crime sentencing. These penalties included everything from extra time in prison to the death penalty.

That same year, the US House of Representatives introduced the Hate Crimes Sentencing Enhancement Act. It was later approved by the Senate as part of the 1994 Act to Control and Prevent Crime, also known as the Clinton crime bill, a sweeping piece of legislation that included a ban on automatic weapons, the establishment of sex offender registries, and a widening of federal crimes that could be punished by the death penalty. Under that new bill, capital crimes included hate-motivated murder that occurred on federal land—including national parks. However, in the years after passage of the bill, its provisions had never been employed or constitutionally tested. In 1996, Congress passed the Church Arson Prevention Act, which made it a crime to damage or destroy religious property because of the race or ethnicity of the people associated with that property. It wasn't until 2009 that Congress passed the Matthew Shepard and James Byrd Jr. Hate Crimes Prevention Act, which expanded federal hate crime laws to include any crime that causes—or attempts to cause—bodily injury because of a person's race, ethnicity, sexual orientation, gender identity, or disability.

The fearless work of survivors and advocates like Claudia Brenner prompted this legislation. After she and Rebecca Wight were shot in 1988, their assailant, Stephen Roy Carr, argued that it was the women's sexuality that had provoked him to attack. Specifically, Carr's attorney crafted a defense for him based on his history as an abuse survivor. He argued that Carr's mother, who was gay, along with her various partners, had harmed Stephen in every possible way, including sexual assault. He'd been ridiculed throughout his school years. Women had rejected him again and again. While in prison for the assault of an elderly woman, he'd been raped by another inmate. His mother, meanwhile, had begun a sexual relationship with another woman. All this, argued Carr's attorney, had clearly damaged Carr and turned him into an emotional tinder box just waiting to be ignited. Brenner and Wight's decision to make love at their remote backcountry campsite—an act Carr's attorney described as "flaunting their sexuality"—was the match that lit the fuse.

Attorneys call this type of argument a provocation defense, which essentially contends that the victims of a crime so provoke the person who will ultimately commit the crime that the defendant can't possibly be held accountable for those actions. Sometimes attorneys will use this defense to explain why victims of assault turn on their abusers, as when a woman who endures years of physical abuse finally retaliates against her husband, for instance. It's an argument used most famously, perhaps, by the defense team for Lorena Bobbitt, who stood trial in 1993 after cutting off her husband John's penis with an eight-inch kitchen knife. During the trial, Bobbitt's attorneys pointed to multiple 911 calls she'd made during their marriage, along with reports from their neighbors in Manassas, Virginia, saying they'd repeatedly seen her looking bruised and beaten. Those same attorneys also called John's friends to testify that he'd bragged about forcing her to have sex. After six hours of deliberation, the jury of seven women and five men found Lorena Bobbitt not guilty, citing her "irresistible impulse" to strike back at her abuser.

Stephen Roy Carr's team attempted something similar. The morning of the fatal shooting, Claudia Brenner and Rebecca Wight had encountered Carr at an AT shelter. When Claudia Brenner took the witness stand, Carr's lead attorney accused her of teasing Carr and putting on a show. "You opened up your blouses and showed him your breasts, you meant to taunt him," he insisted. He asked her under oath if she and Wight had been "fondling each other" or "walking hand in hand." He asked her to define oral sex. Ultimately, none of his questioning worked. Carr accepted a deal for life in prison without parole. But the impact on Brenner was profound. In the days she'd spent in the hospital immediately after the attack, Brenner had tried to hide much about her relationship with Wight, for fear that the state police investigators wouldn't take her seriously or work to find Rebecca's killer. By then, the state troopers investigating the case had gleaned that theirs was at least a sexual relationship, and they were pursuing a theory of the crime that involved a jealous ex-boyfriend. "A man could get really pissed off if his wife or lover ran off with a woman," one of them later told an author writing about the case. "I remember asking myself, 'is that what we have up here?'" Had Claudia Brenner also died, that might have remained the trooper's theory throughout their investigation. But because she survived, she was able to assist law enforcement not only by directing authorities to the crime scene almost immediately but also by telling troopers about her encounters with Carr prior to the shooting. Nevertheless, everything about Carr's defense seemed to suggest that the assault was somehow her fault.

In 1990, Congress passed the Federal Hate Crimes Statistics Act, which required the Department of Justice—including the FBI—to maintain data about crimes that had been perpetrated because of an individual's race, gender, sexuality, religion, or ethnicity. The year before, the National Gay and Lesbian Task Force had issued a sobering report: Eighty percent of LGBT people surveyed said they had been verbally harassed or abused. Nearly 50 percent said they had been threatened with violence. Seventeen percent said they'd actually been assaulted. In the wake of that report, the task force held a press conference on the steps of the Capitol Building. Claudia Brenner was one of the featured speakers. She spoke passionately about the impact of her assault and the lingering trauma it had created both for her and her community. Since then, she has remained a powerful advocate both for LGBTQ and victims' rights.

In 2018, Brenner collaborated with documentary filmmaker Austin Bunn on the short film *In the Hollow*, which commemorated the thirtieth anniversary of the attack. It was the first time she had returned to both the AT and Pennsylvania's Michaux State Forest. I must have watched the film a dozen times before I contacted Brenner. In so many ways, it was her memoir that started me on the journey of writing this book. I wanted to understand what the intervening time between Carr's attack and her return to the trail had been like. To my mind, those years are where the real impact of a hate crime lies.

Brenner owns and operates a successful architectural design firm in upstate New York. I phoned on a Friday afternoon, assuming a receptionist would answer and I could leave a message, allowing Brenner time to think about the interview request. Instead, Claudia herself answered the phone. She was exceedingly gracious and patient as I stammered out my reason for the call. We talked for over an hour that afternoon. She spoke candidly about what the world had lost with the death of Rebecca Wight, both in terms of her talents and the reverberating impacts of her murder.

"The outdoors is where Rebecca felt connected," Brenner told me. "And for a lot of gay and lesbian people, a lot of women, that connection has been destroyed."

Brenner said she's always viewed their attack as a hate crime, and that belief has been strengthened by seeing the lingering effects of Carr's violence on both the larger LGBT community as well as on many straight women.

"The nature of hate crimes is that it has a big effect not only on the people who are the victims but also on anyone who feels vulnerable because they relate to people like me," she said. "My level of safety in the outdoors was taken from me. I don't see how I could ever overcome that sense of vulnerability since you can't really prepare for a horrific attack. And you can say that these attacks don't happen very frequently, that they're the exception to the rule, but my attack did happen. Julie and Lollie's murder did happen. And that makes all of this very, very real."

Brenner told me she's heard from countless other women that they feel the same: a level of safety was taken from them the moment Carr first pulled the trigger of his .22 gun. "And if that isn't the very essence of a hate crime, then what is?" she said.

It's a question many of Julie and Lollie's friends continue to wrestle with. Liz, one of the lead guides at Woodswomen, told me their deaths created a total sea change in the industry that has yet to be righted, even today. It wasn't that she and others were any less safe in the wilderness than they had been a few months before, but the murder of her friends had brought the possibility of violence to the forefront.

"And it wasn't just women," Liz says today. "That summer, I met a thru-hiker who told me he had to stop in Virginia: that he just couldn't bring himself to step inside Shenandoah. He was so freaked out, he hitchhiked to West Virginia and kept going northward. He told himself he'd go back and do Virginia later—when it was safe to be there."

By these measures, the murder of Julie Williams and Lollie Winans might legitimately be considered a hate crime. But the way both the congressional bill and the enhanced sentencing guidelines are written is very specific: both insist that a crime must have been motivated by a victim's

minority status and that their assailant selected them because of that status. What made the government so sure that criterion compelled Darrell
Rice to kill Lollie and Julie? Tim Alley had been very clear that neither he
nor his FBI counterparts had found any evidence of homophobic beliefs
or tendencies in their investigation of Rice: "political bullshit" had been
Tim's precise assessment of the hate crime designation when I had asked
him again about his thoughts on the matter.

In his press conference statements, John Ashcroft insisted Rice maintained a hatred of gays and lesbians that had compelled him to commit
murder (the formal indictment against Rice also rested on this assertion).
What had caused the gap between investigators and the Department of
Justice? Certainly, it was true that in late 2001 and early 2002, the Office
of the Attorney General was under intense pressure to demonstrate it was
serious about hate crimes. Both the Southern Poverty Law Center and the
FBI had reported that crimes against Muslims, Arabs, and people perceived to be of either orientation (including Hindus and immigrants from
South Asian countries) had increased by a factor of fifteen times since
9/11. I had to wonder if in the minds of some people at the Department
of Justice, the high-profile murder of two young, successful, attractive
women simply provided the best optics with which to prove they were
taking hate crimes seriously.

To find out, I reached out to John Ashcroft. After leaving his role
as attorney general, he'd returned to private practice. Ashcroft did not
respond to my first three email requests nor to the messages I left with his
assistant. My fourth email attempt elicited this brief response:

> I regret to say that I have insufficient memory of the events and
> discussions to provide any accurate recounting of the situation.
> Best Wishes, John Ashcroft
> Sent from my iPad

At the risk of stating the rhetorically obvious, I'd think the first-ever
federal hate crime death penalty case would leave more of an impression.

I sent multiple FOIA requests to the Department of Justice, asking for any internal communication regarding the decision to seek the death penalty against Rice or any other documents regarding the case against him in general. I was told no such records exist.

IN THE SPRING of 2019, a US district court clerk emailed to say the records for *United States v. Darrell David Rice* had arrived in her office from the Philadelphia archives. She estimated it would cost about seventy-five hundred dollars to photocopy and mail them. Over the course of our conversations, we'd discovered that she had grown up visiting her extended family at a beach just down the road from where I live in Maine. She said she thought she could hang on to the boxes for a week if I could get down to Charlottesville to see them myself. I called Kayla Raftice, my research assistant and a second-year student at the University of Maine School of Law, and asked how soon she could get on a plane. She laughed and said immediately. So I booked two last-minute tickets, maxing out my credit card, and then swung by the beach and bought a box of saltwater taffy for the clerk. The next day, Kayla and I were on a 5:00 a.m. flight to Washington, DC. After we picked up our rental car, I drove her down Route 29 to Charlottesville, following the route Alicia Showalter Reynolds would have taken. The highway is a lot more built up now, lined with vinyl-sided housing developments and strip malls containing Starbucks cafes and urgent-care facilities. But pockets of that desolate, rural emptiness remain.

"Spooky," Kayla pronounced. "Lonely. Like something out of a noir movie."

When we reached the courthouse, we negotiated unsuccessfully with the two elderly security guards about bringing our laptops and cell phones inside. Reduced to notebooks and pencils, we finally made our way to the clerk's office. There, she'd lined up the six dusty boxes containing the hundreds and hundreds of pages of documents related to the case against Darrell Rice.

"I remember him," she told us. "Creepy guy."

The clerk apologized, saying she needed to be in court, and left us alone with the documents. We didn't have much time. Kayla offered to work on sorting through all the legal motions. I began working on the discovery materials. The legal gods' gift to journalists and reporters, discovery rules mandate that the parties in any federal case may request and obtain any nonprivileged document, evidence, or information that is relevant to their case before the matter goes to trial. Because those documents, unless they are sealed by a judge, remain public, whatever the prosecution had against Rice, then, should have been in those boxes.

Kayla and I both quickly concluded there was little of substance in the boxes. What we did find were lab reports confirming that none of the hair taken into evidence belonged to Rice, nor did his fingerprints match any of those lifted from the scene. We found confirmation of the days on which he had alibis. And we found reams of motions related to that Spectrum LGBT Center phone call.

Rice made the one-minute call at 10:30 a.m. on Tuesday, May 28. Ten minutes later, he called his supervisor and said he'd be late for work. As Tim Alley had told me and Brenda Blonigen, that first call became the linchpin in the prosecution's case. Tim hadn't mentioned that the call was also pivotal to the defense. The main telephone number of the Spectrum Center was 415-457-1115. That was the number printed on Jane Spahr's business cards and the one she gave out to everyone other than her domestic partner. The number Rice called was 415-457-8644, her direct line. The prosecution's argument was that the only way Rice could have had that number was if it had appeared in Julie's journal. The defense disagreed: 415-457 were the first six numbers of the Grateful Dead Hotline, and 8644 were the last four digits of the telephone number of MCI Systemhouse, the company where Rice worked. Rice, a self-professed Deadhead and superfan, was also a self-admitted regular user of marijuana. According to his defense team, he'd been high that morning and conflated the two numbers. That he called his own office's correct number ten minutes later, they asserted, was proof of the honest mistake.

An entire box of documents was dedicated to this disagreement. Legal motions explored the nuances of purchasing Grateful Dead merchandise, when and where the band toured, the 1995 death of Jerry Garcia, and whether or not anyone actually went to spinoff shows headlined by surviving Grateful Dead members. (I've been to one or two. I have thoughts.) They analyzed passages from Spahr's anthology and interviews with Rebecca Strader, the Presbyterian minister who had led the LGBT Bible study Julie attended in Burlington and the woman who later outed Julie and Lollie. Strader admitted she did not have Spahr's direct line and did not know anyone else who did. As Tim had already told me, no one could place Julie and Spahr together, including Spahr herself.

What the prosecution did have was one jailhouse informant who said Rice had admitted to killing the women because they rebuffed his advances, purportedly telling him, *We don't like men.* Another jailhouse informant reported that Rice had referred to them as "lesbian hors [*sic*]." After news of these informants reached investigators, they asked one of the men to wear a wire to see if he could get Rice to confess a second time. Rice did not. But the indictment and pretrial documents for the prosecution repeatedly stated that during that recorded interaction with the informant, Rice had clearly stated, *I hate gays.*

Two hours into our speed-rifling through the boxes, Kayla grabbed my arm. "Look at this," she said.

The defense team had requested the full recording of Rice's interaction with the jailhouse informant and sent it to a noted academic expert for analysis. What came back was the entire transcript of the jailhouse encounter. The defense team had reprinted that transcript in one of their motions, and it painted Rice in a very different light:

Informant: They didn't, they didn't ask you that that was an awful strange coincidence that you was there this year and then last year this happened?

Rice: Yeah. They looked at me with a slanted eye.

Informant: Slanted eye? (laughs). Yeah.

Rice: But I think that the bodies had been dead for a week. Like they found them, like the day after that.

Informant: Yeah.

Rice: Think they were dead about a week.

Informant: Yeah. And that was the two females?

Rice: Uh huh. Then they asked me if I hate lesbians.

Informant: Lesbians?

Rice: That made me angry. And I was like—nooooooo.

Informant: Oh they was trying to get you to open up to them and say, *yeah, yeah, yeah, I killed them—*

Rice:—yeah, like, *I hate gay people.*

Informant: Yeah.

"They ignored the entire context of that conversation," said Kayla, incredulous.

"Or omitted it on purpose," I added, rereading the document. Even after everything I had learned over the past two years of research, Rice's actual statement stunned and stupefied me. Back in 2002, the nation had been told again and again that Darrell Rice was a violent, misogynistic homophobe who had sought out the women because of their sexuality. Instead, he was apparently a guy angry about that characterization. And the US government had never bothered to correct the misapprehension that literally millions of newspaper readers and TV news viewers had been consuming. The realization left me numb with rage.

Without the *I hate gays* statement, there was little indication that this murder fit the federal definition of a hate crime. Without that statement, it also wasn't entirely clear what Rice's motive would have been for killing the women either. Kayla and I tried to keep focused on reading what was left in the boxes. As our time was running out, Kayla passed me a motion to dismiss the case. Rice's team pointed out that the prosecution had no physical or forensic evidence linking him to the crime. He had an alibi for the day the women were killed. Despite psychological profiling, multiple interrogations, and an expensive undercover operation involving an expert counterterrorist FBI agent, the government had never elicited a single statement suggesting Rice's guilt, let alone a full confession. The defense team wrote passionately about what their client had been unfairly denied in the years since his arrest—fresh air, sunlight, the chance to find love. "Never—in our collective experience—have any of us had a client who has been more maliciously and falsely prosecuted and trashed," they wrote in a subsequent newspaper editorial. "After all these years, we count him as a friend as well as a client, and he is welcome in our homes and around our children."

Kayla whistled. "Wow," she said, studying the document. "They really, really liked him."

We began packing up our things. Each day that we'd worked together on this project, I'd asked Kayla what percentage chance Rice seemed guilty. Early on, our numbers had ranged as high as 95 percent. As we walked to the courthouse elevator, I asked her again.

"Twenty or twenty-five," she said, without hesitating. "Probably lower."

15

WHY DO SOME CASES GET SOLVED almost immediately while others grow cold? In the case of Claudia Brenner and Rebecca Wight, the fact that Brenner survived and had interacted with her assailant meant she could work with a sketch artist to create a likeness of Carr, which led to his arrest (the Mennonite community he'd been staying with recognized him when one of its members saw the sketch on the local news). That alone might not have been enough to convict him, but Carr also left shell casings at the scene, which were matched to his gun.

In the case of Molly LaRue and Geoff Hood, Paul David Crews had left behind at the crime scene his duffel bag, along with a bus ticket and a slip of paper with his known alias. A week after the murder, he was apprehended in Harpers Ferry, in part because he was carrying Hood's gear. Inside Geoff's pack, Crews had stashed the knife and gun he'd used to kill the couple. His DNA was obtained during the posthumous rape kit performed on LaRue.

Randall Lee Smith, who pled guilty to the 1981 AT murders of Robert Mountford Jr. and Laura Susan Ramsay, was already widely known in his Virginia community as "lyin' Randall," the withdrawn guy known for getting into scraps and committing petty crimes. After he killed Mountford and Ramsay, he stuffed both bodies into sleeping bags and partially buried them. He also took great care to hide or bury many of their belongings—he even ripped the film out of her camera, which had a picture of him on it. He might have escaped notice of the authorities entirely, but he abandoned his truck in South Carolina. Although he took the license plates with him, he left behind the VIN tags, along with a cryptic note on the dash.

Virginia State Police obtained a warrant and searched the house Smith shared with his mother. There, they found bloody clothes as well as a sleeping bag and rain jacket that appeared to belong to Ramsay. Back in South Carolina, authorities found Smith squatting in a makeshift camp deep in a coastal bog. He claimed not to know who or where he was—or why the police were interested in him—but state psychiatrists ruled him a faker (my word) and argued his behavior was all a ruse to avoid trial. In the end, Smith got his way: instead of going to court, he pled guilty and received a lesser sentence of two concurrent fifteen-year terms.

After his controversial release in September 1996, and despite the correctional officer's public assurance that Smith would never return to the trail, he was back in the AT corridor almost immediately. Neighbors repeatedly complained to authorities that he trespassed across their property to get there. Hikers reported disturbing exchanges with someone there who claimed to speak for the forest. But at least for that first decade, Smith managed to avoid arrest. Then, in May of 2008, Smith shot two fishermen who were camping just off the AT—and not far from the Waipiti Shelter, where Mountford and Ramsay were killed. The two injured fishermen managed to escape in one of their cars. As they were being rolled into surgery, police approached them with a photo of Smith. Both men easily identified him. Smith, meanwhile, had stolen the second vehicle the fishermen had used to get to the campsite. In his haste to drive away, he flipped the truck. Police found him pinned in the vehicle. They also found the gun used to shoot both men—and speculated that it may have been the same weapon that killed Mountford.

Smith never stood trial for the second shooting either—he died in prison two days after the car accident. But agents continued to investigate the crime. Up on the trail, park service investigators, including Tim Alley, found a cache of different weapons, including women's underwear,

fishhooks, and more than twenty knives and meat cleavers. Smith's neighbors say he left the caches to help him protect the woods from hikers, who
he believed were mistreating the area.

In each of these cases, the assailant left enough physical evidence to
ensure a conviction. It is also true that from the beginning the cases themselves were overseen by state police forces that could dedicate homicide
detectives, along with mobile crime labs and trained evidence technicians.
That wasn't the case, of course, with Lollie and Julie.

Theirs is not the only unsolved murder in the area. The FBI has also
yet to solve the 1986 case of Becky Dowski and Cathy Thomas, the young
women brutally murdered at a wilderness area on Virginia's Colonial
Parkway, about 150 miles southeast of Shenandoah and also administered
by the NPS. Friends of Dowski and Thomas would later say that the two,
a lesbian couple, visited the parkway frequently: it has a series of picnic
places and recreation areas that are perfect for a leisurely afternoon or
quiet nighttime rendezvous (at the time, it was also known as a safe place
for homosexual hookups in the otherwise very sexually conservative
patrician south).

Because of the location of the crime, this particular case became the
joint purview of the FBI and NPS. The subsequent medical examination
reports for Cathy and Becky concluded that they were first bound and
strangled with rope before their throats were slit. The examiner speculated that both women were either unconscious or perhaps even dead
when their assailant cut them from behind. No signs of sexual assault or
robbery were found; however, cigarette butts were discovered in Thomas's
vehicle (neither woman smoked). No arrests have ever been made.
However, not long after the murder of Lollie and Julie, some FBI agents
working that case began drawing parallels between their deaths and the
killing of Becky Dowski and Cathy Thomas: they noted the similarities in
the choice of victims (two young, athletic lesbian women), the location
of the crime (secluded NPS property), and the cause of death. In more
than one newspaper story, both named and unnamed FBI agents speculated that the pair of double murders might have been committed by the

same person. Journalists also picked up on the similarities and, at multiple press conferences, including Ashcroft's announcement of the indictment of Darrell Rice, and they grilled officials about whether the two crimes might be linked.

Bill Thomas is Cathy's older brother. After her death, he went on to a successful career in the Hollywood music industry, but he remains forever haunted by her murder. He has been a loud and staunch advocate both for victims of violent crimes and for the further investigation of his sister's murder. I first encountered him on an online discussion board dedicated to the two crimes. At the time, I was flying to a conference in Portland, Oregon, and I spent the entire flight reading Bill's posts about his sister. I appreciated the patience with which he entertained questions and some-times cockamamie theories from true crime aficionados as well as the obvious passion he had for solving his sister's murder. He seemed palpably frustrated with the investigation undertaken by the FBI and NPS. I sent him a direct message through the discussion board. Within an hour, he had emailed me back. By the time I'd reached the conference hotel, we'd set up a phone call. By the end of that call, he'd invited me to visit him and his partner at their rural farmhouse in western Connecticut, a four-hour drive from my home in Maine.

These are the kinds of visits that made my partner, Ray, insane. We'd settled into an uneasy understanding about them: with the help of a patient private investigator, I always did as much background research on a person as I could. I'd already visited Ken, Lollie's former fiancé, that way, along with other friends of the two women. Bill Thomas had been so public in his quest to find his sister's killer that I figured he couldn't possibly have ulterior motives. On the phone, he'd spoken candidly and emotionally about the loss of his sister and offered to share three decades of research with me. And, on that discussion board, his avatar was his MINI Cooper. It all seemed so innocuous.

"We need to discuss a safety plan," Ray texted from his base a few days before the trip. That night, we sat down, and he grilled me about how I intended to minimize risk. His concerns increased my own apprehension about the trip. Connecticut, where Bill Thomas lives, requires people to maintain state permits to carry loaded pistols in their vehicles. Even if I had such a license, and despite multiple handgun courses now under my belt, I still wasn't comfortable with the idea of carrying a gun around with me. Ray knew that, and while he didn't say it out loud, I'm not entirely certain he would have liked that idea either. In the end, we agreed that I would enable the location tracker on my phone, text Ray just before entering the Thomas house, and then message him again as soon as I felt like things were okay. He told me that if he didn't hear from me in twenty minutes after I texted to say I was at the house, he was going to call the police.

I arrived at Thomas's farmhouse around lunchtime, lugging a box of photocopies, pictures, and dog-eared books. I pulled in next to Bill's MINI, took a deep breath to still my thrashing heart, and tried to act blasé as I knocked on the door. Inside, it was clear I had nothing to worry about. Bill's partner, Pamela, a painter, had made us soup and tomato bruschetta. Their kitchen hummed with happy, artistic energy. As Bill and Pamela set the table, I assured Ray everything was fine and felt a little foolish for being so anxious in the first place.

After lunch that day, we moved to the farmhouse's parlor to begin comparing notes. Bill lit a fire. Their dachshund, Oliver, curled up in my lap and immediately began to snore.

"We were a traditional New England Catholic family," Bill told me. "My father was a navy veteran and an Annapolis alum. Cathy was in one of the very first Naval Academy classes that admitted women; she and Dad were the first father/daughter legacy in the university's history." After she graduated, Cathy became a commissioned officer and served on several ships, including a submarine tender. She was tough, with a black belt in at least one martial art, but she was also kind. The early 1980s were long before any iteration of a military "don't ask, don't tell" policy. Homosexuality was still punishable by dishonorable discharge or even prison time in places like Leavenworth. Cathy Thomas had long known she was gay, Bill told me. She was open about her sexuality with her family (another of their siblings was also openly gay); she'd had a few clandestine relationships while in

college and during her first commission. When she and several other lesbians in the navy fell under scrutiny by the Naval Criminal Investigative
Service for their sexuality, Cathy made the decision to resign.

"It was a heartbreaking decision for her," Bill recalled. "She'd only ever
wanted to dedicate her life to military service." After leaving the navy,
Cathy sank into a real depression. Meeting Becky was part of what eventually brought her out of it. While at the Naval Academy, Cathy had been
a Russian scholar. She began applying to doctoral programs in international relations. "She figured if she couldn't serve in the military, she could
still serve the country in the foreign service," said Bill. Cathy and Becky
began dating the spring of 1986. "Cathy talked about her all the time," Bill
told me. "It was a solid, happy relationship. She was planning on bringing
Becky to see us at Thanksgiving. Everyone in the family was thrilled."

Bill struggled to remain composed as he continued his story. "We were
all looking forward to finally meeting Becky. We never got the chance." He
brushed away a tear. "And my father went to his grave never knowing who
killed his daughter."

Bill's grief turned to real anger. "The FBI has botched my sister's case at
every turn," he said, his Irish complexion turning red. "They destroyed her
rape kit. They've misled us. They've lied to us." Take the wad of hair found
in Cathy's hand, Bill explained. "When you talk to the FBI, sometimes it
exists and sometimes it doesn't. It's never been tested. When I ask why,
I get all kinds of answers." Once, he said, an agent told him they hadn't
bothered sending the sample to the lab because it was animal hair. "In
the process of being strangled, my sister what? Pets a dog? Or maybe her
attacker was actually a raccoon?" Bill demanded. He said that other times
he'd been told the hair—which is described as brown in some reports—
belonged to his strawberry-blond sister.

Becky Dowski and Cathy Thomas were the first of four couples killed
on and around the Colonial Parkway between 1986 and 1989. Known col-
loquially as "the Colonial Parkway murders," the crimes are sometimes
attributed to a single killer, though none have been solved. The surviving
families have joined forces in trying to raise awareness about the cases

and to push for more attention and resources from law enforcement. Bill Thomas often serves as their spokesperson. "We've demanded answers. We've called *bullshit*. We've involved the media every way we know how. Nothing seems to push along the FBI," he told me.

We spent the rest of the day and then evening breaking down our two cases and trying to look for any evidence that they might share a killer. One commonality among the Colonial Parkway murders is that the victims' vehicles were often found with the driver's-side window down and with the driver's wallet out and open. That has led multiple people to speculate that someone in law enforcement—or posing as law enforcement—was the killer.

"It would certainly explain how they managed to subdue Cathy and Becky, who was also a strong college athlete," said Bill. He speculated that the two women had pulled off into a secluded picnic area that night. Perhaps a person posing as a ranger had apprehended them, maybe even handcuffed them. Based on forensic evidence, it appears that they were killed at the picnic area and that their assailant then stuffed the women's bodies into Cathy's car and drove them to the lookout, where their attacker attempted to light the car on fire and then pushed it down an embankment. Four of the law enforcement rangers who worked on that case in 1986 had transferred to Shenandoah National Park by 1996 and were assigned to Lollie and Julie's case as well, including Tim Alley, Clyde Yee, and their supervisor, Ken Johnson. At least two of the four were considered suspects by the FBI. (Agents went so far as to get a warrant to search Johnson's vehicles; he also willingly gave hair and fingerprint samples. The FBI found no evidence he was involved and later ruled him out as a suspect.)

Long after the sun had set, Bill Thomas and I were still at it. Eventually, we both had to accept that neither of us knew enough about the cases to conclude much of anything. Even though he is Cathy's surviving relative and the family's spokesperson, Bill has been denied access to almost all the FBI's information on the case. Because Darrell Rice's case had made it to a federal court, I actually had more information about Julie and

Lollie's murder than Bill could obtain on Cathy's. What he did have wasn't enough to explain what had really happened at that campsite or who was responsible. I asked Bill about the experience and emotional impact of not knowing so many details about his sister's death.

"It was especially hard on our family at first because we had no way to focus our anger and loss," he told me. "For a while, I tried to put it behind me, but that didn't work either. In a lot of ways, closing Cathy and Becky's case has become my life."

Bill said that a big reason he left Los Angeles and moved back east was so that he could be closer to the investigation. Since then, he has been tireless in his attempts to shine a spotlight on the unsolved crime, appearing on multiple TV shows, in magazine and newspaper stories, and at CrimeCon, the high-profile convention for armchair sleuths and true crime fans. It's emotionally draining, he admitted, but he also feels like it's worth it. I asked him what finally closing the case would mean for him. He said he has met other surviving family members who want a kind of biblical vengeance for the people who killed their loved ones. He empathizes with that sentiment, but it has never been his motivation. Instead, he said, his motivation has always been a quest for answers.

"I don't believe that the sun will come out and always shine and everything in my life will be rosy," Bill said. "But I think there will be real satisfaction and peace in at least understanding why this happened to my sister." He paused and swallowed hard. "All we've ever wanted to know is why she had to die."

He looked at me over the frames of his glasses. "What about you? What's brought you down this path?"

I thought about that question for a long time before I spoke. The truth was that I was still parsing out that answer for myself. In the beginning, I had just wanted to preserve the memory of two extraordinary women and outdoor leaders. I also continued to believe that the case could be solved if it could just get the right attention. But my motivations had also become more complicated in recent months. As far as I could tell, the federal government had made Darrell Rice a stooge for its campaign to seem tough on hate crimes. That didn't make him guilty or innocent, of course, but I'd become increasingly skeptical of the theory that he had done it. And the deeper I dug, the more incredulous I was becoming over how authorities had handled this case—and the more I was starting to recognize that their missteps and omissions seemed part of a larger systemic problem in our justice system. Add to all this the fact that our country, despite concerted efforts from strong and vocal people, continues to suffer from an even larger collective problem of overlooking, excusing, or otherwise dehumanizing violence against women and marginalized people. I wasn't quite sure how to articulate a lot of that yet, so I stuck with what I knew to be true. *I guess I'm just tired of being scared*, I told Bill.

16

A FEW WEEKS AFTER MY VISIT to Connecticut, Bill Thomas called me. "How about a road trip?" he asked in his morning drive-time radio voice. I asked what destination he had in mind. "Albany, New York," he said. "We can carpool." I told him I thought I was going to need a little more information first. "Check your email," he boomed. There, already in my inbox, was a registration form for the annual meeting of the American Investigative Society of Cold Cases, a consortium of law enforcement officers, behavioral scientists, and forensics experts, to be held on the campus of St. Rose College later that month. "Albany?" I complained. "There's no easy way to get there. And I'm on deadline for a story." Bill wasn't taking no for an answer. "You can write during the off time. Book a room at the conference hotel. We can hang out over meals and compare notes." It had already become clear that Bill and I were the archetypal odd couple. He's a big talker. I'm an introvert who loves my quiet time and who becomes increasingly rude when I don't get it. "All right," I conceded. "But I'm driving my own car." He laughed. "Suit yourself. I'll see you there."

On the morning of the first conference session, I found Bill sitting alone in the second row of a gilded ballroom at St. Rose. He was dressed in a tweed jacket and wearing clunky hipster glasses in a wash of very loud colors. Even if we hadn't already met, it would have been easy to pick him out in a sea of law enforcement officers who mostly wore khaki pants, the requisite polo shirt, and sidearms.

The American Investigative Society of Cold Cases is the brainchild of Ken Mains, a veritable celebrity in the true crime world. A former marine

intelligence operative turned cop, Mains made a name for himself first
working as an undercover FBI narcotics agent and then as the progenitor
of one of Pennsylvania's first cold case squads. In 2013, while investigating an unsolved double murder, Mains became, in his words, "stuck." "It
is a detective's worst nightmare," he writes in his memoir, *Unsolved No
More: A Cold Case Detective's Fight for Justice.* "It is a horrible feeling. You
feel lost, desolate, failed and alone. I felt I had nowhere to turn for help
because no single person or group entity had invested the time and passion I had into the case." Mains is also a sports fan. He decided that what
he needed to break open his stuck case was the criminology version of
a dream team. And so he contacted the world's best detectives, forensic
psychologists, crime scene investigators, DNA experts, and more. By 2013,
they had become the board of Mains's organization, the AISCC. Together,
he and his board have advised on over one hundred cold cases, including
high-profile murders like those perpetrated by California's Zodiac Killer.
Along the way, Mains has been an unflinching critic of homicide investigation in the country and one of the first to call attention to the ways in
which an inability to account for bias has led both to wrongful convictions
and unsolved crimes. It's become his life's work, which he's tackled with
a series of television shows and books. I'd watched several of the former
before the conference. Depending on the situation, Mains can look like
a Hell's Angel or a geeky A/V enthusiast. That morning, as he kicked off
the conference, he appeared somewhere in between. A blue sport coat
hid Mains's impressive collection of tattoos; he'd trimmed his beard and
slicked his hair back into a tiny ponytail.

   In addition to law enforcement, the audience that day comprised a
number of surviving family members like Bill Thomas. Even in the second row, with my back to most of the audience, I learned very quickly
that the bereaved are easy to pick out by the raw emotion in their voices
and the gut-wrenching specificity of their questions (*Yes, but what if he
stabbed her sixty-five times in the chest? Or But what if she had already
taken out three restraining orders and he was still showing up for the kids*).
Regardless of what brought them there, each of the audience members sat

spellbound as a parade of international experts worked their way through digital presentations and grim statistics. The only reprieve was the pervasive graveyard humor: the last slide of a presentation made by a forensic psychologist, for instance, read THANK YOU FOR NOT VOMITING.

But for all the attempts at levity, the news delivered by these keynote speakers was sobering. Currently, at least 250,000 active murder investigations in the United States don't just remain unsolved; they have also gone cold, which is to say that they are no longer being investigated. Every presenter at this conference believed that figure is actually much higher—and that it doesn't even begin to account for the number of cases in which an innocent person has been found guilty. The national trend for all violent crime investigations is just as concerning. Despite huge advances in technology and investigation techniques, the murder clearance rate is still dropping: In the 1950s, the overwhelming majority—nearly 70 percent—of murder cases led to an arrest and conviction. Today, murder clearance rates are as low as 30 percent in some areas. According to studies completed by the International Association of Chiefs of Police, the NPS has the lowest clearance rate among law enforcement agencies nationally.

One big problem, Mains told me during a break, is the lack of resources for law enforcement. "Again and again, cold case leads don't come in while new cases build up," he said. "Eventually, a detective has to tend to those other cases, so the cold ones go into a drawer and then a vault." Once those cases move off a detective's desk, said Mains, it's really hard to get any attention for them. As a result, the overwhelming majority of cold cases will never result in a conviction. But there are also advantages to a cooling-off period, and time can work to an investigator's benefit. "Loyalties and allegiances change over time," Mains said. "We think differently as we age. Cold case detectives can use that to their advantage." Sometimes what a case needs more than anything is a changing of the guard—a handoff from one investigator to the next.

"Skepticism is also a powerful weapon," added Mains. "Far too often, investigators who have worked a case for a while will become entrenched in their own theories. As a result, they'll literally funnel every new piece of evidence through their account of the crime. And if a piece of evidence seems to call that theory into question, they'll downplay or even disregard it." It's a phenomenon known as confirmation bias—as humans, we are predisposed to favor any information or opinion that affirms our preconceptions. In the world of homicide investigation, confirmation bias can cause investigators to explain away evidence or refuse to have it tested, so certain are they that it will not help solve the crime. In the Cary Stayner case in Yosemite, for instance, the FBI investigators focused almost exclusively on the theory that Carole Lund, her daughter, and the friend were killed by a loved one, because statistically that is usually the case. When that didn't pan out, they focused only on those employees of the lodge who had criminal records. Because Cary Stayner did not, he was cleared. In the meantime, Stayner went on to kill his fourth victim.

Scholars have only recently begun to understand just how widespread confirmation bias has been in thwarting justice, particularly for the victims of violent crimes. A recent study found that 80 percent of all wrongful convictions occurred because of demonstrable confirmation bias on the part of both investigators and prosecutors. This bias included everything from misjudging witness reliability to preventing laboratory testing of evidence—what researchers say is nothing short of a complete breakdown of logic and inquiry. And, said Mains, confirmation bias can be especially pernicious because it often occurs at such a subconscious level that the experts don't even realize it's happening. New eyes—even amateur eyes— are an important corrective for that kind of bias, said Mains.

I asked him what he would recommend someone like me do. "Start at the beginning and investigate the case all over again. Assume they got it wrong the first time," he said, finishing his coffee. "Doubt leads to inquiry. And inquiry leads to the truth."

OVER THE COURSE of the conference, Bill Thomas and I cornered every expert we could find. Most of the people we spoke with were familiar with the cases. That included Laura Richards, a criminal behavioral analyst who consults regularly for the FBI and England's Scotland Yard.

She and Bill Thomas first met when he appeared on *Real Crime Profile*, the popular true crime podcast she hosted with former FBI profiler Jim Clemente (he and Thomas have since collaborated on a TV series about the Colonial Parkway murders). Richards told me she thinks there are definitely enough similarities between these two cases for them to be at least considered together. In the case of the first Colonial Parkway and the Shenandoah murders, she said, it's not just the victim selection and modus operandi (MO) of the crime but also the number of things that were done to the victims. "In both cases, we have them being bound, being gagged, having their throats cut. These three acts together, the sheer togetherness of them, stands out to me as a linkage," she said.

Richards also said she was as interested in what investigators didn't find as what they did. "It's not just about the commission; it's also about the omission," she explained. "In both cases, you'd expect it to be sexually motivated. It's almost always about power and control and sexual motivation when women are killed. But neither sets of women, as far as we know, were sexually assaulted. They weren't robbed; it doesn't look like a drug deal gone wrong. That narrows it down in terms of the reason they were targeted." The same, she says, is true between the cases of Lollie and Julie, on the one hand, and Alicia Showalter Reynolds and Anne McDaniel, on the other. All four victims have notable similarities, another hallmark of a serial killer. Take, she said, by way of example, serial killers like Ted Bundy. They often have a particular type of victim they target (in Bundy's case, mostly white women between the ages of eighteen and twenty-four, almost all brunettes with dark eyes, many of them college students).

Richards cautioned me not to make too much of the differences in these cases either. Intentional murderers—particularly serial killers—begin their criminal careers with a fantasy period, she explained. "Serial killers tend to rehearse different parts of a killing fantasy, rather than try it all at once," said Richards. Bundy, for instance, began with low-level crimes like disabling women's vehicles before advancing to attempted abduction and, eventually, murder. It wouldn't be at all a surprise, said Richards, to see a murderer progress from killing one woman to two, or to shift from strangling to another form of killing. And, she added, most serial killers change their MO over time. "Perpetrators learn over time and develop countermeasures," said Richards. "If one victim screams, next time you're going to bring a knife or a gun to keep them quiet." Dennis Rader, the serial killer who gave himself the nickname BTK (bind-torture-kill), for example, began his homicide career trying to suffocate people with plastic bags. After that, he tried strangling them but said later that doing so took too much time and effort. And so he then transitioned to shooting his victims, which meant he could spend a lot less time in their house.

"Would a serial killer transition from, say, slitting throats to strangling their victims," I asked Richards. "Absolutely," she said. "There's so much less potential DNA evidence left that way." There are also plenty of cases of killers who just shook up their techniques along the way, she added. Take David Carpenter, the so-called Trailside Killer. Between 1979 and 1981, he murdered at least seven different women, all of whom were hiking on trails in state and national parks outside San Francisco. The first two women were found naked and kneeling, with a single shot to the backs of their heads. The third was tied up with wire. Two were raped; three were not. Later, Carpenter said he just got bored killing people the same way. Gary Ridgway, the Green River Killer, managed to kill more than forty women in a twenty-year period—making him the deadliest of all known American serial killers. The length of that spree was due to Ridgway's efforts to throw off authorities by altering his crimes. He even went so far as to pour battery acid on his arm to hide a scratch left by a victim and to collect other people's cigarette butts and leave them at the scene of his crimes. He'd clip the nails of his victims to remove any trace of his cells and leave their jewelry in public restrooms, hoping other women would begin wearing the pieces as their own. On multiple occasions, Ridgway became a suspect in some of these homicides. Each time, he always passed the requisite polygraph test. That, say forensic psychologists familiar with his case, is because Gary Ridgway was obsessively concerned with his own self-preservation above all else—his need to kill so defined him that he was able to structure his entire life, including his mental processes, in a way that would allow him to continue to do so undetected.

Regarding Julie and Lollie's case, Laura Richards felt confident that the murderer had become proficient over time. "Whoever killed them took countermeasures to confuse investigators and managed to leave so little evidence that the crimes remain unsolved all these years later," she said. "I can't say for certain that their deaths are linked to the others in that area, but it certainly does seem that whoever killed them had plenty of hate." I asked her if that made theirs a hate crime. She said she was reluctant to put labels on the case without knowing all the facts. "But I will say I don't think this is the first time the person has done something terrible to women," she conceded. "You don't just wake up and do this. I think there was probably a whole sequence of things beforehand. This person has deep-seated anger and resentment toward women." And that, she said, makes their killer all too similar to many others out there. "Women and girls being killed, women and girls going missing—it's a major problem we still aren't addressing," she said. "In our culture, the lives of women and girls seem to be not worth so much—particularly to law enforcement."

17

AFTER THE COLD CASE CONFERENCE, any attempt I'd made to create healthy boundaries between me and the investigation into Julie and Lollie's murder crumbled. As a reporter, I've always gone down plenty of rabbit holes, but now I found myself in new subterranean territory and unable to think about anything else. I began turning down other writing assignments. I'd regularly stay up well past midnight, tracking down possible witnesses and suspects or trying to confirm minutia like the uniforms worn by Skyland busboys in 1996 (black pants, black button-down shirt, and a black apron, in case you're curious). Then, the next day, I'd monopolize dinnertime conversations or group trail runs, breathlessly recounting each hunting expedition and how little it had yielded—with little awareness about whether or not my audience even cared to hear each detail. When I discovered that the duct tape used to bind Julie and Lollie was a highly specialized and hard-to-find size (1.5 inches instead of the standard 1.88-inch width you'll usually find in a hardware store), I spent weeks trying to track down who would have that size and why. I enlarged the images of the crime scene Tim Alley had sent me, staring for hours at the tangle of gear outside the tent, looking for clues. When I found a UV image taken of Julie's sleeping pad that appeared to show the outline of a pair of human calves in leather ankle restraints, I scrolled through dozens of pornography sites specializing in fetishes and binding. I became distracted thinking about the women who appeared in the bondage films I watched and wondered what had led them to consent to acts that looked undeniably painful—and sometimes down-right degrading. At one point, I even went so far as to hire a psychic medium to see if she could communicate with Julie and Lollie directly (she couldn't, but she did tell me that I had the energy of a wild pony and that my guardian angels thought I should probably take a break and get some rest).

That June, Ray and I celebrated my birthday with a camping trip on a remote island in Maine's Casco Bay. We'd paddled all day to get there and arrived on the tiny patch of granite exhausted and content. We set up our tent and toasted with a shot of tequila on the shore before making dinner. After sunset, I built a fire out of driftwood and stared out into the surrounding darkness. We were so far from everything. Ray went to bed, and I stayed up watching the fire burn down. Then I spread around the charred remains of wood so that they'd be swept away by the high tide and then crawled into the tent. Musty, rust stained, and barely still water-proof, that tent had been my constant outdoor accommodation since I first purchased it in 1998. However, as I zipped up the blue-and-yellow fly that night, I didn't feel the familiar comfort of settling into a nylon cocoon. Instead, I felt panicked and deeply claustrophobic, as images of Lollie lying dead in a strikingly similar tent ricocheted through my head. It didn't matter that I was sleeping beside Ray, a big, muscular guy who knows how to keep his cool in a crisis. It didn't matter that a tiny island in the Gulf of Maine is quite possibly the safest place in the country to spend a summer night. I was terrified, haunted by the images of Lollie's body in *her* blue-and-yellow tent. I thought about how the other victims must have felt, jolted awake and, in some cases, trapped inside their own tents, not knowing who or what awaited them outside. And then I began to hyper-ventilate. I tried every technique I knew to slow my breathing, but nothing worked. I was too ashamed to wake up Ray and admit how scared I was. Most of all, I think I was worried that, even awake, he wouldn't be able to stop someone intent on killing us. And that was a revelation I wasn't prepared to embrace. Instead, I spent the night sitting upright, nervously cataloging every tiny noise, certain someone was about to arrive by boat and murder us both.

The next morning, in the light of day, my panic attack seemed kind of ridiculous. But even knowing that, and that none of what I was feeling was all that rational, I packed up the tent, vowing never to sleep in it again.

BACK HOME, IN the safety of our bed, my nightmares were slowly giving way to frustration. I'd lie awake not so much worried that someone was inside our house as agitated that I couldn't make the case against Darrell Rice fit together. Tim Alley didn't believe Rice killed Julie and Lollie because they were gay. He believed Rice became enraged when they denied his advances and wanted to punish them. As Laura Richards made clear, there are a disturbing number of crimes today that fit that exact description. It's what theorist Kate Manne describes in her book *Down Girl: The Logic of Misogyny* as an extreme example of the policing and enforcing of women's subordination by punishing those who flout "patriarchal law and order." Misogyny, she contends, works by creating threatening consequences for women who violate or challenge those perceived patriarchal norms. Today, there is still a subset of white men who view the wilderness as exclusively their domain and actively employ misogynistic or racist techniques in a misguided attempt to maintain that. Each year, message boards and Facebook pages dedicated to the nation's most well-known long and scenic trails offer indelible reminders of this: female backpackers spreading the word about which male thru-hikers have been harassing them, accounts of attempted sexual assault, epithets written in logbooks or shouted from shelters.

It wouldn't be a stretch to argue that whoever killed Lollie and Julie wasn't even rebuffed by them sexually, that he just thought they'd grossly overstepped by having a great time backcountry camping. Maybe he wanted to punish them for invading his domain. Maybe he wanted to make sure other women would stay away. But even knowing that Darrell Rice had assaulted Yvonne Malbasha, I was having a hard time believing that any version of those ideas would have motivated him to kill. Rice had willingly told investigators, prosecutors, and even his own defense attorneys that he assaulted Malbasha because he wanted to wreck her day. He freely admitted that his attack did more than that. But the gulf between that assault and a premeditated double murder still seemed too wide to cross. Rice expressed regret about the 1997 incident. His former girlfriends said he was kind and, if anything, not all that interested in sex. That didn't sound like a person who would kill two women and stage a vibrator at the scene. Was I just succumbing to my own version of confirmation bias? Was it because I just didn't understand how criminal minds really work? All I knew was what my sources told me. Maybe then, it was time for me to follow Ken Mains's suggestion: I needed new eyes, more eyes, on the facts of the case.

The next morning, I sent a lengthy email to Ann Burgess. Born in 1936, Burgess took her doctorate in psychiatric nursing and co-founded one of the country's first hospital-based crisis counseling programs for trauma survivors. Her early research specialty was working with rape survivors. In the early 1970s, the FBI was just launching its Behavioral Science Unit, which sought to understand the minds and motivations of rapists and killers. Of the ten agents assigned to this new unit, special agents John Douglas and Robert Ressler soon took the lead in compiling interviews with serial predators to understand their motivations, planning, and execution of crimes. When a particularly complex rape case came before the unit, they asked Burgess to consult. She arrived there somewhat horrified to realize that the Behavioral Science Unit had no codified methods to homogenize and analyze their data. Over time, she provided the academic mechanisms and research methodologies to systematize and interpret their information.

At age eighty-three, Burgess was still teaching full-time at Boston College in the summer of 2019. She'd recently been made something of a pop-culture icon when the TV show *Mindhunter* created lightly fictionalized versions of her, along with Douglas and Ressler, as their main characters. I worried that the huge success of the show would have made her inaccessible, but she responded to my email the same day with an invitation to visit her at the college. A week later, she met me in the faculty parking lot, dressed to the nines in a well-coordinated Brooks Brothers blouse and scarf and driving an ancient, rusting Jeep Cherokee. Her mannerisms were precise to the point of seeming curt, and as she unlocked her office in the School of Nursing, she explained that she had allotted me forty-five minutes to discuss the case. As we ran down the time, I was certain she'd dismiss me. Instead, she invited me to help prepare platters of lunch meat for the Iraqi war veterans she would be meeting with later that afternoon—part of a new project she had undertaken to assess exercise and competition as a means of overcoming PTSD and other effects of war. Standing at a small counter space in a stuffy conference room, we rolled slices of ham and turkey as we discussed the nuances of the Shenandoah crime.

"It certainly sounds like a complex crime," she agreed. "I wonder what my forensic psychology students would have to say."

I returned to the campus on a Tuesday evening that fall to find out. I have been a career attendee of college classes for almost thirty years. I've never seen anything approaching the enthusiasm I witnessed in that lecture hall. Students began arriving forty minutes early, jostling to get the best seats. Ten minutes before class was set to start, the place was already standing room only. Attendees had brought personal pizzas and subs in takeout wrappers, cafeteria trays with their half-eaten dining-hall dinners. They brought along their friends and roommates who weren't even enrolled in the course but had become fans of the TV show.

Burgess knows how to sustain the attention of undergraduates. She'd structured the course based on episodes of *Mindhunter*. She began the three-hour lecture with a clip from the show and then provided the real psychological background on the killer depicted in that episode. As she lectured on the specific elements of each crime, brutal images of murder victims flashed across the auditorium's large screen. Most of the students continued blithely eating their dinners, setting down forks or sandwiches just long enough to take the occasional note. That evening, Ann was focusing on why predators commit violent sex-related crimes. She stressed that all criminals have a motive and that in the moment of their crimes that motive truly feels to them like justification for all manner of violence. She explained the *opportunist*, who often put little planning and forethought into the crime (and thus often leaves plenty of evidence), and the *power-assertive* criminal, who prowls like a predator, constantly looking for excuses to use force. She explained the *power-reassurance* offender, who is motivated by feelings of inadequacy and a robust fantasy world, and the *sexual sadist*, who just really gets off on thinking through different ways to torture people.

"Crime is never senseless from the criminal's point of view," Burgess reminded her students.

To demonstrate, she played the video of an interview between John Douglas and Robert Ressler, and Jon Simonis, the so-called ski mask rapist, who assaulted more than eighty women from 1978 to 1980. In the interview, Simonis told the agents he was motivated less by sexual gratification and far more by the adrenaline high he felt. "Crime was my drug. I got so much more adrenaline from that than racing cars or climbing mountains," he told the agents. "My intention was to inflict fear. I enjoy watching their suffering."

For me, there was something so dissonant about watching Simonis and some of the serial killers Ann showcased that session. They were all attractive and clean-cut. They were highly articulate and nuanced as they explained their crimes, as if committing them was the most rational decision in the world. Simonis seemed delighted to provide Douglas and Ressler with his autobiography. In the taped interview, he explained his criminal progression as if he were listing off bullet points on a résumé: He began peeping at fifteen. By age twenty, he was exposing himself to women and making obscene phone calls. At twenty-three, he committed his first rape. As his crimes escalated, Simonis became more and more efficient. He fine-tuned his rape kit, always keeping handcuffs, rope, and a knife at ready access. *Why did it take you so long to get caught?* asked Douglas. "I learned from my mistakes," Simonis calmly replied. "It was a game of cat and mouse with the police, and I knew I had to create good patterns to win." He explained that he deliberately spread out his crimes across different states. He became adept at getting rid of evidence. He was so proficient, in fact, that three other men were arrested and convicted for some of his crimes. Watching Simonis, I realized that someone like me could spend hours or days or even years with someone like him and never sense that he was a violent offender.

"He's a super criminal," Burgess told her students with what almost sounded like a hint of admiration. "He's really, really good."

Burgess had devised a worksheet for her students not unlike the rubric she created early on for the FBI's Behavioral Science Unit. On it, she asked students to assess the motivations of various criminals she had discussed, along with other details, like whether their crimes were organized or disorganized. In advance of my visit, we'd made a special document outlining possible scenarios that would explain who killed Lollie and Julie.

For the last hour of the class, I raced through a tick-tock account of the crime as we knew it and what Tim Alley had told me about the subsequent investigation. I offered the students what Burgess and I had decided were probably the four most likely suspect scenarios, based on what we knew of the investigation, namely that: (1) Darrell Rice had, in fact, killed the two women; (2) it had been a ranger or park employee; (3) a local poacher or homesteader was responsible; and (4) a yet unnamed serial killer murdered the women. Burgess instructed the students not to leave the auditorium until they'd completed the entire questionnaire.

Afterward, as we wandered the parking garage looking in vain for her Cherokee, she seemed almost giddy about the prospect of collating their responses. "As soon as I have all the data, I'll send them your way," Burgess promised.

A week later, a fat Priority Mail envelope arrived containing almost two hundred completed questionnaires, along with a note on a monogrammed card: "Very interesting. —Ann."

Of the scenarios presented, most students selected the park ranger or employee, followed by the unnamed serial killer. A local homesteader came in a distant third and Rice, an even more distant fourth. Again and again, the students reasoned that Rice didn't seem to have the capacity to commit what they felt was a highly organized crime. Reading their responses, I wondered if I had somehow unduly slanted my telling of the story. Had I focused too long on the similarities between the Colonial Parkway and Shenandoah murders? Had I overplayed Tim Alley's assessment of Rice? I hoped not. I still had no theory of my own about the case. But I was becoming increasingly dismissive about any theory that included Rice. I knew I couldn't put it off any longer: I needed to talk to his team.

Tim Alley's assessment of Rice's attorney still weighed heavily on my mind. On my drive home from Boston, I texted Bill Thomas. "Thoughts on Deirdre Enright?" He responded right away. "She's always heard me out and seemed willing to help." Enright served as the director of the University of Virginia School of Law's Innocence Project, so I called a good friend, a fellow journalist who covers death penalty cases and asked if he felt comfortable querying his contacts at the national Innocence Project about her reputation. The next day, he forwarded the response to me: "She's one of the good guys," it read.

First thing that morning, I composed a lengthy email, asking Enright if we could talk. My phone rang that afternoon. "Kate," said a rich alto voice, slowly drawing out each syllable. "Hel-looooo."

PART III

18

DEIRDRE ENRIGHT AND I SPOKE for several hours on that first call. She made it clear she couldn't say much beyond what was in the court documents until she had spoken to Darrell Rice and the rest of his legal team, but it was plain even then she remained passionate about the case. She spoke at length about her own investigation and what it was like taking her four young children—all still in car seats—to the scene where Lollie and Julie were killed (she told the kids it was a picnic, and in her defense, she did bring lunch). She spent hours talking to veterinary physiologists about whether or not a dog that hadn't eaten in a few days would lose enough weight to slip out of her collar (they say she wouldn't). She once woke up her husband in the middle of the night to see if zip ties the length of ones found in Darrell Rice's truck could bind a woman's wrist (they can't—and after complying, her husband, also a capital defense attorney, told Deirdre to go back to bed; instead, she drove to a big box store to buy more ties so that she could be sure).

In the past five years alone, Enright and the Innocence Project team worked to free fifteen people wrongly convicted of crimes ranging from rape to murder. When NPR's *Serial* attempted to unpack the case against Adnan Syed, convicted in 2000 of killing his girlfriend, Hae Min Lee, they contacted Enright (in one of the episodes, she includes a detailed account of Rice's case as an example of what to look for in an innocent client). At the end of our first conversation, Enright promised to be in touch as soon as she'd heard back from Rice and the rest of his counsel.

A few days later, she called again. "Darrell's excited about the book," Deirdre told me. "And the team is glad to talk."

After John Ashcroft announced that Darrell Rice's had become a capital case, his court-appointed lawyer successfully lobbied for reinforcements. Given the high-profile nature of this particular case, the federal judge overseeing the matter called up some of the best defense attorneys in the region. They included Gerald (Gerry) Zerkin, who defended Earl Washington, an innocent man who had been on death row for nearly twenty years after being convicted of raping and killing a woman in Culpeper, Virginia, in 1982. Washington, who has an IQ of 69, was coerced into making a false confession by police. Initial forensic testing revealed that the assailant's blood was marked by a rare plasma protein. After it was determined Washington didn't carry that protein, the state altered its forensic report to make it appear as if the tests to identify the protein were "inconclusive." In 1993, DNA testing of semen evidence from the case ruled out Washington as the contributor; however, state legal mandates prevented Washington's defense team from introducing that evidence, even though their client was on death row. It wasn't until 1999, and after the zealous legal advocacy of Zerkin, that the state conducted additional DNA testing in the case. Washington was partially pardoned and released from prison in 2001.

In 2006, Kenneth Tinsley, who was already serving a life sentence for another rape, admitted to the 1982 rape and murder. At that time, Earl Washington received a full pardon and two million dollars for his wrongful conviction—nearly twenty-five years after he was arrested. Zerkin was widely celebrated for his work exonerating Washington, which was one reason he was tapped by the federal government to represent the so-called twentieth 9/11 hijacker, Zacarias Moussaoui, in the death penalty phase of his trial. It was an appointment Zerkin accepted until the bitter end, despite months living away from home and a defendant who repeatedly referred to him as "Jewish Zealot Zerkin."

Also on Darrell Rice's legal team was Claire Caldwell, a former prosecutor who had become a highly regarded defense attorney. Along the way, the team also enlisted Enright, who had served as a staff attorney for the Mississippi Capital Defense Resource Center and who had just begun work at Virginia's Capital Representation Resource Center. It was, in short, a dream team of its own.

By the fall of 2019, Zerkin had retired from full-time practice for health reasons. Cardwell had been elected and was serving as a judge for the Richmond General District Court. Nevertheless, Enright had somehow wrangled both of them into taking a day to meet with me at a swanky law firm on the top floor of a Richmond high-rise. She arrived like a blond gust of wind, toting behind her a cart of evidence boxes, along with a dozen bagels and six different kinds of deli salads. The meal would have fed a gaggle of thru-hikers. But, as I was about to learn, for all her tough-ness—and it exists in spades—Deirdre Enright also has an irrepressible nurturing impulse. One way it manifests itself is her great desire to feed people. The four of us picked at marinated vegetables and tabbouli and potato salad for hours that day.

It was fifteen years since the case was dismissed without prejudice, but the three attorneys were still able to discuss the nuances of their work in admirable and frankly surprising detail. It was also clear that little of their frustration over the handling of the case had abated.

For Zerkin, that animus had begun before he even set foot in the courtroom. Prior to an indictment that includes the death penalty in any federal case, the Office of the Attorney General is required to submit that case to a Department of Justice committee on capital cases for review. That same committee reviews the attorney general's case as well as any coun-terarguments presented by the defense. Ashcroft's office skirted that entire process, Zerkin said (the Department of Justice declined my requests to confirm whether any committee review took place).

Zerkin also said that while it is not uncommon to begin work on a capital defense team with next to no information about the case, a defen-dant's possible guilt, or the prosecution's body of evidence, that informa-tion was particularly lacking in this instance, especially since Rice had not confessed.

"At first, I think we all assumed that the government must have had a solid case," Gerry told me that day.

Enright nodded. "When they asked me to come on as a consultant, my colleagues told me I was crazy—the case against Rice was too strong. I almost believed them."

Instead, she agreed to meet with Rice at the prison where he was serving his time for the attack against Malbasha. "I started with all the personal questions, and the guy just seemed like such a sweetheart. The idea of him accomplishing this crime was so hard to see. So I tried to get him to reveal his pissed-off side," she said. "I started asking prying questions and getting aggressive, but nothing. Instead, he just seemed clueless."

It was only during the process of discovery, when the government is compelled by the courts to present their arguments, that Enright and the rest of the team began to realize how thin the case against Darrell Rice really was.

The landmark 1963 Supreme Court case *Brady v. Maryland* requires federal prosecutors to disclose all exculpatory evidence prior to a trial. In 2002, after the government began its case against Rice, it provided the defense with about seventy-five hundred pages of documents, along with audiotapes and videotapes. Deirdre Enright began to piece together that those files were only a fraction of the key documents involved: one document would reference another not included in the files, or a twenty-seven-page file would be missing half its pages. Enright began keeping a list of what was missing. In court, she'd request the missing pages.

"The prosecution kept telling us we had everything. I kept insisting, 'That's not possible. Look at my list,'" she told me. In time, she said, prosecutors would come back to say they thought the documents might be in one office or another. She began keeping a running list of those other locations and what might be there. Eventually, someone from the US Attorney's Office made mention of a storage shed being used to house evidence. It was the first that Enright—and the rest of the legal team—had heard of this location and what might be inside.

As it turned out, the "shed" was actually a four-hundred-square-foot unit at Charlottesville Self Storage, located not far from the jail where Rice had first been housed. The prosecution initially told Enright she wouldn't be able to visit. She insisted she would. "They were like, 'Oh, but it's too hot there,' and I'd reply, 'Oh good, because I love the heat.' Or they'd say, 'It's far too cold: you'll be too uncomfortable,' and I'd say, 'I'd love some brisk air.' Finally, they told me I couldn't visit unattended, so I asked for a chaperone. They appointed Tim Alley." On the first day Enright arrived at the self-storage facility, Alley was waiting for her. He assumed she wouldn't want to spend much time there. When it became clear she was in it for the long haul, he arrived the second day with a lawn chair and a book (Tim Alley tells the story the exact same way, one of the few times he and Deirdre Enright are ever in agreement).

"The shed was packed," Enright told me. "I had to move a ton of things just to get inside. It was totally unorganized and stuffed with boxes and file cabinets. Behind the file cabinets was a whiteboard upon which someone had written in black marker: 'Time of death: 5/28, plus or minus 30 hours. Not for release.' It was clearly their war room." As soon as Enright realized just how much evidence was in the storage unit, she requested copies. The government said it would be too onerous to provide them. So instead she loaded her minivan with a portable copier, boxes of paper, and all the extension cords she could find. She strapped a ladder to the roof so that she could access the only electrical outlet in the unit, which was on the ceiling.

"The whole case was in that shed," she told me, pointing to the boxes she had wheeled into the conference room. "This isn't even a third of it."

The three attorneys laid out their case and answered all my questions about what I had read in the court clerk's office. Afterward, we began to talk about next steps. Enright asked what I wanted to see from the boxes. I laughed. "Everything, of course." She told me it had been years since she had been through it all. Now, as the director of Virginia's Innocence Project, she volunteered her students to help catalog the boxes first. "I'm still Darrell's attorney," she reminded me. "I have to make sure I'm doing my due diligence by him."

I asked what that meant—if there was a chance she thought he might be guilty. "Absolutely not," she said. I looked at Claire and Gerry. She nodded in agreement. So did he.

"In over forty years of defense work, I've had exactly three clients I absolutely knew were innocent," Gerry said. "Earl Washington was one. Darrell Rice was another."

How, I wondered, could the case have ever made it so far if Rice was innocent?

"It happens all the time," said Gerry.

As far as Zerkin is concerned, there is a direct correlation between the notoriety of a case, the stakes for the prosecution, and the pressure they feel to get a conviction—sometimes at any cost. The Shenandoah case, he theorized, was particularly problematic because it was so high profile: the violent double murder had put the entire country on edge and called into question the safety of our national parks. The federal government was under intense pressure to solve the case and assure Americans they were secure in the nation's wilderness areas. Time and time again, the investigation failed to turn up a viable suspect. "Then Darrell dropped himself into their laps and they tried to force everything into that box. It's not just bad police work," Zerkin concluded. "It's bad police work on steroids."

CLAIRE CALDWELL HAD to get back to court. Gerry Zerkin offered to stick around to help deal with all the boxes of evidence. "There are some things I can give you now," Deirdre told me. "You'll definitely want these," she said, sliding to me a folder marked CRIME SCENE AND AUTOPSY PHOTOS. I didn't actually know if I wanted them. I hadn't even decided if I wanted to look at them. But I knew enough to take them. "Oh, of course," I said, trying to sound nonchalant. I asked if I should just take shots of the images with my phone. "No, I trust you," Deirdre said. "You'll give them back."

She asked a secretary who was staying late if we could use one of the firm's photocopiers for other documents. Together, we copied stacks of FBI lab reports and eyewitness statements. I had a suitcase full by the time we were done. "Whom do I owe for these?" I asked. "Nobody," she said. "The partners here believe in this work."

We loaded up a dolly with all Deirdre's boxes while Gerry threw away our used plates and napkins. The three of us rode the elevator down to the bowels of the parking garage. Deirdre couldn't remember where she'd parked her minivan—a common plight, apparently, of exceptionally gifted criminologists. She, Gerry, and I spent more than half an hour pushing the loaded dolly as we looked for her car. The sun had long since set, and she insisted on driving me back to my rental car. Once we found it, she leaped out of the minivan and gave me a big bear hug. "You're never going to get rid of me now," she joked. I admitted that that was exactly what I was hoping she would say.

"Here," she said, thrusting copies of Julie and Lollie's last journals into my hands. "You're going to need these, too."

I made the hour-long drive to Charlottesville, looking in my rearview mirror, wondering if there was a chance I was being followed. Tim's prediction that Deirdre would alert Darrell Rice to my whereabouts was still ringing in my mind as I pulled into a grocery store to grab some snacks for dinner. I walked from the rental car scanning the parking lot, trying to determine if anyone was watching me. Not a single person noticed or seemed to care that I was there. Mollified, I found my hotel and settled into my room with a coffee mug full of wine and the final chapter of Lollie and Julie's story. And then, with the literal turn of a page, there they were at last: the voices of the two women who had filled my thoughts for so long, despite the fact that we had never spoken a word.

19

AFTER LEAVING WOODSWOMEN at the end of the summer of 1995, Lollie Winans returned to Unity College to complete her degree. Her friends all agree she couldn't stop talking about Julie that semester. Whenever Julie would call, Lollie would put her friends or roommate on the phone: *Say hi to Julie,* she'd command them. Whenever Julie sent her a new mixtape she'd made, Lollie would pop it in her car's tape deck and play it over. And over. And over again. On a trip to an outdoor recreation conference in Pennsylvania, she played one of Julie's tapes on a continuous loop for the entire drive there and back. *Julie made this,* she reminded her suffering passengers, as if it hadn't already been abundantly obvious.

Julie visited Unity a few times that fall, but the social scene there was hard for her. The parties seemed so raucous, so different from what she was used to. Meanwhile, back in Vermont, life was also proving infinitely more challenging than she'd imagined. She and Derek had found a two-bedroom apartment above a diner in Richmond, a small town tucked into the western foothills of the Green Mountains, about twenty minutes from Burlington. Richmond is a sleepy, rural community. It's a fine place to raise a young family, but if you're a single twenty-something, it can feel pretty isolating. Julie struggled to find a job, mostly living off the dwindling savings she'd built up from the summer at Woodswomen. There were glimmers of joy, like when old friends would visit and they'd dance in the kitchen to Rusted Root or collect leaves on long walks in the woods. Periodically, she'd hop onto the AT for a day hike and some contented contemplation. But for most of that season, Julie holed up on the single mattress she kept shoved against the wall in her bedroom and wondered if she'd made the right choice moving there.

As the temperatures continued to drop, Julie hit an all-time low. She loved Lollie—she knew that. But she was also struggling to define herself, to find her own feelings and trust her intuitions. She wrote in her journal that she was lonely and missed physical touch. She felt estranged from the universe—from her family and friends, from God. She contemplated graduate school but couldn't conceive of it beyond a basic idea ("How? Where? Why? What?" she wrote about the prospect in her journal that October). It seemed like everyone else had their lives together. So why didn't she?

Lollie was beginning to experience her own doubts. She didn't know if she was ever going to be cut out for a long-term relationship, and she confided to Julie that the prospect scared the bejesus out of her. Their phone conversations grew more terse. They stopped visiting each other. Then, just after Halloween, Lollie suggested they take a break. "Lost the woman I love because I couldn't hack it," Julie wrote in her journal that November. To her friends, she tried to keep a brave face. *But it's okay, I'm going to be fine*, she wrote to her best friend from St. Cloud. *Every now and then, God scrapes a little bit of frost off my windshield and peeks in to see if I'm okay.*

In the safety of her bedroom, Julie tried to puzzle out what was next. She knew she was gay. She was terrified about what that meant for her relationship with her family, her god. She struggled to embrace a future where the two most important facets of her identity seemed to be at odds. How do you maintain a spiritual commitment when it seemed like every church offering fellowship was also opposed to—and even oppressed— her very identity? Her journal entries became more contemplative, more lyrical.

As the holidays approached, she found a seasonal job at Waldenbooks in Burlington. "Working in the basement of a mall is something I'm definitely not cut out for," she wrote to a former professor. But it was a start. In her journal, Julie noted successful moments of chitchat—with customers, with her colleagues. She found a therapist she liked and trusted. Their first meeting was the day before Thanksgiving. She told the therapist she wanted to work on her self-esteem—how to define herself, how to be intimate in a relationship. She began writing letters to God.

On December 6 of that year, Julie took a risk. She called Lollie: told her she loved her and wanted her back. Lollie didn't respond at first, Julie later recounted in her journal. So Julie said it again. Lollie told her she was hesitant. She said she wasn't sure she had a relationship in her—that she didn't know if they could meet each other's needs. But her response was enough of an overture for Julie and gave her reason to hope. Her subsequent journal entries reflect the joy that so often comes with hoping: that maybe things will work out; that maybe you don't have to say goodbye—not yet, maybe not ever. I know this hope. Even if it has no basis in reality, it can fill our hearts with so much warmth and assurance.

Not long after that phone call, Julie and Lollie met up for the weekend to hash out their relationship and how to go forward. On a single sheet of paper in Julie's spiral notebook, they wrote down all their hopes and fears. Their handwriting is distinct and upside down in places—you can see that one woman was taking down notes as the other spoke, that they were maybe sitting cross-legged and across from one another or sharing the corner of a small table. Lollie recorded Julie saying she worried that after a commitment ceremony, they'd get caught up in the day to day and not focus on their relationship. Lollie admitted that she feared being publicly affectionate as two women and that the strain of a gay relationship in an intolerant culture would pull them apart. Lollie wrote down that she was bisexual. They both wondered what would happen if one of them ever wanted to be with a man. They put an asterisk by the question "What does a relationship mean to us both?" The biggest word on the page is "TRUST." It's the one word I can't tell who wrote, almost as if it came from them both.

The next week, Lollie flew back to Michigan to spend Christmas with her mom, Laura, and Laura's partner, Terry. She warned Julie it was best to call during the day, when the adults would be out of the house. Besides, it wasn't going to be a long trip—just a couple of days was all she could tolerate. Then she'd head back to Unity, maybe try to find a temporary job or just loaf around until the semester started up again.

Julie flew home to St. Cloud on the winter solstice. The night before she departed, she dreamed of her wedding to Lollie. Julie wore a white dress. Lollie brought a million groomsmen. But no one stood next to Julie in support. It was her worst nightmare, she wrote in her journal the next morning. And it brought into real relief what was at stake as she sought to navigate her identity. What would it mean, she wondered, to never be celebrated as a woman starting a family with the full support of her community? To never have a legally recognized marriage? Or one that would be embraced by all the people she loved?

Back at home, she dug out the key to a childhood chest and retrieved all her old journals. She spent the afternoon curled up with them, reliving a high school relationship with a girl at her school and her subsequent sexual awakening. Rereading the pages about the fear and doubt and shame she'd experienced was exhausting. The next day, she wrote to Lollie that she felt "lethargic & lonely/unsettled" and very much like a lost child: "It has been very important to me, to remember who I was. But so painful to see my baby heart poured out with no place to go. No place but destruction and denial of myself." She wondered which of her high school experiences had left a bigger mark: being a survivor of date rape and knowing that someone forced her into sex or forcing herself to deny her real sexuality. "I am still not sure if I, a lesbian woman, am blessed by God and have the right to live my life as God made me," she wrote to Lollie. She never sent that letter. Instead, the next day she and her dad and sisters traveled to their woodland cabin. That night, she persuaded the others to take a snowmobile ride so that she would have the place to herself. She called Lollie. It was a risk, she knew. But Lollie answered and sounded so legitimately happy to hear from her. As the year wound to a close, they both agreed: they were back together—and stronger than ever.

THAT WINTER, JULIE spent several weeks at Unity while she completed a Wilderness First Responder course, an intensive field-based program that teaches rescue medicine and backcountry evacuations, outdoor leadership, and how to survive in extreme environments. Several of Lollie's college friends and classmates were in the course as well. They all agreed that Julie was great and hugely competent in the backcountry. March 9 was Lollie's twenty-sixth birthday. She celebrated first with friends at Unity and then in Vermont, at a club called Toast, where she introduced Julie to Ken, along with some of her old friends. It was a rowdy night with some external drama, the details of which no one quite remembers—probably an alcohol-induced squabble or something like that—but regardless, no one really had the time they needed to talk. *Julie*, Lollie wrote to her friends right after. *I have so much more to tell you about.*

Ken remembers liking Julie, thinking she was quiet and reserved and a little out of place in the jam band scene, but an honestly kind and real soul. He knew the idea of a deeper relationship was freaking out Lollie. She told him she still wasn't sure what to do about the coming summer. He offered her a spot on his farm to park a camper van or trailer. She said she'd think about it.

Julie confided in her journal that the night at the club was a rough one for her. She felt more out of place than Ken had realized. And if she was being honest, she was also a little envious of the easy intimacy Lollie and her friends seemed to have with one another. After returning from the holidays, Julie had begun her coming-out process. She wrote to an old friend from Minnesota, telling him that she was a lesbian and was in a loving relationship. His reaction was far from what she hoped—*condescending and judgmental*, she wrote back to him. She objected to his characterization of her sexuality as a "lifestyle choice" and Lollie as a "temptation" and a "vice." She was hurt and offended, yes. But her letter also had a newfound tone of confidence and even defiance, a refusal to be put down. "I am moving from a cave to a mountain top," she wrote to him. She'd begun involving herself in Vermont politics; she attended activist meetings and called the state's senators to support hate crime legislation and LGBT issues, like partner adoption rights and funding for HIV/AIDS work.

Julie had also begun attending the LGBT group run by Rebecca Strader at a progressive Presbyterian church that met on the University of Vermont campus. There, for the first time, she began to feel like she had a real community, one based on honesty and fellowship. Each week, they'd meet in a small room—usually in the basement or a disused nursery—to read some of the emerging theology and polemics that sought to reconcile sexuality and the Christian faith. Julie brought her journal to each of these meetings, jotting down observations and arguments proffered by other participants as well as her own thoughts. She wrote that she was proud to be finding her voice as a lesbian woman. In her journal, she began referring to herself as a "dyke" and "queer." She said she knew this newfound embrace of a sexual identity was making Lollie uncomfortable. Lollie had told her she wasn't interested in labels, and she also worried about what happened to people who came out publicly. That January, Fred Mangione, a gay man in Texas, had been brutally beaten to death by two men identifying as neo-Nazis. The story had made national news and had made the potential dangers of publicly owning one's sexual identity feel very real.

Meanwhile, back in the Richmond apartment, Julie's relationship with Derek was crumbling. There were the usual roommate gripes: she didn't do the dishes; he never invited her out with his friends. But the real underlying tension for him, she wrote, was his impatience with the slowness of her coming-out process. It took a huge toll on their friendship. By the end of March, they'd decided not to renew their lease.

Easter was the first Sunday in April that year. Julie's parents were already encountering challenges with their own relationship. For the second holiday in a row, they decided to celebrate separately. Tom took Julie and one of her younger sisters to Sanibel Island in Florida for the week. They rented a boat; Julie insisted she was captain. To her dad and her sister, she seemed the same sweet, brazen girl they'd always known. Inside, she was churning. Her plan had been to tell them about her relationship with Lollie at the end of the week. But the unexpected death of a dear family friend forced Tom back to Minnesota before Julie had time.

Back home, she and Lollie committed to living together for the summer. Julie was nervous: previous roommates had told her she was hard to live with, that she could seem cold and indifferent and recalcitrant. But she was also excited. She'd found a job conducting water-quality tests for the Lake Champlain Basin Program, an impressive nonprofit organization that partnered with state and federal environmental agencies and had sweeping reach in New York, Vermont, and Quebec. The two women located a place to rent in Huntington, a village of 1000 residents tucked in some of Vermont's most dramatic mountains and adjacent to the AT. Lollie found a fellow Unity student to sublet her apartment back in Maine, and she got a job at a children's day camp not far from their new place. On their off days, they could step outside their door and onto endless trails. It was perfect, they both agreed. They planned to move in the first day of June.

In the meantime, Julie was still struggling with how to tell her family what this relationship really meant to her. She drafted a letter to her mother in the weeks before Mother's Day. Like any other good draft, there are cross-outs and arrows and inserts as she sought to find the right words. But one paragraph is crystal clear. In it, she writes about the process of coming to terms with her own identity and how liberating it felt to embrace her own sexuality: "The winter ice and snow have turned to rain and the streams are overflowing," she wrote. "Buds are bursting and the trees and spring have arrived!"

Along with the letter to her mother, Julie intended to include a copy of *Deep Water Passage*, a memoir by Ann Linnea, a US Forest Service naturalist and lesbian who was also the first woman to complete a solo circumnavigation of Lake Superior by kayak. "This book has been very inspirational to me in my journey these past few months," she wrote in the letter's conclusion. "I hope you enjoy the book. I love you, mom!"

In that same notebook, Julie also mapped out her calendar for the rest of the month, day by day. She wrote in Lollie for May 3–4. As it turned out, they would have a lot to talk about.

That same weekend, Lollie threw a party at her house in Unity. Julie didn't drive over; she still didn't really like parties with the Unity crew.

Lollie ordered a keg, and even though the weather was still cold and raw, she and her friends set up their drums in the backyard and threw a Frisbee back and forth. The photos from the night are so impossibly happy: everyone starting out on the lawn, Lollie in a zip-up plaid hoodie and her trademark railroad conductor's cap—puffy, blue-and-white striped denim, with a KEY IMPERIAL patch on the front. In one photo, she has her arms flung wide around two friends; in another, she is snuggled up and laughing with two others. The whole crew is casual, bundled, beaming. There's Taj, first leaning against a pretty young woman in an oversize cowboy hat, then proudly lined up with three guys in trucker hats and scruffy beards. As the night goes on, the humans are dressed in more layers to ward off the chill. There's Lollie with a jacket and round John Lennon sunglasses on the lawn, laughing so hard her face is blurred. Inside now, holding an oversize mug, leaning into another friend, looking a little tipsy but no less happy.

That next morning, Lollie woke up to that same friend beside her in bed. The memory of what happened after that last photo was taken was a little blurry for both of them. Had they fooled around? A little? A lot? They couldn't quite piece it together. But Lollie panicked. She didn't want to hurt Julie. After her friend left, Lollie called Julie and told her everything. Lollie said she didn't know if anything had even happened the previous night. If it had, it was just a party gone too far—two good friends, just having one last good time. Julie was crushed. "She is great," Julie conceded in her journal later that evening. "But I hate all the things that make her great more than I love them right now. Her ease in talking with friends and casual manner of shooting the breeze—her presence and honesty. Those are all things I am now afraid of. I see how they work against me."

Julie turned to the Bible, jotting down verse after verse in the upper margin of her spiral notebook—so many words that the writing gets smaller and smaller as it trails off the edge of the page. Each of the passages she chose overflowed with nature imagery and mentions of streams and rivers, like this one, from Psalm 1:3: "And he shall be like a tree planted by the rivers of water, that bringeth forth his fruit in his season; his leaf also shall not wither; and whatsoever he doeth shall prosper."

Eventually, Julie and Lollie agreed to meet halfway, in the shadows of New Hampshire's White Mountains, for a quick two-day trip. The trees were still bare, the ground a mat of leaves that had spent months compressed by the weight of snow. In one photo Lollie took that weekend, Julie is wearing a long-sleeve shirt with the cuffs rolled up to her elbows. She's sitting on a mossy hummock, hugging Taj, whose tongue is hanging out in one of those goofy, perfect dog smiles. Julie is leaning way in, her cheek pressed against the top of the retriever's head. They're both looking at something far out of the frame. They're happy.

Back at their respective homes, the two women began planning how to spend the few weeks they'd have before they both started summer work. *Maybe a trip to New York City*, they decided. Lollie began worrying how Taj would fare there. *Shenandoah*, they finally decided. *We'll all be good there.*

MAY 12, 1996, was Mother's Day. Julie wanted to send that letter she had written. She didn't. She thought about coming out to her mom over the phone, but she couldn't find the words. Instead, she wrote the shortest entry in her journal that year:

Mom. Mom. Mom.

Mother's Day.

Mom.

That weekend was also commencement at Unity College. Wilson Hess, the college's president and the former dean at Sterling College, saw Lollie in the school's administrative parking lot before the ceremony. Most of her friends were graduating that term; she still had a semester left. But Hess recalled that the beatific smile on her face made it seem like she was the center of the upcoming ceremony. She told him she was so excited. She'd just received a 4.0, her first semester of straight A's. The internship at the summer camp in Vermont came through. *And Wilson*, he remembers her saying, *I've met this amazing woman and we're in love. We're going *backpacking before my summer job begins.* Here was this former eighteen-year-old hellion turned grounded adventure therapist. And she was just aglow, *shining*, Hess remembers. He remembers what he told her, too. *Lollie, you're there. You've arrived.* "She couldn't have been happier," he says now. "She was in a state of pure joy. One of tremendous satisfaction. She was the whole person we all hope to be. She was there."

After the graduation ceremony, Lollie spent her last day at Unity at a party hosted by her friend Ann. Lollie arrived, as she almost always did, with a six-pack of Corona. She talked about the trip to Shenandoah, about her summer with Julie. At some point—no one quite remembers when—she slipped out the door. It was the last time any of them saw her again.

Once in Vermont together, Lollie and Julie holed up in the latter's bedroom, mostly avoiding Derek and getting ready for their trip. On May 16, Julie and Lollie attended their first couple's counseling session in Burlington. They still had a long way to go to make this relationship work, they knew. But they were committed to doing so. The therapist gave them some exercises intended to build trust and intimacy to work on during their trip. She suggested they go slow, take some real time to get to know each other as partners. Either that same day or the next, Lollie called her mom. Lollie would write in one of her last journal entries that it was a disastrous conversation—another in a seemingly endless loop of Laura chastising Lollie for being irresponsible with money and Lollie feeling defeated, despite her best efforts to prove she was an adult. Laura's words stung. *Didn't Lollie understand just how much wealth she would one day inherit? What was she going to do? Fritter it all away on concerts and her friends?* Lollie continued journaling about the impact of that conversation on her for the remaining days of her life.

As the two women prepared to leave for their trip, Julie told Derek she'd be back around the twenty-eighth to finish packing up the apartment. They drove to Burlington and spent seventy-nine dollars on trail food. Lollie called her friend Ted, a student at Warren Wilson College in North Carolina. She told him they were headed south. *Maybe we could meet up after Shenandoah*, she offered. She phoned Lyrica, her best friend from Sterling, who was still living in Burlington. Lyrica was out, so Lollie left a message on her answering machine. *I can't believe we're going to be living in the same town again,* Lollie gushed. *Julie and I are going backpacking for a week. I'll call as soon as we get back. It's going to be a great summer!* It was the happiest Lyrica had ever heard her.

20

THE PRECISE NARRATIVE of how Julie Williams and Lollie Winans spent the last week of their lives will always be incomplete. The journals Deirdre Enright gave me sketch out a few chapters. Other threads can be gleaned from some of the credible eyewitness accounts offered after the women died. Still other moments are lost forever.

The dates and times on their initial backcountry permits indicate that Lollie and Julie arrived at Shenandoah National Park late in the afternoon on Sunday, May 19, 1996. The entire region was on the third day of an unexpected heat wave: record-setting temperatures were well into the nineties with humidity and heat indexes to match. Already, local schools had canceled classes for Monday. Back in New England, the women had been waking up to frosted windshields. The heat outside the ranger station, then, must have felt especially intense. Their next stop was Pinnacles, a sweeping overlook around mile 36 on Skyline Drive. They stopped there and asked someone to snap a photo of them. In it, they're still wearing their road trip clothes: Julie has on her leather sandals and a pair of brightly patterned cotton shorts; Lollie is in her ratty Keds and a white cotton T-shirt. She's sitting cross-legged on the overlook's retaining wall, her arm half slung over Julie's shoulder. Julie's leaning in, her arm around Lollie's back, her whole body pointing at an angle toward Lollie. They are wearing nearly identical glasses. Julie's hair is down and loose. They look excited and maybe a little self-conscious.

Just past the overlook is the Pinnacles picnic area, which includes a sprawling parking area, along with a large pavilion and bathhouses containing toilets and sinks. The AT cuts right across the grounds, a fact the park has always been proud of. APPALACHIAN TRAIL. ELEVATION HERE 3400, reads a large wooden sign. ENJOY A SHORT HIKE ALONG A PORTION OF THIS FAMOUS TRAIL, A 2000-MILE FOOTPATH FROM MAINE TO GEORGIA. There, the two women changed into wool rag socks and leather hiking boots. Lollie grabbed her striped conductor's cap. They shouldered their massive packs, made heavy by Nalgenes filled with water, as well as food and gear for several days. The air was still heavy with humidity; temperatures remained blazing hot. That evening, the couple hiked a short ways and found a stealth campsite just off the trail.

The morning of Tuesday, May 21, was still boiling hot—the last full day of the weeklong heat wave. Several park visitors and employees recalled seeing the women at an overlook just south of Skyland that morning, trying to dry out their gear near the 4Runner as Taj lay in the shade nearby. One witness said Julie had confided that Taj was already struggling on the trip: the dog was having a hard time sleeping with all the ambient forest noise at night and that she wasn't able to keep up on the longer hikes.

Late that morning, Jeff and Amy, a young couple from just outside Baltimore, departed the Skyland resort at mile 42, crossed Skyline Drive, and walked down the White Oak Canyon Trail, just south of the Bridle Trail. The former is a gorgeous path—about nine miles if you do the whole thing out and back—and one of the most popular in the park, with six dramatic waterfalls along the way and plenty of places to take a dip. By noon that Tuesday, temperatures were already in the midnineties, so Jeff and Amy were taking it slow, pausing here and there as the trail descended eastward. They hadn't gone all that far into the Whiteoak Canyon when they stopped for water in a shaded clearing. There, they sat on a large boulder, overlooking a shallow patch of whitewater on one fork of Cedar Run, a tributary of the Rapidan River.

As they lingered, Lollie and Julie emerged from the woods, Taj wandering behind them. Jeff and Amy are divorced now. After reading the accounts they provided the FBI, I spoke with them first individually and then together. They differ slightly in their recollections: he remembers

Lollie and Julie loaded down with their packs; Amy thinks they were camping nearby and just came to purify some more drinking water. But the rest of their recollections are pretty much identical. Jeff is a Yale alum. He says Julie reminded him of his classmates there: well educated, attractive, affluent. Lollie, he says, looked like none of those things. Julie, he and Amy both agree, was shy; she hung back from the little group, didn't say a lot. Lollie, on the other hand, was gregarious, maybe even a little forward, like she was the spokesperson of the couple. She and Amy had similar cameras—they talked photography for several minutes—and then the two couples took turns taking photos of each other. Amy's is time and date stamped, so she's sure of when it happened.

At some point that day, Lollie also took a photo of Julie: in it, she's wearing a bright blue sports bra and baggy hiking shorts, her T-shirt wound through the belt loops. You can tell it's still blazing hot—Taj is hunkered down and panting nearby, her belly in a cool patch of mud—but Julie is beaming, a big, surprised smile, like she hadn't realized Lollie was watching her. She's holding a metal pan of water in her right hand, the same Cedar Run rapids behind her. Probably, then, Amy's right; they must have been camping nearby, preparing to boil water for a meal.

The two couples ran into each other later that day as well, back up at the Skyland resort—around 4:00 or 5:00 p.m., maybe a little later. Jeff and Amy both remember seeing the two women lying in the grass outside the busy lodge late that afternoon. Amy thinks Julie had her head in Lollie's lap; Jeff can't remember if they were that close or not. Both agree that they said hi to the women as they walked by. At first, Lollie and Julie seemed guarded and ignored the other couple. But after the women realized who it was, they immediately became more friendly. Jeff and Amy also both recall that there were a lot of other hikers around—the AT goes right through there, so it's a popular spot to grab a burger or a beer or sponge off in the bathrooms. They don't remember if Julie and Lollie spoke to any of them.

The following day, Wednesday, May 22, began as hot as the previous ones, but big thunderstorms broke the heat wave in the late morning and were followed by steady showers, which lasted well into the night. Wednesday was also the day Julie and Lollie met Barb Stewart when they ducked into Thornton Gap to renew their permits. The ranger station is ten miles away from Skyland by way of Skyline Drive, which is more mileage than Julie and Lollie had been completing in a day. Later, when rangers inventoried Julie's car, they found a copy of *USA Today* dated May 22, which suggests that they drove to the entrance station (and stopped somewhere along the way that sold the paper). The permits Julie and Lollie completed at Thornton Gap that Wednesday confirm they intended to stay in the park through Monday, May 27, and that they planned to spend their last night at Nicholson Hollow, just north of the Stony Man Overlook at mile 38 on Skyline Drive. After they renewed their permits, Lollie and Julie swapped out some clothes in the 4Runner and decided to hole up in a lodge to wait out the rain. I can't say which lodge for certain: it could have been back at Skyland. It also could have been the now-defunct Panorama resort, which is right at Thornton Gap. Either way, Julie called her mom, Patsy, from inside. She told her they were having a great time—trying to stay dry, hanging out with some other hikers, that sort of thing. Patsy says she has spent years trying to recapture the details of that conversation, or at least Julie's last words before hanging up. She still can't: she had no way of knowing it would be the last time she'd talk to her daughter.

Around 5:00 or 6:00 p.m. that day, multiple guests at Skyland reported seeing the women and Taj descending down toward the AT, past the stables at the south end of the resort. A woman who remembered chatting with them earlier in the week asked if they were going to set up their tent near the lodge. Julie responded that it wasn't a good idea to ever camp near a built-up area. The witness got the impression the two women were going to try to get several miles down the trail that night. Three additional witnesses recalled seeing them around the stables and refilling their water bottles that day and the next. On either Thursday or Friday, the two women hiked Pollock Knob, around mile 43 on Skyline, and posed for a photo at Crescent Rock Overlook a mile south of there. Several members of a park trail crew remembered meeting the women at the overlook: Taj had been off leash, and the supervisor reprimanded the women. Otherwise, Julie and Lollie seemed cheerful and maybe just a little subdued about the lousy weather. They stayed at the overlook for a few hours, trying to dry out their clothes and gear. During that time, the trail crew and the women started chatting. Lollie said she attended Unity; Julie mentioned that she'd worked at Big Bend. She and the crew members traded park stories.

By Friday, May 24, they'd gotten no farther than Hawksbill Mountain, located at mile 45 off Skyline. They were clearly in no hurry. The weather was still a little crummy—mostly overcast, with a chance of showers each day. Around 11:00 a.m., a surprise thunderstorm sent the women, along with several other park guests, scurrying for cover in the Byrd's Nest, a three-sided stone shelter with a rusting tin roof and stunning views of the western valley.

Two of the other visitors seeking refuge in the shelter were a thirty-something couple from Lancaster County, Pennsylvania. He remembered petting Taj for a while before stepping outside the shelter to watch the lightning. His wife stayed behind and chatted with Lollie and Julie. Both women, she recalled, had spent most of their time in the Byrd's Nest Shelter writing. Julie also nibbled on a bag full of peanut butter crackers. The eyewitness recalled telling the women she was curious about what they'd been eating throughout the trip and whether or not they were losing weight. When the rain stopped, her husband paused just long enough to take a picture of the Byrd's Nest—he thought it was such an amazing coincidence that the shelter had been right there when they needed it. In the photo, Lollie is stretched out on the floor of the shelter on her stomach. She's wearing her trademark hat turned backward, along with a navy-blue sweatshirt and green pants. She's writing in a bound notebook and looks content. Taj is curled up behind her, against the back wall of the shelter. Next to Lollie, Julie sits on a tree stump, a little knock-kneed as she supports a small book and a pen in her lap. She's wearing a blue rain jacket. Her head is turned in the direction of the Pennsylvania man's wife. Her face is in profile, but you can tell she's smiling.

That afternoon, Lollie made what appears to be the last entry in her journal, a letter to Laura Winans in which she apologized for the volatile conversation they'd had just before Lollie left Vermont. "I know that the money I will have one day is a reality," she wrote, "but it's also a heavy and depressing topic for me because it will mean my family is gone, which is something sad and that I can never look forward to." She signed it with the openhearted affection she was famous for among those who knew her best:

Take Care!
I love you!
Love always,
Lollie

AFTER THE BODIES of Lollie and Julie were discovered on the Bridle Trail, Karen Malmquist Fleming, the dispatcher who had helped with the initial investigation, came forward. She recalled observing two young women with a retriever mix and heavy backpacks thumbing a ride near Hawksbill Mountain, just after 5:00 p.m. on May 24, 1996. According to Karen Malmquist's statement, she pulled over to see if they were okay. The women told her that their dog was tired and that they were hoping to get back to Skyland. Malmquist recalled helping the women load their packs into her car. They didn't talk much during the drive, Malmquist said, nor did they provide any identifying information about themselves. Instead, they were studying a map, trying to decide where to go. Malmquist said she had the impression that their vehicle was parked nearby. She also recalled that the women originally wanted to be dropped off at the southern entrance to Skyland but later changed their mind and asked to be dropped at the north end, in the Stony Man parking lot. When they got out of her car, the two women still hadn't decided where they would spend the night.

When pressed by rangers, Malmquist couldn't remember what the women's dog looked like, but she was pretty sure it was light colored.

A law enforcement ranger showed her photos of Julie and Lollie, along with Taj. She said she couldn't be certain they were the women she picked up but that they looked familiar. The ranger drove her back to the area around Hawksbill. She told him she also couldn't say for certain where she picked them up. He showed her additional photos of Julie and Lollie, but she said she still couldn't be sure if they were the women she had picked up. Nevertheless, the ranger wrote that he was certain she had made a positive ID. "All descriptions of two girls, dog, and equipment, plus location, match known info," reads his subsequent report. "As a result, it is believed there is a very high level of probability the two girls given a ride by Malmquist were victims."

Malmquist's report established what became the investigation's official place last seen: the Stony Man parking lot, 5:26 p.m., May 24, 1996. The prosecution's theory was that Darrell Rice had been in the parking lot when the women were dropped off there. The idea was that he had observed Julie and Lollie as they continued looking at their map and then finally settled on the Bridle Trail. As the women began to hike down the path, he grabbed his murder kit and then followed them, waited until they set up camp, and then killed them both.

Multiple aspects of this theory have always bothered me. First, there is no evidence that Rice was in the park that day. Entrance station cameras recorded him entering the park over the next two days. It could have been the case, of course, that he drove through the one entrance station where the cameras weren't working, but that seems unlikely since the others were closer to his father's house in Culpeper, where Rice had been staying. The other aspect that has always frustrated me is the location and nature of this particular parking lot, which is about a third of a mile from the Skyland lodge, where we know Julie and Lollie had been hanging out during their trip.

The Stony Man parking lot is just that: a small horseshoe-shaped parking lot with spaces for maybe thirty cars, tops. Brenda Blonigen and I had spent hours sitting there during our visit, trying to figure out why anyone would ask to be dropped there. We couldn't come up with a single reason.

If it were me, and I still hadn't figured out where to spend the night, I would have asked to be dropped at the lodge itself. I'd order a beer or a coffee while I looked at the map; I'd take advantage of the opportunity to use real toilets and wash my hands with real running water, maybe grab an ice cream cone on the way out. I don't know many hikers who wouldn't do the same, especially if they'd been out for a week first in demoralizing heat and then even more punishing rain.

On my way back to the airport from Charlottesville after another visit with Deirdre Enright, I returned to Shenandoah and parked my rental car in the Stony Man parking lot. It was late autumn, but the park was still plenty busy. I watched a few families wander back from the nature trail contiguous to the lot, grab something out of their coolers, and drive away. I watched a man pull into the lot driving a camper and sit in the truck of his cab while he had lunch. That was pretty much the sum total of activity I observed. After a few hours, I made the third of a mile walk to Skyland to grab a salad from the coffee shop there. Other than a few cars leaving the lodge, I didn't see any activity on the road until I was just steps away from the resort. I returned to my rental car and grazed on iceberg lettuce and ranch dressing. As I did, another family or two cycled through the nature trail. That was it. It seemed so unlikely to me that the two women would have lingered there or that Darrell Rice would have been camped out at 5:30 p.m. on a Friday evening, having come with a murder kit, looking to target a victim he could later follow into the woods and kill unseen.

I also didn't understand why investigators were so quick, on the one hand, to buy the eyewitness accounts of people like Karen Malmquist Fleming and Jeff and Amy, the couple who had seen the women at Whiteoak, but not witnesses who offered equally, and in some cases *more* credible accounts of seeing the women after May 24. In fact, the only explanation I can imagine is that there was some reason investigators needed the date of death to be on that specific day.

As far as I could tell, the medical examiner's determination that the women had died on May 28 has never been called into question. Certainly, in all documents generated during the first year of the investigation, the

FBI and NPS made regular mention of the twenty-eighth as the prob-
able date of the crime (it was even written on that board in the storage
unit). During the first year of the investigation, several eyewitnesses came
forward to say they had encountered Julie and Lollie after May 24. They
included three cyclists who had stopped at the Panorama lodge to get out
of the rain on the morning of Sunday, May 26, 1996. One of them, Ron,
was a forty-one-year-old backpacker who had completed thru-hikes on
both the Appalachian and Pacific Crest Trail. He'd also run a hostel on
the AT for years, where he became conversant in backcountry gear. In the
summer of 1996, Ron reported to the FBI that he watched Lollie and Julie
step off the trail and walk up to the lodge that Sunday. He'd noticed them,
he said, because of the weight of their packs and the women's athletic
body types: neither was compatible with the gaunt build of calorie-deprived thru-hikers and their ultralight packs, so he knew they must be
section hikers. He saw them tie off Taj to a railing and drop their packs in
a dry spot before heading inside. He correctly remembered the color of
the women's rain gear, including both their jackets, neither of which had
ever been publicly reported. Nevertheless, Ron told me when I called him
recently, he had a terrible time trying to get the FBI's attention.

"At the time, for my day job, I worked across the street from FBI headquarters in Washington," he told me. "I could literally look out my window and see their computer screen savers." He said he made repeated
offers to walk across the street for an interview. The FBI did not return his
calls. Some months later, the agency sent a field agent from Harrisonburg,
some three hours away. Ron correctly identified the women and Taj in
a photo array. He told the agent that the women were carrying internal
frame packs and described each backpack in detail. At least one of them
was definitely wearing glasses, he recalled. Taj seemed well behaved but
tired. The women looked a little grumpy about the rain. No mention of his
eyewitness account shows up in any of the prosecution's court documents.
The defense team was made aware of his account only when Deirdre
Enright found it in the storage unit, along with a stack of other eyewitness
accounts from that weekend.

That stack also included multiple employees at Panorama, who had made credible sightings of the women that day. One, a waitress, corroborated the time that Ron said he saw the two women arrive, even though she and Ron had never met, let alone spoken about the case. She described Julie and Lollie in detail: Lollie, she said, was wearing an engineer's hat turned around backward, glasses, and a corded necklace. She had on a dark-colored watch, turned so that its face was on the inside of her wrist. Julie, she said, was "bone-skinny" and had tiny white fluoride spots on her teeth. That Sunday morning, the waitress recalled, Julie spent a lot of time trying to dry out her clothes in the restaurant restroom. The waitress remembered Lollie saying that she was finishing up college in Maine. When the waitress observed out loud that Lollie looked a little old for college, Lollie had laughed and said that, yes, she was twenty-six. She also recalled Lollie saying that they planned to meet up with some people the next night, Monday, May 27.

When first interviewed by the FBI and park service police during the summer of 1996, the waitress produced the ticket from what she insisted was the women's order: Julie had French toast and hot chocolate; Lollie ordered pancakes and lots of coffee. Both breakfasts came with a choice of sausage or bacon. As the waitress remembers, Julie initially said she didn't want it, but then Lollie asked if the waitress would wrap up the meat for Taj. The waitress said that she brought the bacon back to the women in aluminum foil and that they also asked for four pre-packaged muffins they intended to eat later. They paid for breakfast with a twenty-dollar bill.

The manager of the Panorama resort was also interviewed that month by the FBI and park service police. He told agents that he remembered talking to Julie in the lodge's gift shop on the afternoon of either Saturday, May 25, or Sunday, the twenty-sixth, and that she was wearing a dark blue rain jacket, shorts, white socks, and hiking boots. He recalled that she was accompanied by a "heavier-set woman" who appeared to be the same age. Another unrelated witness recalled that the women tied Taj off on a railing before entering the Panorama lodge around 3:00 p.m. that Sunday afternoon. Finally, those same investigators also spoke with two longtime park volunteers and senior members of the Potomac Appalachian Trail Club, the organization that oversees the section of the AT that cuts through the park. One of the women was a retired dog groomer and thirty-five-year veteran volunteer at Shenandoah, where she also worked as a camp coordinator for the Potomac Appalachian Trail Club. She insisted that she and a fellow volunteer met Lollie and Julie on the Stony Man Nature Trail, back near Skyland, around 10:00 a.m. on May 27. She remembered their dog as a light-colored golden retriever mix. She also recalled specific details about Lollie's hat. She told the agents she was an amateur seamstress and always noticed fabric. For her part, the other volunteer remembered that Julie was carrying a dog leash and was wearing a rain slicker. She said she couldn't remember the exact color, but it definitely wasn't orange or yellow or red—that would have stood out to her.

After the indictment of Darrell Rice in April 2002, both the two park employees and two trail volunteers were reinterviewed by Clyde Yee, one of the law enforcement rangers who had also worked the Colonial Parkway case. Yee also reinterviewed Karen Malmquist Fleming, the dispatcher who said she may have dropped the women at Stony Man on Friday, May 24. Although Fleming continued to state she couldn't be certain it was Lollie and Julie she had picked up at Hawksbill, Yee concluded in his subsequent report that her account was credible.

In her 2002 interview with Yee, the Panorama waitress recounted a nearly verbatim version of the account she had given to agents and rangers in 1996. Nevertheless, Yee wrote in his 2002 report that he questioned the legitimacy of the waitress's story. He speculated that she was influenced by her supervisor, the manager of Panorama, and that her descriptions were based on posters that had hung around the park or news media coverage rather than any actual interaction with the women (he gave no reason in that report about why he believed this was the case). When Yee suggested to the waitress that she was only remembering photographs of the women, she disagreed: they were wearing different clothes than those in the now widely seen photographs, and they had clearly been out in the rain. Yee remained dismissive. In his 2002 report, he also discredited her account by noting that the two women were vegetarians and thus would never order breakfast meat, which ignored the waitress's repeated insistence that she wrapped up the meat for their dog. When two of the private investigators hired by Rice's team visited her that same year, she said that she felt bullied and intimidated by Yee. She said that he had dismissed all her claims because she couldn't remember the exact name of the women's dog.

Yee also visited the man who had served as the manager of Panorama in 1996 and who recalled meeting Julie in the gift shop. The manager also stuck to his original story: he had spoken with Julie on a wet and rainy weekend day in late May, and she had been wearing a blue rain jacket and possibly a fleece pullover at the time. Yee asked him to recall the particular shade of her rain jacket. The manager said dark blue. *Wrong*, said Yee. *It was royal blue*. Next, Yee showed the manager a photo of Julie in her shorts and sports bra. He asked the manager if he was sure that that was the woman he'd met six years earlier. The manager said yes. Yee asked the manager if he was certain there weren't any physical differences between the woman he remembered and the person in the photo: *like maybe their weight, for instance?* The manager conceded that the woman in the sports bra could have been ten pounds thinner than the woman in the bulky rain jacket, but that it was hard to tell. Yee ruled the manager's eyewitness account uncredible, saying that Julie was fit and trim to the point of being skinny and that a difference of ten pounds was surely indication that the manager had met someone else.

That same week, Yee also visited Emma Garthoff and Zella Dingus, the two Potomac Appalachian Trail Club volunteers. Both distinctly remembered meeting Julie and Lollie. One produced her daily nature center journal, which cited Lollie by name on May 27. Yee discredited the volunteers' 2002 eyewitness accounts as well. In the case of Zella Dingus, he wrote she had misremembered the correct shade of denim that had been used to make Lollie's hat. Emma Garthoff, on the other hand, had incorrectly recalled that Taj weighed around seventy pounds (the retriever mix clocked in around fifty pounds, say Lollie's friends).

In his 2002 report, Yee also seemed to suggest that the woman's emotional response to the murders was to blame: "GARTOFF advised that after finding out about the homicides, SHE felt violated and as if SHE HERSELF had been raped," Yee wrote in his report. "SHE advised that SHE cried for weeks afterwards."

Emma Garthoff and Zella Dingus both passed away before I could speak to them. But they told Rice's investigators they felt intimidated by Yee and unfairly pressured to recant. Regarding their estimate of Taj's size, I'll say that in advance of a recent vet appointment, I underestimated my own dog's weight by ten pounds. As for the Panorama gift shop manager's uncertainty about Julie's precise weight, let me offer this: when Brenda Blonigen and I sat down with Tim Alley, he noted on three separate occasions that Julie and I had the same build and weight. At that time, I weighed twenty pounds more than Julie did when she was in Shenandoah.

I don't know why Yee chose to disregard these five witnesses, and Yee isn't saying: my repeated attempts to reach him by phone, mail, and through other rangers have all gone unacknowledged. But if Emma Garthoff and Zella Dingus were correct, then the case against Darrell Rice begins to crumble, since we know he was back in Annapolis on the morning of May 27.

It is also true that Clyde Yee's park service career ended with significant credibility problems. From Shenandoah, he was transferred to the Grand Canyon area. While there, he received at least one letter of reprimand for insubordination. His supervisor also reported that he was dealing with multiple "serious problems" Yee had created in other cases. In 2004, for example, Yee was involved in a raid on a Native American trading post. A subsequent investigation by the Department of the Interior's Office of the Inspector General (OIG) found that Yee falsified information in order to obtain the warrant used to search the trading post, including an erroneous account of criminal activity there. That same report also found that Yee exceeded the authority of the warrant and that he improperly handled money and other evidence seized during the search. According to the OIG report, this mishandling included changing the locks on the evidence room without his supervisor's authorization, thereby destroying the chain of custody and preventing other investigators—including his supervisor—from accessing the evidence.

Yee refused to speak with the OIG until he was granted immunity from criminal prosecution. The NPS agreed and determined to pursue "administrative remedies" for his missteps. A short time later, Yee and his wife, also an employee with the NPS, were transferred to another park.

Paul Berkowitz, another law enforcement ranger at the Grand Canyon, was the whistleblower who first reported Clyde Yee in the trading post case. Berkowitz says there's a term in law enforcement for what Yee did at the Grand Canyon— "noble cause corruption," which Berkowitz described to me as "an approach to law enforcement where a desire to put bad guys in jail is used as justification for bending the rules." It's a catch-all term for ethically questionable workarounds, like embellishing reports or concealing evidence that threatens your case.

Berkowitz believes that noble cause corruption remains rampant in the park service. In his book *Legacy of the Yosemite Mafia*, Berkowitz points to systemic issues, like an agency-wide cover-up of the murders of multiple rangers that went on for decades, along with individual cases in which specific rangers suppressed evidence or provided false alibis for one another. One reason, he said, is the park service's mission and the kinds of "idealistic employees" it tends to attract. Some rangers, he said, think little of covering up incidents—including crimes—in order to protect their park's image or to cover for someone who they believe is otherwise a "good guy." Their supervisors willingly overlook or forgive violators, reasoning it is a professional courtesy for a job otherwise well done.

Paul Berkowitz has his fair share of critics in the National Park Service, among them Shenandoah rangers who worked the double-murder case with Clyde Yee and who contend that the whistleblower had no right to publicly denounce Yee's work or character. But after doing my own research into ranger misdeeds, I have to wonder if we, as a country, might benefit from more people like Berkowitz. In the past twenty-five years, dozens of incidents have come to light in which NPS rangers conducted searches without warrants, continued to interrogate suspects after they requested attorneys, and used aggressive apprehension techniques. In one case, an individual died after being tased by a ranger when the man failed to leash his dog. In another, an unarmed man sitting behind the wheel of his car was shot by a ranger. In that case, the NPS settled with the family out of court. In 2007, a federal judge found that Bobby Fleming, one of the two rangers who found Julie and Lollie's campsite, had committed an "unreasonable violation" of a female driver's Fourth Amendment rights when he pulled her over and subjected her to field sobriety tests without cause. Other whistleblowers have come forward to say that their supervisors prohibited them from investigating crimes in national parks or later covered up evidence that crimes ever occurred. Internal investigations in recent years have found huge deficiencies in training and oversight of NPS law enforcement officers and their supervisors.

For its part, the FBI has always been an agency that has suffered from a poorly stated mission or focus. Since the 1990s, the agency has increasingly been pulled in the direction of counterterrorism work, stretching its already thin staff. The agency's effectiveness in solving violent crime has also been called into question in recent years, and studies similar to those conducted at the NPS have found grave issues with everything from the integrity of the FBI's lab work to their ability to manage data to their willingness to submit documents for mandatory review by the Government Accountability Office.

Meanwhile, a recent study by the National Registry of Exonerations found that at least 2,663 innocent people have been exonerated of criminal convictions since 1980. In more than 50 percent of these cases, official misconduct (including witness tampering, concealing or fabricating evidence, and inappropriate interrogation techniques), directly contributed to the false convictions. The study found that this level of misconduct is particularly problematic in cases involving violent felonies: of the more than nine hundred individuals exonerated for murder in the last forty years, a full 72 percent of cases were found to have included misconduct on the part of law enforcement or the prosecution.

None of this means that investigators and prosecutors deliberately botched or compromised the 1996 Shenandoah murder case. But it does make me wonder why they are so certain that they didn't.

21

AFTER MY FIRST VISIT with Darrell Rice's legal team, Deirdre Enright and I began a long stretch of weekly phone calls as we worked to unpack the case against Darrell Rice and the investigation that proceeded it. *Damn you for dragging me back down this rabbit hole*, she'd joke at the start of each conversation. *Why won't you just let me sit around and watch reality TV like a normal person?* I'd retort. Nevertheless I had, in Tim Alley's words, "drunk Deirdre Enright's Kool-Aid." I no longer saw any reasonable argument for Darrell Rice's guilt. And after speaking to both the surviving eyewitnesses and Paul Berkowitz, I had escalated from frustrated to incensed about how the case had been managed.

I couldn't understand—I still can't understand—why authorities were so certain Lollie and Julie had been killed on May 24, a date for which Darrell Rice had an alibi (several friends confirmed that he had had them over for dinner that evening). To my mind, there must have been something crucial about that day: something more than just a dispatcher's saying she thought she had dropped them off near the Bridle Trail then. But Deirdre wasn't so sure. Rice, we both knew, had an ironclad alibi beginning the morning of May 27, 1996. If the eyewitness accounts and the medical examiner's ruling concerning the women's time of death was accurate, Darrell Rice couldn't have killed them.

"I've always thought they just wanted to walk back the date as far as they could to give themselves some wiggle room," she said. "They just needed to keep the date as far away from the twenty-eighth as they could."

"Was the twenty-eighth ever in question?" I asked.

"Kate, it was on a giant board in the shed," Deirdre reminded me. "You've seen the medical examiner reports and the photos. There was basically no decomposition on the women."

I hedged. I hadn't yet opened the folder containing the crime scene and autopsy photos. In fact, I'd been deliberately putting it off.

I promised Deirdre I would go back and look. After we hung up, I went to my office and pulled the manila envelope out of the drawer where I had hidden it. By then, it was nearly dusk, but I refused to turn on a lamp for fear that the added illumination would make what was inside that folder too vivid and real. Instead, I sat down, cross-legged, in the center of the room and forced myself to look at each and every image. The wounds sustained by Julie and Lollie were unimaginably grotesque. I found myself apologizing repeatedly to the women as I pulled my knees to my chest and rested my forehead there, weeping over what I saw. It felt prurient and invasive and frankly wrong to view Julie and Lollie naked and bound and bloody without their permission. As the darkness grew around me, I struggled to understand why. I had sat through a series of images at least as graphic in Ann Burgess's lecture hall. Was it because, over the course of three years, I had come to love Lollie and Julie and the joy they infused everywhere they went? That photographs of them lying dead was painful confirmation of what the world had lost with their murders? Maybe. Certainly, I'd come to know their friends and family and doubted they'd think sitting on my office floor with such graphic images spread around me was all that good or defensible an idea. But there was something else, too. Despite the awfulness of their injuries, Julie and Lollie still looked very much like people, not like the decomposing assemblage of tissue and bones Burgess had used in her slides or I had seen in my work on other cases.

I went back to the medical examiner's report. The date of May 28 was firm there. I spent a day reading peer reviewed articles about the accuracy of potassium vitreous eye tests. By all scholarly accounts I found, the procedure is a sound one for determining a date of death. I stewed over what seemed to be the almost utter absence of observable decomposition in the photos. There were visible fly eggs on Julie's gag, yes, but that was it. Their bodies had been recovered June 2, 1996. The state police officer who transported them didn't think they had been refrigerated that night. Wouldn't the two women look more . . . dead?

I began emailing forensic anthropologists. *I have some questions regarding human decomposition and how bodies interact with the natural environment*, I wrote, hoping I didn't sound like a sociopath. Nick Passalacqua, a professor at Western Carolina University, responded. The founder of the journal *Forensic Anthropology* and a former deployed forensic anthropologist for the Defense POW/MIA Accounting Agency, Passalacqua now splits his time between the classroom and western North Carolina's body farm, a highly euphemistic descriptor for what researchers call a Forensic Osteology Research Station, or human decomposition research facility. The second of its kind in the world, the facility was established in 2007 to study in real time the decomposition of human bodies in a variety of scenarios as well as the systematic recovery of human remains, working almost entirely with bodies donated by people in their wills or by their remaining loved ones.

Passalacqua was friendly to the point of gregarious and had the conversational ease of someone who knows they know what they are talking about. He spoke candidly about his experience working on cases with law enforcement and the different approaches between forensic archeologists like him and police work. "Law enforcement isn't really trained to think of the outdoors like field anthropologists and archaeologists are. All our work is about finding and delineating spaces outside where no clear boundary is present. Law enforcement are trained to look at confined spaces, like living rooms. I've seen a lot of evidence get lost that way."

We talked at length about the things that might affect the decomposition process. Temperature, of course, is a big one, as are other meteorological factors like precipitation and even wind. "There are so many weird variables," Passalacqua explained. "Certainly, the colder it is, the longer it takes for a cadaver to go bad. Insulated clothing or a sleeping bag might slow down how long it takes the body to cool, and that could actually accelerate the decomposition process. Shade and even a cooling breeze can make a difference. But things will still go bad. The body has a ton of bacteria inside it, and blood has a lot of stuff in it just waiting to decompose." He spoke about insect activity, including which flies lay their eggs when and where and how maggots do their work—details that, if told here, would most certainly haunt your dreams. In the end, though, Passalacqua said the work done by forensic anthropologists is really too imprecise to help parse out days or even hours. "Most often, we're dealing with bodies that have been out for weeks or months or years," he said. "We're looking for major decompositional changes."

I asked if there was any way to gauge the difference of, say, four days in a case.

"I mean, you could go buy a bone-in roast and leave it on your kitchen counter for a week and keep track of how gross it gets," he offered.

That last suggestion may well have been facetious. But conversational subtlety has never been one of my strongest talents, and I had grown increasingly zealous about this case with each passing day. Now I was fix-ated on the date of death. If May 28 truly was correct, then it seemed certain that someone other than Darrell Rice had killed Lollie and Julie. Using Passalacqua's idea as a starting place, I began to hatch a plan for my own decomposition study: namely, that I would buy a couple of very large pork roasts, loosely wrap them in quilted nylon to simulate a sleeping bag, and then keep track of what happened over a week. By then, it was midau-tumn in Maine and so cooler than it had been in Shenandoah during May 1996. But I nevertheless hoped I would learn something.

The more I began to settle on the details for this amateur experiment, the more I began to lose my nerve. I texted two of my most trusted friends to ask their thoughts: *Is this at all disrespectful to Julie and Lollie?* I typed. *I'm worried I might offend their family and friends.* The consensus response was that solving the case would make any offense worth it. I wondered about appropriate logistics for setting up my experiment. Our neighbor-hood had recently found itself with something of a backyard rat problem. *Maybe I could just put the roast atop a tall ladder,* I typed. *Can rats climb ladders*? What resulted was a full day's worth and thousands of words dedicated to the extended subject, which included the funerary practices of Tibetan Buddhists as compared to the Zoroastrians, the physiology and mental acumen of rodents, the merits of bear boxes and greased flagpoles. At no point did any of us stop and reflect on how truly nuts all this was. Along the way, it occurred to me that I hadn't even considered what Ray would think of the plan. We were in our second day of a chilly argument that had included, among other things, how to handle the neighborhood rat problem. *How upset would you be if a rump roast was left to decompose for a week in a pan on a ladder in the backyard (where presumably dogs and rats wouldn't be able to get at it)?* I texted. *Not sure why you would do that, but fine with me*, he responded and then returned to whatever actually defensible project he had been working on.

I drove to the nearest butcher store and bought the two largest bone-in roasts I could find. One, swaddled in an old down coat, drove with me to a stretch of woods that abuts a former superfund site turned national wildlife refuge. There, I walked about a thousand feet and tucked the roast under a loose pile of downed limbs. When I returned the next day, it had disappeared and all that remained was the torn jacket, now a hundred feet away. The other went into a roasting pan, which I placed atop the arched arbor in our garden. Our dogs knew it was there at once. By the end of the second day, the flies had found it as well. Tiny eggs, each looking like a grain of rice, had begun to accumulate, particularly around the bone of the roast. On the third day, it began to pour rain, but the flies kept at it. Friends had begun texting, asking about the roast's progress. I responded with close-up photos. They quickly stopped asking. Some swore off meat.

By the fourth day, maggots had begun to hatch and squirm. The roast had begun to turn green, and its odor was palpable long before you opened the gate from the driveway to our backyard. Neighbors began to inquire if everything was all right at our house. I began unconsciously wriggling and brushing off my arms and hair, worried maggots were there, too. By the fifth day, the external surface of the roast had turned black and hard. A putrid brown liquid seeped from small cracks. Inside, the meat was teeming with maggots. I'd seen enough. I double bagged the roast and the pan and threw both in our garbage can. Even inside the closed can, it still reeked—my own porcine version of a tell-tale heart.

Did I actually learn anything? Maybe. The only decomposition noted on Lollie was a slight discoloration under her fingernails. On Julie, the only signs were the loosening of skin on her hands. What I saw on that roast far exceeded that level of decomposition within the first few days. And while there are a million reasons that would prove my experiment unscientific and probably worthless in terms of determining any human being's time of death, to my mind it did seem to confirm the medical examiner's determination. Certainly, it lent no credence to the theory that the women were killed four days earlier than had been concluded. And while I knew none of these conclusions would stand up in court—or even Nick Passalacqua's lab—they at least gave me some solace that I was doing everything I could to make some progress on the case.

Or at least that was the story I told myself at the time. The truth was that I had become feverish, if not altogether frantic, in my attempts to advance the case. I had already asked for and been granted one extension for completing the book. Now it, too, was ticking away, and I worried that I had precious little to show for the extra time. Deirdre Enright had already been more than generous granting access to her files: I had far more evidence and key documents than a writer covering a case like this would ever normally be granted. But it still wasn't enough to say who had killed Julie and Lollie, and somewhere along the way I had decided I couldn't rest until I could make that pronouncement myself.

IN 2007, DARRELL Rice was released from prison, having served his sentence for the assault on Yvonne Malbasha. In the years immediately afterward, he attempted to restart his life in eastern Maryland; however, all the publicity surrounding the Shenandoah case had simultaneously made him both a pariah and perennial cause célèbre for local media outlets and true crime followers alike. Eventually, he moved out west, where he worked whatever odd jobs he could find, sometimes on organic farms in exchange for room and board and, other times, holing up at homeless shelters or disused shacks offered to him by sympathetic back-to-the-landers. A probation violation not long after his prison release (he tested positive for marijuana and admitted to looking at a pornographic magazine owned by his brother-in-law) resulted in a court-ordered ban of social media and personal electronics, including a smartphone, so it had become difficult for his friends and family to keep tabs on him. Even Deirdre Enright often didn't know where, precisely, Rice was much of the time. But he stayed in regular enough touch that no one worried too much about his well-being.

When I first contacted Enright about this book in late 2018, she sent Rice an email asking him to call her. It was their usual means of communication: she'd send him a message, knowing that at some point he'd find his way to a public library with free computer access, and that he would then call her when he found someone willing to loan him a phone. After that first conversation about my request, they spoke a few more times. Rice told Enright, along with his sister and several of his longtime friends, that he was hopeful the publication of the book might finally result in the vindication he'd wanted for so long. By the fall of 2019, we had begun making plans to sit down for a lengthy interview together, a prospect Rice said he found "pretty cool." On a subsequent call, when Enright asked Rice where he was and how he was doing, he sounded content but a little vague: *he'd been busy pulling garlic at a small farm in southern Colorado*, he said. He said that the hippies who owned the place were super chill, and that he had plenty of time to ride his bike and listen to Grateful Dead bootlegs.

Then, just a few days later, Rice called Enright again. He was back in Charlottesville, Virginia, and clearly agitated. He worried the government was after him again. *Could she help?*

Deirdre Enright is as unflappable as they come. On one occasion, she spent hours patiently reprimanding an intellectually impaired client and threatening to return his Christmas gift after she received word that he had attempted to sexually assault his cellmate. On another, she gently explained to the family of a recently executed prisoner that no, they could not collect his body using the family's station wagon. But Darrell Rice's sudden appearance in Virginia rattled her. She called me that same day, her voice filled with an anger that belied concern. As far as she could piece together, a Virginia-based private investigator long interested in the Shenandoah case had persuaded Rice to make the twenty-eight-hour drive with him back to Charlottesville. The entire time, that man had peppered Rice with questions about his involvement. It worried Enright immensely that an investigator would take the time for such a long road trip, and it made her wonder if authorities were again attempting a case against Rice.

This prospect remains a distinct possibility. Despite the best efforts of Rice's legal team, back in 2004, the federal judge in the Shenandoah case agreed to dismiss the charges against Darrell Rice without prejudice, thereby allowing the government to continue to build its case against Rice and bring it back for trial whenever prosecutors saw fit. According to records kept by the Innocence Project and other human rights organizations, fewer than ten federal capital indictments have been dismissed in the past thirty years, and Rice's is one of only a few dismissed without prejudice. Because the government is at liberty to again bring charges against Rice, his legal team's abiding concern has been that Darrell will again be tried in the case—and that, this time, it might actually end in a jury verdict.

There was no way of knowing it, but that strange phone call from Rice to Enright in late 2019 would be the last she, his friends, and family would hear from him. At the time, Enright had encouraged Rice to return to Colorado and helped him drum up the money for a bus ticket. She, along with everyone else in his circle, assumed he was safely on his way back to the garlic farm, where he could spend the season in relative peace. No one knows if he ever made it or where he might have ended up in the interim.

It would take months of phone calls to various shelters and soup kitchens, followed by formal inquiries to psychiatric facilities and then the dreaded calls to county morgues, before anyone realized just how missing Rice really was. But even before all that, the sheer appearance of that investigator and his insistence that Darrell drive with him to

Virginia was more than enough to worry Deirdre Enright and the rest of Rice's legal team.

The next time she called me, she had a new proposal. "I've been thinking," she said. "The way the courts dismissed the charges against Darrell is almost tantamount to double jeopardy. I think that alone warrants the Innocence Project's reopening this case. I'm putting together a team of students. You should come down." I tried to temper the adrenaline-fueled hope that offer created: we would be starting at the beginning and going through those boxes containing evidence only the government and Rice's legal team had ever seen. Somewhere in there, I hoped, lay the key to this case.

As 2019 wound to a close, I booked a flight. Enright's assistant began scanning documents. Three files comprising about twelve hundred pages landed in my inbox before I departed. "This should keep you busy until you can get down here," Deirdre wrote.

22

THE DOCUMENTS SENT TO ME by Deirdre Enright included everything from alternative suspect lists to witness interview transcripts to FBI lab reports. But what most surprised me at the time were the lengths the FBI went in an attempt to elicit a confession from Darrell Rice. At the heart of these efforts was a four-year-long sting operation that undoubtedly cost a significant amount of money, even by federal agency standards (although just how much the FBI won't say, despite my repeated FOIA requests). And the sheer complexity of this operation far exceeded anything I would have thought possible, outside of a Hollywood thriller.

In late 1998, the Richmond FBI field office applied for and was granted both the permission and funds to employ an undercover agent in their pursuit of Rice. To serve in that capacity, FBI headquarters tapped Mike German. A graduate of Northwestern University School of Law, German had spent several years investigating white-collar crime for the FBI before becoming an undercover agent in 1992. A self-described "popular and successful agent" and the author of two books, German characterizes himself in his most recent memoir as "known and respected throughout the bureau." He spent several years infiltrating white supremacist groups around Los Angeles before being transferred to Washington State. There, he famously persuaded members of a notorious militia group to handcuff themselves during a sting operation. (He says he told them he was going to instruct them on how to get out of handcuffs after being arrested. They bought it.)

By 1999, German was working out of the Providence, Rhode Island, FBI office. The agency, he contends, was already in a state of disarray:

"unmanageable, unaccountable, and unreliable," he writes in his 2019 book *Disrupt, Discredit, and Divide: How the New FBI Damages Democracy.* Rice was due to be sentenced for the assault on Yvonne Malbasha in early March of 1998. German arrived in Charlottesville several days prior and met with lead investigators in the Shenandoah case, along with members of the FBI's Behavioral Analysis Unit (formerly the Behavioral Science Unit) and a contract forensic psychologist, who had prepared an extensive profile on Rice. They advised German at length on the best way to get Rice to crack. Part of that education included the creation of a persona: Mike McCarthy, a low-stakes marijuana mule and devotee of the Grateful Dead who had become estranged from his wife and dog, who loved backcountry camping, and who had come from an abusive home. All those attributes, the behavioralists contended, would immediately endear him to Rice.

They were right.

On March 11, 1998, Rice was taken to Charlottesville for sentencing. His court-appointed attorney had told him he'd probably spend a couple years in prison. Instead, the judge gave him eleven, arguing that Rice's truck had been used in the crime and, thus, he had committed assault with a deadly weapon. Both Rice and his lawyer were both shocked by the sentence. When Darrell returned to the holding cell, he found Mike McCarthy, dressed in a Grateful Dead shirt and eager to chat. German waxed on about Chris McCandless, the Generation X nomad made immortal by Jon Krakauer's 1996 *Into the Wild.* German repeatedly turned the conversation to Shenandoah and Skyline Drive. Rice told him the park was rich in history, particularly Native American history. He said he'd royally fucked up when he assaulted Malbasha. He said he and his friends had hiked the Whiteoak Canyon Trail the weekend of the search operation for Lollie and Julie and had been stopped by a ranger asking if they had any information about the missing women. He said that, afterward, when they learned about the murders on TV, they were all spooked and distraught; they'd followed the case closely ever since.

German pressed the issue. He asked for details—where Julie and Lollie had been found, if they had a dog, that sort of thing. Rice got multiple details wrong: he said he thought they'd found the women on the western side of Skyline Drive and that one of them had been tied to a tree. He didn't know if they'd been raped or if their dog had survived. He heard the assailant had urinated on the women (after that assertion, the FBI agents listening to the conversation immediately ordered lab tests looking for urine on the evidence; they found none).

German speculated about how it must have felt to stumble on the crime scene. Rice said he couldn't imagine how awful it must have been: he'd only seen one dead person before, and it was someone who had accidentally overdosed at a Dead show. German wondered aloud what kind of person could have committed the kind of crime that ended the lives of Williams and Winans. Rice speculated that their killer must have been badly abused their entire life to do something so terrible. *Either that, or they had to be totally insane, like Jeffrey Dahmer,* he said. "I don't want to be part of that category of crazy," he told the undercover agent. German said he kind of identified with Dahmer and that he, too, liked dissecting things. In response, Rice said he wondered about the kind of severe trauma that would prevent someone from exercising basic impulse control. He said he knew he'd been on a fine line with Malbasha: "I was thinking about running her off the road. Nasty things going through my head. But I just didn't do it. I catch myself saying, 'Well, I'm stupid to want to hurt somebody,' really, ya'know. I wasn't out to hurt nobody," he told the agent. German kept at it for another hour. He didn't get any further than that assertion. When the marshals came to transport Rice back to prison, German promised to keep in touch by mail.

The FBI timed his first letter to coincide with the third anniversary of the murder, as originally determined by the medical examiner's findings:

05/28/1999

Hey, Darrell,

Well, I hadn't planned on it, but here I am at Shenandoah National Park. I had plans to go to a music festival with friends this weekend, but they didn't get enough tickets so I couldn't go.

I had already given my car and the dog to my ex for the weekend so I was kind of stranded by myself. I knew I would be crawling the walls if I was by myself all weekend, so I decided to rent a car and come down to check out some of the trails you mentioned. I almost didn't make it. The POS (piece of shit) car I rented only had 4 cylinders and sounded like it was going to explode before I got here. I was kind of surprised they charged to get into the Park. Is there a way to get in without paying? I got lucky and got a room at the Skyland Lodge. Kind of pricey, but nice enough. There was a cancellation right when I got here so I got in without a reservation. I left most of my camping gear in the trunk of my car when I gave it to the ex, so I would have been sleeping in the car if I didn't get a room. I'm going to go out and check out some trails before it gets too dark.

I just spent a couple of hours on Stony Man. Good name. Great views. I even saw a black bear—first time I ever saw a bear in the wild. I was very surprised to see one so close to the lodge. Do black bears ever attack people?

I helped a girl change a flat tire in the parking lot. She wasn't too bad looking, and was a fellow New Englander. I think she's staying in the lodge, so maybe later . . .

I ate at the lodge restaurant. I'm usually a vegetarian, but there wasn't much on the menu and I was really hungry so I had the turkey dinner. Great food. The blackberry ice cream was good too. I'm sure I'll work it off tomorrow.

5/29/99

I got up early, grabbed a quick breakfast and did the White Oak Canyon Trail. I see why you liked it so much. Apparently there hasn't been much rain this year so the falls were kind of low. I got some pictures I'll send you. I hiked all the way to the bottom where the trail ended. I must have actually left the park because when I turned around two Park Service guys tried to charge me an entrance fee again! I went round and round with them and finally they let me back in.

The hike back up was definitely a workout. I saw a lot more people on the way up. Some people have no business going outdoors. A lot of foreigners, too. I got off the trail to light a bowl, but I could still see the trail and a pool beneath one of the falls. It's amazing the things people will do when they think nobody is looking! This would have been a great trail to bring my dog on and I was feeling very sorry that I left her with the ex. She would have really liked it. The bitch is probably going to keep her cooped up inside all weekend.

I am starving! I missed lunch and they don't start serving dinner until after 5:00 p.m. I hope a Powerbar will tide me over. A fat lady that worked at the Lodge was wearing a button that said "Take back the Trails", which had something to do with that thing you told me about that happened a couple of years ago. I asked her where it happened, because I thought it would be cool to go and check it out, but she acted like she didn't know. Yeah, right. That's probably the most important thing that ever happened in the Park, and she works here but doesn't know where it happened. Give me a break!

Dinner was good but I had a run in with that girl whose tire I changed yesterday. I saw her going to take a walk after dinner so I asked her if she wanted company. She got all nasty. She said she already had a partner and wasn't looking for another one. Fuck her. Where was her partner when she needed help yesterday? That's so typical of women that they can be so nice when they need something from you and then turn around and hurt you after they get it. I almost lost it. I wanted to scream and hurt her back but there were too many people around so I just left. I don't know why shit like this always happens to me. I just want to explode. Does this make sense? If I find her car I'm going to key it up good. Maybe she'll learn not to treat people like they are nothing. I saw her again later on and just stared at her. She acted like she didn't notice but I know it creeped her out. I just wanted to scare her and ruin her night.

5/30/99

I went back out to the top of Stony Man last night to light up so I could mellow out some. There was a full moon and I tried taking a picture for you, but I don't think it will come out because my camera has an automatic flash. I probably looked silly trying to take it. Hopefully the other pictures will come out.

At breakfast I saw the fat lady again. She didn't say anything to me but I could hear her talking about me behind my back. I just pretended that I didn't hear her.

I'm going to take a little time on the drive and then head home. I can see why you like this place so much. It's just like you said, not spectacular but special. I can definitely see myself coming back here. It's not really that far out of my way and it's definitely worth it. Gotta go now.

Later,

Mike

German enclosed a series of photographs, including one he had taken of himself at Whiteoak Canyon.

Rice responded a week later, offering dating advice and counseling calm, saying he'd learned the hard way after assaulting Malbasha:

Hey Mike,

Good to hear from you . . . Shenandoah has got to be one of the wimpiest Natl. Parks. It gets more wilderness like more south. But you can always look in the valley and see lights of civilization at night. There are a couple of places me + my friends could take you still that are cool (one or two). These friends have been going to W.V. and this Hemlock Wildn. Area near Carlisle Pa. Described

it as the total non–Skyline Drive experience. So you can get a
sense how that park is kind of like Central Park for Wash D.C. It
gets so back when the trees turn color. Last few years its been too
dry or too wet for good tree changes. We have to hook up and do
some things, start at Shenandoah then work our way to (over a
period of time) the Canadian Rockies. I still think I'll get a better
deal with the gov. You mentioned the Black Bear. Its probably the
same one I ran into twice. It seemed young then 2 yrs ago. I doubt
there are many there. I hear Black Bears are more aggressive than
others like Griz and Brown. But the one I saw had no intention
of checking me out. Back to the real nuesance, people. You
know the stuck-ups are going to stay at Skyland. You are lucky
to have gotten a room tho. They do exactly what you did, hardly
anything. I hate that dining room experience tho they used to
have Buckwheat Pancakes. All I can say about that girl's attitude
is it was a front. She didn't have a companion, and that was her
way to keep it so. Don't let it bother you, that's why I never ask so
you are one step closer than I'd ever be. My dad has gotten lucky
up there finding a friend so its not women in general. My advise
is ask to join for coffee or a meal before going for the Home Run
of a walk in the woods. It might take a few meetings. To me its
not even worth it, so stay alone. Usually I am too exhausted from
cycling and would be a bore. So I eat and light up, what more to
ask for. That fat lady probably did not know where the killings
happened. Keeping an eye out and remembering faces is most
likely her job. Your question to her gave her meaning and purpose
in her life. Keep your cool dude. Don't go off and scare some
chick for revenge. That's what I was doing, tho she didn't make
me angry. It was a lifelong dose of talking behind my back like
the fat lady did to you that set me off. I ended up with Abduction
(attempted) with intent to rape for throwing a soda can at her and
making remarks about her breasts. That girl with the tire is just in

protection mode. How quick the mind can think. The only way
Ive got in free to the park is coming in the middle of the night.
To get back in you need a receipt. That 10$ or so is for seven days
I think. My dad used to get a Golden Eagle Pass and give it to
me. Any Natl Park/Mon. in the country for a year. The bottom of
White Oak trail is a popular hike up into the park, maybe those
guys were legit. We have a great place between two of the falls to
hang out along the water. It's a tiny fall with a pool but nobody
will see you pretty much from the trail. That water is always
really cold. They are doing lots of construction this summer up
there. I have no idea where on the drive or what attractions will
be tied up. I'd still think there are better places in the east to go.
My friends love Smoky Mountain Natl. down South. That's really
crowded too. Maybe a wilderness area or Natl Forest will do better
for hiking, camping, and bike riding. My situation is crawling
but maybe the next letter I'll let you know more whats going to
happen . . .
Keep on Growing,
Darrell

Rice concluded the letter with a quick sketch of a marijuana leaf and
Kilroy, the iconic graffiti face first made popular by World War II troops
and later by science fiction writers.

The correspondence between these two men continued for three years
and totaled more than thirty letters. In each of his, German attempted
to make inroads on any possible confession. He wrote in one that Cary
Stayner confessed to the Yosemite killings, then reflected on how similar
the two sets of crimes seemed. He asked again and again where, exactly, the
Shenandoah murders took place. He raged against women. In response,
Rice advocated for finding peace in nature, in the beauty of the stars. He
offered tips on meditation. He asked McCarthy if he might be able to send
a couple copies of *Club*, an adult magazine akin to *Penthouse*. German

wrote back that he could send some raunchier stuff—maybe some BDSM or hard-core rough stuff, but Rice politely declined, explaining that that had never been his thing.

In November 1999, German visited Rice in prison, still posing as Mike McCarthy. He told Rice he was planning on going back up to Shenandoah to see if he could try again to find the murder scene. "You might think I'm too weird about it," he admitted to Rice, "but I just thought it would be cool to camp there, you know. Smoke a bowl and get karmic there. I just think that would be neat."

Rice said he didn't understand what seemed neat about it. News of the murder had really rattled him and his friends. As far as he was concerned, the only thing to be had from that section of the park were nightmares. He advised German not to go up asking about the murders: he said when he'd posed the same question after attacking Malbasha that he'd immediately become a suspect. Getting nowhere on that subject, German tried circling back to the story of Cary Stayner. He spoke at length about the story of Steven Stayner, Cary's younger brother who had been kidnapped and held as a sexual hostage for years. Rice said he couldn't understand why that would make Cary murder three women: after all, the bad stuff had happened to Steven, not Cary. German disagreed: *Somebody just says or does something on the highway*, he offered, *and you just kind of snap*. Rice told him he needed discipline and self-control. He suggested German try yoga. *It's just stretching*, objected German. *Try meditating in the park*, Rice offered instead. "Hear all the sounds. Try to hear everything. Close your eyes and hear the wind," Darrell said. German replied that he had heard of a park in the desert where the wind blows and nothing decomposes. *Bodies just mummify there.* Rice said that sounded weird—and a little gross. By the end of the visit, they'd still gotten nowhere.

After that interaction, the FBI took more extreme measures. In June 2000, the agency concocted a new scenario. Mike McCarthy, they determined, would commit a similar crime to the murder of Julie and Lollie and also in Shenandoah National Park. To make the story believable, they fabricated issues of the *Washington Post* with what appeared to be legitimate news stories detailing the murder of two unidentified women and a forest fire believed to have been perpetrated by their killer in an attempt to destroy evidence of the crime. Mike McCarthy sent Rice the clippings, along with an ominous assertion that he had to flee the country. The Richmond FBI then enlisted the agency's Sensitive Operations and Support Group with the task of obtaining a postcard from Copenhagen, Denmark, and creating a postage cancellation stamp that would make it appear as if the card had been addressed and sent from there. On the postcard, McCarthy alludes again to the crimes and his responsibility for them.

After he got that postcard, it would take Rice nine months to reply to the undercover agent. When he did, he explained that he was "worried and dismayed" about McCarthy's actions—that they ate at him and left him unsure about how to respond to his friend. McCarthy responded, "Simply retaliating when pushed is natural, and must be accepted." The agent cited the Oklahoma City bombings as the other end of the spectrum—a case where multiple innocent people, including children, were killed. "But fate has a hand, and people die everyday. That's just the way of the world." He concluded his letter by again alluding to the Shenandoah case and saying he hoped they would have more time to discuss it again.

The epistolary relationship between German and Rice continued up until the latter's indictment in 2002. German never succeeded in getting Rice to say anything at all that would connect him to the murders. But Deirdre Enright was right: he did do a fantastic job of persuading Rice that the two of them had become bosom friends. When she found the McCarthy undercover file in the storage shed, she told Rice that Mike McCarthy was actually Mike German, an undercover FBI agent. Rice vehemently disagreed. She showed him some of the documentation surrounding the sting.

"Darrell was crushed," Deirdre told me. "It was one of the only times I ever saw him visibly emotional about the investigation." I get it. By the time I'd read these letters, I was still doing my best to maintain a healthy skepticism about Darrell Rice's innocence. But the four years of interactions made it hard. Rice was never angry, never resentful, never anything but reflective, warm, and kind. That doesn't prove someone's innocence, of course, but for the first time in this project, my heart really went out to him.

As far as Mike German is concerned, any negative emotional or legal impacts of his undercover work are just part and parcel of the job: "Most experienced undercover agents I knew recognized that our techniques were extraordinarily intrusive and could easily be used to entrap the innocent," writes German in *Disrupt, Discredit, and Divide.* "We weren't shy about acknowledging the deceitful nature of the work. One undercover school instructor liked to start each class by saying, 'Our job is to establish deep, trusting relationships and then betray them, and if that makes you uncomfortable, leave now.'"

What he doesn't say is why none of these highly honed tactics worked with Rice. I wrote German and asked him that question; his personal assistant responded and said that as much as he'd like to, German just couldn't discuss the case.

23

ON TUESDAY, JUNE 25, 2002, an interstate all-points bulletin was issued for Richard Marc Evonitz, a thirty-eight-year-old white male from Columbia, South Carolina. A day earlier, he had kidnapped fifteen-year-old Kara Robinson. The day before that, she'd woken up after spending the night at her friend Heather's house in West Columbia, a small commuter suburb not far from the state capital. It was hot that day, even by South Carolina standards, and the two young women had planned on spending the afternoon at a nearby lake. Heather's mom had asked Heather to water the flowers before they left, and Kara said she'd do it while Heather took a shower. Hose in hand, Robinson watched as a green Trans Am slowly rolled past the house. A few minutes later, it returned and parked at the base of the driveway. Robinson's first thought was that it must be a friend of Heather's mom. The man who got out of the vehicle looked like he was in his late thirties or early forties. He was heavyset, with a goatee, and he carried a disheveled stack of magazines. The man, Marc Evonitz, asked if there was someone in the house he could speak with. Robinson told him she was just visiting. Her friend, she said, was inside showering. Evonitz asked if Heather's parents were home. Robinson said no, they were at work. Evonitz said he had some free magazines to leave for them and made a show of shuffling them around. From the stack, he pulled a small handgun. He shoved the barrel of the gun against Robinson's neck. *Why don't you get in the car?* he said, calm and polite. Robinson resisted. *Why don't you come with me?* Evonitz insisted again. He led her to the Trans Am and opened the driver's-side door. In the backseat was a large plastic storage bin. He told Robinson to get in. Then he shut the lid and began to drive.

Inside the storage tub, Robinson knew any detail could be the one that would save her life. She memorized the model number on the plastic lid; she made a mental map of each stop and turn. She felt the car accelerate on a straightaway and knew they must be on the interstate, headed out of the city. Eventually, the car exited the highway and stopped in a wooded area. Evonitz stepped out of the car and opened the tub. He bound and gagged the teen and then drove on.

Next, at Evonitz's apartment, he ordered her to follow him into a bedroom, where he instructed her to lie on the bed. He left the room and returned a few minutes later with a notebook and a pen, then proceeded to interview her.

What was her name? Hair color? Age?
When was her last period? Had she had sex before? Given oral sex?
Received it?
Had she smoked marijuana? Did she like it?

Then he explained the rules. When he removed the gag, she absolutely should not scream. He'd want her to talk dirty and would give her a list of words to use. He pulled a sheet of paper from the notebook and commenced to write. He removed the gag and asked her to read the words and phrases aloud, then wondered if she had any questions. She said no. He left and fetched her a bottle of Gatorade, told her to drink up and stay hydrated. He raped her repeatedly, then forced her to shower. He brought her back to the living room and put on a Kirstie Alley movie for her to watch. He continued to assault her, sometimes using a vibrator, sometimes dressing her in a satin eye cover or different lingerie. Once the movie was over, he brought her back to the bedroom. He handcuffed Robinson and attached the restraints to a C-clamp on his headboard. He tied one of her legs to the footboard with a leather restraint. He gave her a couple of pills, told her it would help with her anxiety. Then he joined her in bed, where they watched the evening news. Afterward, he read a book. She dozed off around 3:30 a.m. When she woke up, Evonitz was asleep and snoring loudly. Kara managed to unscrew the C-clamp with her teeth and undo the leg restraint. She grabbed her T-shirt and shorts. She pushed aside an open closet door and vacuum that were blocking the front door. She unbolted it, and then she ran like hell.

Once outside, Robinson flagged down a car moving through the parking lot. Two men were driving—a father and son, she hoped. She told them she'd been kidnapped. She pointed to which apartment, and then she told them she needed to get to the police. *Roll,* she remembers the younger man saying to the older.

As soon as Evonitz heard the door open, he knew he was in trouble. He didn't try to race after Robinson. Instead, he grabbed the keys to his wife's Ford Escort, a bag full of his favorite porn videos, and several pairs of women's panties. He drove to the nearest Wal-Mart and spent $583 on a combined TV/VCR unit, a copy of *American Pie 2*, and new socks, boxer shorts, khaki pants, and men's vitamins. He next went to the pharmacy and bought razors, blond hair dye, caffeine pills, and a bottle of Tums. He refilled his Viagra prescription. Next, he stopped by a B. Dalton bookstore and bought a few books. He called one of his sisters, asking her to meet him at a nearby McDonald's. There, he told her he was in trouble—that the police were after him. She agreed to rent a room at a neighboring Days Inn under her name. Once inside the room, he shaved off his beard and mustache, and then the two went out to dinner. The next morning, he decided to make a run for Florida, his former home and where another of his sisters lived. While on the road, he called her—told her he'd done something terrible. *I hurt a girl,* he said. She asked if there were others. *More than he could remember,* he admitted. His sister asked how long this had been going on. *A long time,* he said.

Because of Kara Robinson's almost superhuman ability to remain calm and mentally record copious details, even during unimaginable trauma, police were able to identify Evonitz shortly after she arrived at the station. They ran his criminal record and found only an indecent exposure charge from his time as a young navy crewman. "We had not heard of Richard Marc Evonitz," an officer later told the media. "He was not on our radar at all." He definitely was now. Bulletins went out throughout South Carolina and neighboring states. The night of Wednesday, June 26, Florida police spied him somewhere just outside of Sarasota, Florida. They initiated a high-speed chase, but Evonitz refused to relent. They then forced his car over a spike mat, disabling his vehicle. He opened the door, brandishing a handgun. The police sent in a trained German shepherd to pull him from the vehicle. The dog bit his leg and arm, but Evonitz was determined to end the ordeal on his own terms. He placed the barrel of the gun deep into his mouth and pulled the trigger. He died instantly.

Back at Evonitz's apartment, police returned with a search warrant. What they found was deeply disturbing: caches of women's underwear, multiple dildos and vibrators, dozens of types of lubricants. They found bondage devices of every stripe, from nipple clamps to ankle cuffs, along with old floppy disk boxes filled with locks of women's hair. They logged hundreds of VHS tapes of porn, most of it hard core and some of it home-made movies featuring Evonitz himself. In the investigative reports, officers made particular note of the fact that most of the women in Evonitz's pornography collection had shaved or waxed vaginas. To their line of thinking, this seemed like further evidence of his pedophilia. As anyone who's watched much porn knows, it's standard wardrobing for pretty much every adult film star of this period.

They also found multiple weapons, including several guns and knives, and they archived dozens of slips of paper on which Evonitz had been tracking women across the country:

Nora, 5'7". 23. Chicago. Just broke up with boyfriend.
Kami, 16. Syracuse. Looks like Rachel from Friends.
Rhonda Lee. Assistant to a Senator. Age 28. 36D. Average build.
Wants kids.
Erin. 19. Vancouver. Disabled. Thinks I could change her mind
about liking sex.

Based on this evidence, the FBI issued a report, stating in part, "Indications are that Evonitz may have been involved in an unknown number of kidnappings and possible murders throughout the US." By August 13, 2002, the bureau announced it had all the evidence it needed to establish that he had killed Sofia Silva and the Lisk sisters: fibers taken from all three girls were found in the trunk of Evonitz's car. Microscopic analysis of hairs found on all three girls revealed "substantial similarities" to Evonitz. Most damning, forensic agents were able to lift a palm print identified as belonging to Kati Lisk from the trunk of his car. The South Carolina sheriff working the Robinson case told shocked reporters that Evonitz had been an original suspect in both cases, but Virginia law enforcement hadn't had the evidence needed then to obtain court-ordered forensic testing.

After news of Evonitz's involvement in these three murders broke, the FBI issued a second bulletin stating that Evonitz had a preoccupation with drowning, along with forcing victims to wash or shave their pubic hair. His MO also included binding his victim's hands, the use of sex toys—especially vibrators—and wrapping his victims in blankets. As late as 2004, the FBI was still considering him in unsolved murder cases of young women as far away as California. In the meantime, local authorities felt they had enough circumstantial evidence to link him to two 1995 rapes in Virginia. Although agents never pursued either investigation, they did note that in at least one of the assaults, the assailant arrived with strips of cloth that he used to bind the victim, along with duct tape, a knife, and surgical gloves. Some of the Route 29 stalker victims came forward to say they were certain he was the person who had accosted them.

Nevertheless, when asked by local reporters, a spokesperson for the FBI said that Evonitz had received "only a cursory look" in Julie and Lollie's case, despite the fact that he was not at work and no one could account for his whereabouts on May 26 and 27, 1996. The agents told those reporters it was easy to rule him out in that case: Evonitz was at work on May 24, 1996. And he clearly preferred little girls.

THE POSSIBLE CONNECTION between Evonitz and the other murders in the Shenandoah Valley might have stayed unexamined forever, had it not been for an FBI trace evidence analyst who had been assigned to work on the special detail task force that was analyzing Evonitz's role in the Lisk and Silva murders. That expert insisted Evonitz should be considered a strong suspect in the 1996 Shenandoah National Park murders. By the spring of 2003, the FBI lab had already run the hairs found in the duct tape and the gloves found at the scene against Darrell Rice's DNA and determined they were not a match. What the lab had confirmed by way of microscopic analysis was that the glove hairs and the tape hairs were contributed by the same person and that person was most likely Evonitz.

It's worth noting that microscopic hair analysis has fallen out of favor in the world of forensic science. Known more formally as "hair micros-copy," it can be a highly subjective analysis, since the process is conducted by a lab technician who compares microscopic patterns between two hair shafts and then determines the likelihood that those two hairs came from the same person. Although multiple law enforcement agencies continue to employ the technique, detractors are quick to point out historical flaws. In 2015, an investigation into the FBI determined that over 90 percent of its hair examiners overstated the likelihood of forensic matches when under oath as expert witnesses for the prosecution. To date, according to the national Innocence Project, at least seventy cases involving people wrongly convicted of serious crimes were done so based, at least in part, on erroneous hair sampling.

That said, it was hair microscopy that first implicated Evonitz in the Silva and Lisk murders. And the patterns observed between the hairs found at the crime scene and those taken from Marc Evonitz, however subjectively they were analyzed, were clearly strong enough that they war-ranted further attention.

By May 2003, that FBI analyst had persuaded the Richmond office to submit some of Evonitz's DNA for comparison in the Shenandoah case. The subsequent request form, signed by Jane Collins, who was then the lead agent in the case, instructed the lab to compare the DNA obtained from the crime scene hairs with that of both Darrell Rice and Marc Evonitz. On October 1, 2003, the lab sent back its findings: Rice's DNA again did not match that of the hairs. Evonitz, on the other hand, could not be excluded. On October 21, 2003, the Richmond office again requested a DNA analysis of the crime scene hairs. This time, they requested that it only be compared against Rice, and not against Evonitz.

If there is a single moment in this case that most haunts me, it is this one. Like the NPS decision not to announce the murders, this decision seems more than just catastrophically myopic: it also suggests a more deliberate agenda.

At that time, DNA analysis of hair was done entirely with mtDNA testing. Of the 16,569 base pairs in mtDNA, forensic experts had isolated eight hundred pairs most suitable for this kind of comparison. Lab protocol standards stipulated that more than two differences in these base pairs would rule out someone as a contributor. Evonitz had only one. For that reason, based on the FBI's own protocol, he still should have been considered a suspect.

After reading the lab results from Evonitz's DNA test, I contacted at least twenty different leading international geneticists. All said the same thing: that not only could you not exclude Evonitz based on that one base pair difference, but also the location of that difference made it all the more likely he *had* contributed the sample because of a condition known as "heteroplasmy." Deirdre Enright had first uncovered this phenomenon during her research in 2003. At the time, what was known was that a body sometimes misfires a protein in a particular place, stamping a C protein when it would normally stamp a T, for instance. As a result, two hairs taken from a person with heteroplasmy may not be perfect matches to each other, even though they share identical DNA.

In 2003, little was known about rates of heteroplasmy or its pervasiveness. In the intervening years, a body of scholarly work has been dedicated to the subject. Thanks to the rapid rise of ancestral testing and sites like 23andme, we're only now beginning to collect enough sample DNA to understand that heteroplasmy is far more prevalent than anyone could have guessed. Hair samples, for instance, can have rates of heteroplasmy as high as 37 percent. One of the most common places to see that difference is in position 16,217—that same place where the one discernible difference was noted between the hair at the crime scene and the blood taken from Marc Evonitz.

Of the twenty geneticists I contacted, fifteen, including a representative of the European Union's DNA bank and the former head of the US Armed Services Identification program, agreed to look at the FBI lab reports of Evonitz's DNA. Each one said the same thing: that this single difference, particularly given its location, could not be considered cause to rule out Marc Evonitz. They also agree that the place and nature of that one base pair difference in the Evonitz results are the most commonly observed kind of heteroplasmy. Finally, they agreed that it would be highly unusual to see only one difference between samples taken from two different people and that a lab error could just as likely be to blame for that one difference. When we learned that the hairs from the crime scene were actually compared to Evonitz's blood, the experts said the likelihood of seeing a base pair difference in that location was even greater, since they were comparing mtDNA from two different types of tissue.

I also emailed my public affairs liaison back at the FBI lab. She reiterated that the geneticist who had run the tests on all the DNA associated with the Shenandoah murders could not answer any questions specific to that case. *But she'd be glad to consider general questions about mtDNA analysis*, the liaison added. I wrote back and asked the scientist's thoughts on what the other geneticists had said about heteroplasmy. She said she concurred and provided paragraphs of explanation as to why she did.

I thought back to my visit to the FBI lab at Quantico almost exactly three years earlier: *Even if we wanted to, we're not the ones who get to open that vault*, the scientists had told me. *The lab exists in support of the field. All we do is examine what they tell us to.* So why had no one told them to test Evonitz again?

The FBI had asked me not to contact Jane Collins directly, and they once again denied the FOIA request I sent asking about the 2003 tests. So instead, I called Tim Alley. By then, we'd settled into what felt like a casual friendship: he'd talk about his summer cabin in Maine or tease me about my politics, and the exchanges were always warm and meandering. This one was not. As soon as I brought up Evonitz, the conversation ran off the tracks and exploded. Tim railed about Evonitz and amateur detectives and what he knew to be true. As he did, I paced my kitchen, sending my dogs scuttling as I tried to envision a way to defuse whatever warhead I had just detonated. Twenty minutes into the conversation, we both realized what the real problem was. "You're saying that all the work I have done for the past twenty-two years has been a total waste of time," he insisted. I apologized and tried to explain that wasn't the case. But in a way, it was. And we both knew it. Before that moment, I had never understood how much the case, which is really to say how much Lollie and Julie and their families, had meant to Tim and what it would mean if he was wrong.

By the end of the conversation, we were both exhausted. But we'd at least found an uneasy détente. "Send me the information about the heteroplasmy," he told me. "I'll make sure it gets where it needs to be."

I thanked him. But he wasn't done. "Evonitz was a pedophile," he reminded me before hanging up. "Besides, he was never in the park."

24

IN FEBRUARY 2020, the Rice team at Virginia's Innocence Project convened around a large conference room table, preparing for our first official meeting. While we waited for Deirdre Enright to arrive, I tried making friendly conversation. The students seemed formal and polite but distant. My normal nervous get-to-know-you jokes were falling flat. Thankfully, Deirdre arrived a few minutes later with a case of chilled seltzer water and bags filled with takeout from P.F. Chang's. "Try the mapo tofu," she instructed. We of course complied.

Deirdre and I outlined the case as best we knew it. The students had smart questions about legal procedures and the nuances of discovery. She spoke about some of her most recent cases: a client who had been in prison for 28 years for a rape he did not commit; another who was sentenced to 132 years for armed robbery. "We were able to free them because we found evidence they didn't do the crime," she told the students. "In almost every exoneration case, the only way to free a client is to prove someone else is guilty. That's what we are looking for here."

She and I spent several hours outlining the case against Rice and what we had learned about Marc Evonitz.

"They totally dropped the inquiry into Evonitz," Deirdre explained. "And at that point, they had no reason to do that. I really feel like the decision not to test against Evonitz smacks of a deliberate attempt not to tarnish their case against Rice, even if it helps to solve the crime," Deirdre said.

She told them about that Hail Mary attempt to find Darrell Rice's DNA on the women's gags. The FBI knew that there was male DNA on at least one of them, and it was sent to the independent lab for the more sophisticated Y-STR testing. It, of course, excluded Rice as well. One of the students asked if that test had also excluded Evonitz.

"No idea," she told him. "Because the prosecution dismissed the case, we weren't allowed to see the results." Enright and the rest of the legal team had tried to lobby the judge, pointing out that because charges against Rice were dismissed without prejudice, he could find himself back in the courtroom whenever the prosecution decided to take up the case again. For that reason alone, they argued, those Y-STR results ought to be considered part of the ongoing discovery. The judge disagreed.

She outlined the team's strategy for the semester. The most important task at hand, she said, was the attempt to build a strong enough case against Evonitz that the government would have no choice but to retest the evidence in comparison with his DNA.

"That task force the FBI formed to put Evonitz under the microscope was disbanded before it ever really got off the ground," she warned the students. "So as far as I can tell, he hasn't really been looked at for the murders of Alicia Showalter Reynolds or Anne McDaniel or the killing of any other woman over the age of eighteen."

We made a list of witnesses to reinterview and evidence requiring further consideration. Deirdre explained the legal research that would be needed to see if Rice's team even had any standing to request further government action. She talked to the students about spreadsheets and cataloging evidence and how they would divide the content of all the boxes for reexamination. Four hours later, long after we'd finished eating the mapo tofu and everything else in the take-out bags, we were ready to get started.

AFTER THAT FIRST visit, I flew back to New England. On my way home from Boston's Logan International Airport, I made a spontaneous decision and exited I-95 just before the Maine border. There, off the traffic circle in Portsmouth, New Hampshire, is a stretch of bypass locally notorious for its smoke shops and robust offering of adult stores. I parked at the one that had the highest Yelp ratings and went inside. Behind a tall purple counter with a safety-glass screen, the one clerk in the store was helping a variety of customers. I waited until they left and introduced myself and the book project. "You're a journalist?" the clerk asked. "Yes," I assured her, "I am." She told me she was going to need to see my official credentials. In all my years of reporting, she was the first person to ever ask. And I had to hand it to her for even thinking of it. I explained that I didn't have any credentials with me, which rightly made her suspicious. As a compromise, we pulled up my author website. She took comparing the headshot and my face seriously. "Okay," she finally said. "What do you need?" What had struck me most about the disturbing story of Evonitz's final days were all the sexual fetishes it seemed to include—not to mention the sheer volume of sexual props, toys, and pornography in his apartment. I showed her the photos of the vibrator found at Julie and Lollie's campsite and asked her what she could tell me about it.

"For starters, it's a piece of crap," she said, coming out from behind the counter. She took me to the back wall of the store, which was covered entirely in rows and columns of every possible vibrator—dozens and dozens of them. She walked me through the different features of several. "All of these were available by the early 1990s, and most women I knew already owned them." She took the photo from me and studied it again. Then she pulled a few items off the shelf and brought them back to the counter. There, she cut open the packaging. She removed the dildos inside and pulled off their latex coverings. Inside were cylinders that looked identical to the ones in the photo. "Is that even actually a vibrator?" she asked. I told her I didn't know.

She wrote down the names of the leading manufacturers during the 1990s and suggested I give them a call and ask about what, specifically, they were marketing then. It was a great suggestion. I thanked her for her time. She came out from around the counter with her hand outstretched. "I'm Heather," she said. We shook hands. "My mother was murdered twelve years ago," she told me. "We've never gotten any answers."

OF THE COMPANIES Heather jotted down for me, only the folks at Adam & Eve were willing to help. They were particularly high on my list, given that Evonitz subscribed to their catalog in the mid-1990s. The director of public relations offered to send me a copy of all the company's catalogs for that decade. They arrived by FedEx just a few days later. There, I found multiple versions of what looked like the vibrator found at the campsite, leather leg restraints with the same pattern of stitching as what appeared on the UV image taken from Julie's sleeping pad, and all manner of lubricants and oils.

I next contacted Lynn Comella, a professor of gender and sexuality studies at the University of Nevada–Las Vegas and author of *Vibrator Nation*. She confessed to being a true crime fan and said she loved the idea that talking about vibrators could help solve a murder. She offered to look at photos of the one at the crime scene, along with images of dozens of vibrators and dildos taken from Evonitz's apartment. "These products from the serial killer are very, very basic, very cheaply made sex toys, ones that you'd be able to get at the most generic adult store (which weren't known for carrying high quality products, because most of their money still came from porn and video booths)," she wrote back. "Certainly by the mid-1990s, better made, prettier and higher quality sex toys were available and many women already owned them." She also said she was particularly curious about what seemed like modifications made to many of Evonitz's props, basically that he was refurbishing them beyond their original specifications to serve his own kinks. One of the things no one could explain to me is what looked like a lanyard or tubing on the vibrator found at the Shenandoah campsite. Comella noticed it as well. "Could he have hacked that one, too?" she asked. "It certainly looks like others in his collection. Has anyone compared it to those?"

Later that day, I phoned Tim Alley and posed Comella's question. He said he didn't think any kind of comparison had been done.

It also appears that the FBI did not compare the outline of what appeared to be the leather restraints on Julie's sleeping pad to similar restraints found at Evonitz's house. According to the FBI lab reports, the agency also requested that the oily residues found on Julie's sleeping pad and during the posthumous medical exam be tested against only Neosporin and Blistex, both of which had been found in the women's backpacks. The lab ruled out those products. As far as I can determine, the samples were not tested against anything else.

After each of these discoveries, I'd phone Deirdre from my office back in Maine. She reported on her own detective work. By that point, she had begun phoning some of the women listed on Evonitz's scraps of paper. With each call, Deirdre would begin with a variation of *I can guarantee this is going to be the weirdest call you receive all day* before explaining why she'd dialed them. She was warm and candid, and the women always talked to her. Some agreed to speak with me as well. They admitted to having begun flirtations with Evonitz, usually on online dating sites. Others said they cut off contact after he began appearing at their places of work or pressuring them to meet him at interstate motels. They experienced shock and shame and embarrassment learning they'd given their telephone numbers and addresses to a serial killer. Most said they'd never been contacted by the FBI.

Every month or so, I'd purchase another round-trip ticket to Charlottesville on my already stressed credit cards. I'd make feeble excuses to get out of social engagements and paying writing assignments and, instead, hole up in my now familiar hotel for a few days or a week, mostly living on pilfered snacks from the law school faculty lounge. Each day, the Innocence Project team and I locked ourselves in our secure conference room and combed through box after box, looking for previously unnoticed evidence that might finally solve the case. We read countless pages of transcripts and summaries of interviews with Evonitz's two wives, his extended family, his coworkers and friends. His father, we learned, had been abusive. According to family members, when Marc was a young boy, his father tried to drown him after Marc splashed water on some hamburgers at a family cookout. After his parents divorced, his mother remarried a man serving a life sentence for the brutal rape and murder of a twenty-four-year-old woman. That union lasted twelve years.

According to his sisters, Marc began making obscene phone calls at the age of thirteen. Two years later, he began breaking and entering. He had rage issues and was prone to physical violence when angry. At a young age, he began watching sadistic pornography with his father and had a particular fondness for snuff films. He sexually molested his sisters and tried to persuade them to have sex with each other. He claimed to have killed a prostitute in Florida. His first wife told similar stories, that he was particularly interested in rape fantasies and had an explosive temper. He would punch holes in walls and break tables when he was angry; he'd go after drivers who cut him off in traffic. His violence became worse with his impotence in early 1996, and his behavior became more erratic then as well. In September of that year, he abruptly announced to his wife that they had to sell their Volkswagen Beetle, which had been his beloved car. He insisted they trade it in for a Taurus.

At that same time, Evonitz was working for a German-owned grinding company, which sold machines used to sharpen drill bits and other tools. His colleagues said Evonitz was obsessed with Ted Bundy and would regularly pontificate about what he thought the famous serial killer had gotten wrong and right when hunting women. They said Marc regularly made lewd and offensive comments about raping women or wanting to murder one while having intercourse. He stole underwear from the dressers of his coworker's teenage daughters. Even the therapist who counseled Marc and his first wife at the end of their marriage called him "so creepy." She told police she felt uncomfortable and always avoided being alone with him—that she'd diagnosed him as having both a narcissistic and personality disorder, along with multiple adjustment issues.

Along the way, the law school team and I found dozens of mistakes and omissions made during law enforcement's original investigation into Evonitz. In April 1997, the same month Darrell Rice was sentenced for his assault on Yvonne Malbasha, Marc Evonitz printed out a page with

contact information for MCI Systemhouse, the company where Darrell
Rice had worked. Evonitz kept it in one of the locked chests where he also
kept his other trophies, like women's underwear. When I asked investigators about it, they said they'd never heard about it before. No one has been
able to explain to me why it was there and whether Evonitz had any reason
to be interested in or connected to Darrell Rice.

Rangers did run Evonitz's plates against the spreadsheet of license
plates they'd recorded entering the park in late May of 1996, but they ran
his Taurus, which he of course had purchased months after the crime.
They never looked at the Beetle. Nor, as far as we can tell, did investigators attempt to determine if any of the women's underwear or scrunch-
ies or locks of hair belonged to Lollie or Julie. It also appears that they
never tested the fibers found in the duct tape against fibers belonging to
Evonitz, nor did they compare the size of his palm prints to those left
on Julie's sleeping pad—or the fingerprints found on the Wal-Mart bag
and the Mountain Dew bottle. Julie, say friends, didn't care for Mountain
Dew. But couldn't her assailant have forced her to drink it, just as Evonitz
insisted Kara Robinson drink Gatorade?

I called Evonitz's former employer, a German national who did a good
deal of his business in Europe, and asked if there was duct tape on hand
at the company offices. He said no before abruptly hanging up. When I
called around to other grinding companies, I was told by all that it seemed
impossible a grinding company wouldn't have tons of duct tape around.
The owner of a small grinding company in Massachusetts seemed particularly willing to help after learning why I was calling. I asked him why
someone in his industry would have 1.5-inch-wide duct tape, the size used
to bind Lollie and Julie, instead of the standard 1.88-inch width readily
available in stores. "That's not 1.5 inches," he corrected me. "It's 3.8 centi-
meters, a standard metric size. Did your suspect have any ties overseas?"

IN 2005, DOUGLAS Deedrick, who served as the FBI's chief of trace evidence
for the special task force assigned to the Shenandoah Valley killings, told
a circuit court judge that he had wanted to reexamine the evidence from

the Alicia Showalter Reynolds case and compare it to Evonitz's known forensic samples. Beginning in 2002, Deedrick had repeatedly requested that evidence be brought to the lab for testing. In at least one instance, agent Jane Collins requisitioned the DNA evidence and received it. According to court records, it was driven around in her car for a time, but it was never delivered to the lab or subjected to further testing. The judge chastised her for that, but it's not clear if any internal action was taken. By the time Deedrick received the evidence in July 2004, he was just days away from retirement. As of that 2005 court hearing, the FBI confirmed the evidence had not been examined by Deedrick's replacement. In 2007, the FBI responded to legal pressure by Pam Gould, the author of a series of investigative articles into the case against Darrell Rice. At that time, Gould wanted to know about follow-up investigations into Evonitz. The Richmond office confirmed Evonitz's DNA was never checked against DNA obtained during the Alicia Showalter Reynolds investigation, despite Doug Deedrick's repeated requests that the analysis be done. State police investigators also said in court they never checked Evonitz's DNA against that from the Reynolds case. They also never confirmed whether or not he had an alibi for the morning she disappeared. According to a 2018 internal agency memo, an FBI supervisor issued a moratorium on any further testing of evidence related to Marc Evonitz. The FBI will not say why. All my FOIA requests regarding Evonitz's DNA have been denied, including my request to ascertain whether his DNA has ever been checked against the male DNA found on the cloth gags used on Lollie and Julie, and which FBI experts stated they felt certain probably came from their assailant. I also asked if Evonitz's DNA was ever listed on CODIS, the national database that allows for instant matches in new and unsolved cases. That request was also denied. In the letter explaining why my request had been denied, an FBI FOIA officer stated that that information "is not in the public's best interest and thus does not meet the Freedom of Information standard."

The Department of Justice does mandate the collection of DNA from individuals convicted of crimes like Darrell Rice's. Most likely, then, his

DNA was uploaded to CODIS. If it has been, it had not led to a match in any other case.

New methods for extracting skin cells and other trace DNA have emerged in recent years, including MVac, which is basically the world's strongest wet vacuum. Multiple forensic experts who belong to the American Investigative Society of Cold Cases said that that would be exactly where they'd start if they were allowed to consult on the Shenandoah case. They all also said they'd be shocked if the process didn't turn up previously undetected DNA samples most likely left by the murderer. When I asked if the technique had been used in this case, the case investigators willing to entertain my question on deep background said that it hadn't.

Trace evidence is not the holy grail of criminal convictions that TV forensic dramas would have you believe. It is true that advances in science now allow labs to make genetic matches with as few as just a handful of cells. But that sophistication has also come with a problematic legal cost. A few years ago, a father was convicted of raping his young daughter after his semen was discovered in her underwear. Subsequent forensic work found his semen in the clothing of his other relatives as well. It wasn't until experts determined that something as simple as washing a load of laundry was enough to deposit those cells on other people's clothing that he was exonerated. A few years ago, European officials were convinced they had a continent-wide serial killer after DNA taken from more than forty evidence kits pointed to the same individual. It took months before one enterprising lab scientist determined that the DNA actually came from a factory worker who had packaged the swabs used to collect evidence.

However, hairs found in duct tape used to bind murder victims and in gloves found at a crime scene are not exactly trace evidence. And no one I have spoken with has any kind of explanation for how a man who is not Darrell Rice—a man who happens to be a known serial killer, in fact—might have come in contact with Lollie, Julie, a pair of their gloves, and the duct tape used to restrain them. I do know that emerging and even more precise means of comparing hair samples have been touted by the forensic community recently, including a process perfected by Ed Green, a paleogeneticist at the University of California–Santa Cruz. Green developed a workaround for the limitations of mtDNA matching by applying a sophisticated genetic sequencing system that allows him to extract the kind of DNA used in more in-depth analysis. It requires only about a centimeter of hair, and he already has a relationship with the FBI, having worked on previous cases for them. When I called him about the Shenandoah case, he asked to see the lab reports generated by the earlier testing. I sent them to him. We spoke on the phone a few days later. "This is exactly the kind of case we like to take on," he said. "We have availability for a new one. Let's see if the FBI will give us this one." As of this writing, neither he nor I have heard back on that offer.

Similarly, objects like tire irons (which would leave the shape of contusions left on both women, along with the Lisk sisters and Thelma Scroggins and which were placed into evidence from Evonitz's apartment and car) were never swabbed for DNA. I have asked the Virginia State Police what size duct tape was used to bind Anne McDaniels; they would not reply. When I spoke with Sadie Showalter, she was not aware that gloves and cigarette butts were found at the scene of her daughter Alicia's disappearance and where her body was recovered. So far as she knows, neither was compared to Evonitz either, despite the fact that he was a known chain smoker.

I can't say for certain that Darrell Rice did not kill Julie Williams and Lollie Winans. But of the hundreds of experts I've spoken with, only the three agents involved in the initial investigation say they believe he is the perpetrator. Every other profiler, investigator, and scientist says that the preponderance of the evidence makes a strong case that Rice is innocent and that Marc Evonitz is a far stronger suspect. I do know that if Darrell Rice is innocent, his life since 1996 can only be considered a tragedy. I don't use that word lightly. The harshness of his sentence for the crime against Malbasha was in no small part predicated on the belief that he had killed Lollie and Julie. Since his release, he has been harassed wherever he has gone. As soon as residents realize Rice is in their town, rumors begin surfacing that he has done everything from hijacking a school bus and kidnapping the children to leading police on high-speed chases to stealing cars and murdering women. None of this has been substantiated. Much of it has actually been demonstrably disproved, thanks to the ankle bracelet he was forced to wear for several years after he was released. Nevertheless, public outcry continues. When word spread in Durango, Colorado, a few years ago that Darrell Rice had been seen there, social media outlets and local newspapers erupted with the story, citing "several dozen" calls from concerned citizens in less than a week. "All I know is he's not wanted, and we ain't looking for him," the county sheriff told a local reporter working on the story, which was published on the front page of the *Durango Herald*.

Legally speaking, Darrell Rice has a presumption of innocence and the right to live the life of any other individuals who served their time after being convicted of a crime. Instead, public pressure has forced him almost entirely underground. As I write this chapter, he has been missing for nine months. His friends and family say they fear he may be dead: never has he gone more than a few weeks without being in touch with at least one of them. If he is alive, his existence remains clouded by the very real possibility that, at any moment, the government will reinstate his case. Meanwhile, as long as investigators continue to insist that he killed Julie and Lollie, further inquiry into their case appears to remain stalled. And that means neither their friends and family members, nor the many other people impacted by their deaths, will get the answers they want and deserve.

25

AFTER THE COVID-19 PANDEMIC ERUPTED in the spring of 2020, the University of Virginia moved to a virtual campus model, which effectively disbanded the Rice Innocence Project team. Several of the students offered to continue working from their homes, and they've stayed active in the investigation, working with me on case research and sometimes even returning to the Stony Man parking lot and Bridle Trail on their own.

That summer and fall, Deirdre Enright and I continued sorting through boxes and burrowing down one rabbit hole and then another. In our own Hail Mary attempt, we summarized everything we had found, and Enright sent it in a letter to a former federal attorney she knew was sympathetic to the case. We never heard back. But we kept at it.

After one particularly grueling day, we sat on the Enrights' back porch. The family had just adopted a new puppy named Elton John, and I commandeered him as my own that night, tucking him in next to me on my patio chair. As a sultry Virginia thunderstorm built on the western horizon, we ate guacamole made by one of Deirdre's daughters and traded stories about our careers. Deirdre and her husband spoke passionately about their work on capital cases. I wondered aloud how they managed to remain in those very grim trenches for so long, especially knowing that they will watch some of their clients be put to death for crimes they did not commit and witness the emotional despair of so many families looking for answers.

At that observation, Deirdre grew uncharacteristically somber. "Pretty much everywhere I drive around here, I pass the site of a place where another woman's body was found," she told me. "It makes me so very angry."

"Don't you ever just want to get away from that?" I asked. "Find a new landscape that isn't so imprinted with death and suffering for you?"

She shrugged. "Sometimes, especially when I'm particularly tired, I think about leaving all of this and going somewhere new and fresh," she conceded. "But then I think, 'What right do I have to look away?'"

Her response made me think about some of the amateur cold case devotees I've met on discussion boards and at crime conventions over the past few years. One woman, who goes by the username Cleo, has always stuck with me. For nearly a decade now, Cleo has contributed thousands of entries to various true crime discussion boards. On a whim, I once asked her why. She told me she had been raped when she was a young teenager living in the San Francisco Bay Area and that the resulting trauma plagued her for years, particularly whenever local media reported that the perpetrator known only as the East Area Rapist had struck again. In 2001, DNA testing revealed that the East Area Rapist was also most likely the serial killer who would become known as the Golden State Killer. News coverage of that connection brought back much of the trauma Cleo had experienced as a girl. She began spending hours reading websites and list-servs dedicated to the unsolved cases.

"I wanted that guy caught before he could hurt anyone else," she told me. "At first I was too scared to contribute to the forums. I had nightmares all over again. But I also had ideas."

She started doing her own research and reading about violent offenders. She took psychology courses and studied sociopathic and psychopathic conditions. And then she joined in the conversation. "For the first time, I felt empowered," she told me. "And while it maybe sounds odd, the more I learned about the people who do these kinds of crimes, the more I began to trust everyone else."

After Joseph James DeAngelo was arrested for the crimes, Cleo figured that would be the end of her sleuthing. But then she somehow found her way to discussions dedicated to the Colonial Parkway murders, along with

Lollie and Julie's. She, too, decided she couldn't look away. "Once I saw their pictures, I could really put myself right with them," she told me by phone. "It was a moment of particularly powerful empathy."

I think a lot of people, especially women, can relate to that sentiment. I didn't know to ask for help after I was sexually assaulted. It took years of therapy for me to understand that I was both a victim and a survivor. Along the way, and even before I could say those words out loud, I had thrown myself into volunteer work as a sexual assault responder and victim advocate, perhaps intuiting on at least a subconscious level that helping others could somehow help me heal as well. Regardless of whether or not people have been crime victims, so very many of us experience dislocation and fear when we learn about harm befalling other people like us. We want to know that order can be restored after something terrible happens. We want to understand why these things continue to occur and how to keep them from happening to us. We want certainty, which of course is impossible. But we also want justice, and that shouldn't be beyond our reach.

While I was writing the first draft of this manuscript, I tracked down the man who had sexually assaulted me when he was twenty-four and I was sixteen. Now married and with two teenage sons, he lives not far from where Marc Evonitz spent his final years. Scrolling through my attacker's social media account made me question everything I remembered about that incident. His wife posted often about her love for her husband, their faith, and the closeness of their family. Even knowing the overly rosy images so many of us peddle on social media, I still thought long and hard about contacting the man and asking if my memories of that night were all wrong. But I knew in my heart they weren't. And in the end, I decided I didn't want to hear anything he had to say. What really mattered was that I had somehow managed to find my own voice in spite of him.

Writing this book has taken every toll I feared it would. For more than four years, the story of Julie and Lollie and women like them has consumed me. It's depleted my bank account and savings. Along the way, I've compensated with alcohol more than I'm sure is healthy. I put demands on a domestic relationship that were impossible to justify. Other relationships have suffered as well, particularly those with my immediate family after I first began writing about my own sexual assault. But those, to paraphrase Monty Python, are really only flesh wounds.

The day after I submitted my very tardy first draft of this book, a girlfriend and I embarked on a multiday trek in Maine's western mountains. According to the calendar, spring had long since arrived. But the snowpack was still formidable, so we skinned up a section of trail on backcountry skis and made camp at one of the huts atop a ridgeline there. That night, after she and the handful of other campers had gone to bed, I bundled up in my sleeping bag and winter gear and stood outside the hut, gazing into the expansive darkness around us. For the first time in a long time, I felt the same peace and unfettered freedom I had on that first backpacking trip back in college. And in that stillness, I was overcome with the intimate realization that I stood watch, alone, over a slumbering world. I realized only later, back at home, that I had not once felt afraid.

After that trip, I bought a new tent: a green one, the only color I could think of that has no association with the Shenandoah murders. I still haven't taken it on a solo backpacking trip, but the prospect of one doesn't terrify me or leave me with a sense of dread. My dogs and I trail-run almost every morning, and sometimes I can go miles and miles before the thought of the bad things that have happened in the woods begin to surface.

I still wake up with a start, but these days the precipitating emotion is the kind of anger I imagine people like Deirdre Enright experience all the time. I'm angry that amateurs like me or Bill Thomas need to police law enforcement and uncover the deficiencies and mistakes in their investigations. I'm angry that women like the Annes are still too traumatized to hike alone and that every year there is demonstrable evidence that women, African Americans, and nonbinary and LGBTQ people have good reason to wonder if they are safe in the wilderness, which in many ways is still considered a white male domain. I'm angry that since I began writing this book, other backpackers have been murdered and assaulted hiking our nation's trails, including the AT, and that those killers have left grieving families behind. I'm angry about the other people who have been murdered in our national wilderness since I began this project, including a grandmother and granddaughter in Shenandoah National Park. I'm angry that Lollie Winans's parents died before ever learning what happened to their daughter and that grieving parents like the Williamses and Showalters still go to bed at night praying for their own. Then I work my way through the now familiar catalog of women Marc Evonitz kept in his journals and secret chests, the stacks of hotel receipts he preserved from the places those women lived. I think about their families and worry that some of them may have been left to wonder what became of their beloved daughters and sisters. And then I wonder who is demanding answers for all of them.

Acknowledgments

WRITING THIS BOOK was possible only because countless individuals were willing to share their memories, their personal stories, and their expertise. They are far too many to list here, but I am deeply grateful and humbled by each person who responded to a letter, email, or phone call and agreed to talk about some aspect of the Shenandoah case, the nature of crime investigation and forensics, their own experiences with violence, or their continued heartbreak over losing a beloved friend or family member.

I am particularly indebted to Tom and Patsy Williams, who entrusted me with stories, photographs, and writings by their daughter and to Julie's friends and former colleagues who shared their own memories, especially Sarah and Becky, who spoke with me at length for this book. Thanks also to the former staff of Woodswomen and cofounder Denise Mitten, who invited me into their community and shared so much of themselves and their accomplishments along the way. Both of Lollie Winans's parents died before I began this journey, and so I relied heavily on recollections from her friends. I want especially to thank Lyrica, Ken, and Ted for filling in Lollie's childhood and time in Vermont and for extending me some of the same warmth and friendship they gave her. Unity alums Steph and Ann spoke with me for hours on end and were selfless spirit guides when it came to determining who else I needed to speak with and how to find them. I am equally grateful for the assistance of my former colleagues at the college, including Pat Clark, who also served as a mentor to me during my first years there, and Wilson Hess, a true champion of us all. While I was researching this book, two beloved Unity faculty members and particular favorites of Lollie's—Barry Woods and Dot Quimby—passed away. Like many in the community, I continue to miss them both every day.

The research and investigative findings presented in this book were built on the strong and talented backs of individuals who have dedicated their lives to solving this and similar cases. Thanks go to Ann Burgess, who shared her wisdom and the insight of her students, and Bill Thomas, who has become a cherished friend and partner in arms. I am also grateful for the wisdom and time offered by Brenda Blonigen, Claudia Brenner, Terri Jentz, and Annette McGiveney, along with the research help provided by Kayla Raftice. In the course of writing this book, I had the good fortune to spend days at Shenandoah National Park in the company of some of the people who love it the most, including Barb Stewart, Ken Johnson, Bridget Bohnet, and also Sally Hurlbert, who cheerfully responded to the moun-tainous FOIA requests I sent her way. Tim Alley spent hours and hours rehashing every aspect of this case with me and was unflinching in his appraisals and assessments. In the end, we didn't always agree about some of the particulars of the case, but I will forever admire and appreciate his dedication and service on behalf of the park and its visitors. I'm equally grateful for Darrell Rice's legal team and for the staff, students, and faculty at the University of Virginia School of Law, especially Nicholas Cummins, who scanned and organized more documents than one human should ever have to handle, and Paul Lichlyter, who provided invaluable research assistance even after our Innocence Project team disbanded. Deirdre Enright is both a legal legend and laugh riot, and I am a far better person for ever having met her.

I am also grateful for the moral and emotional support of my writing and trail communities. Thanks to Kelly Pietrzak, Christie Rodrigue, Tami Kasoff, Mari Balow, Mindy Slovinsky, Brenda Cyr, and Shannon Bryan for keeping me company in the woods. Thank you also to my Maine community of writers, particularly Brian Kevin, Murray Carpenter, Dave Howard, Lincoln Paine, Mary Pols, and Laura Poppick for your camara-derie and sage advice. Thanks to the editorial staff at *Outside* magazine, especially Greg Thomas, for believing in this story from its inception. And a particularly big toast of gratitude goes to Camille Dungy, Melissa Falcon Field, and Suzanne Roberts for being the world's best adoptive sisters and fiercely fabulous writers.

Finally, and perhaps most important, I want to thank those people who lived this story with me each and every day for more than four years. I feel privileged to have found a home at Algonquin Books and am grateful to the exceedingly talented team there. I count my lucky stars that their inimitable publisher, Betsy Gleick, wanted not only to tell this important story but also to give it the best of her talents and attention, even when I was tardy or recalcitrant. Wendy Strothman and Lauren MacLeod, the geniuses at the Strothman Literary Agency, have been my cherished friends, advocates, and occasional therapists for over a decade now. Every writer should be so lucky to have such smart, thoughtful champions in their court; I am so glad they are in mine.

Notes

CHAPTER 1

17 **"These families have suffered":** Department of Justice, Attorney General Transcript, "Indictment of Darrell David Rice," April 10, 2001, www.justice.gov/archive/ag/speeches/2002/041002newsconferenceindictment.htm.

17 **"sad reminder":** Christopher Marquis, "Man Is Charged in 2 Killings That U.S. Calls Hate Crime," *New York Times*, April 11, 2002, www.nytimes.com/2002/04/11/us/man-is-charged-in-2-killings-that-us-calls-hate-crime.html.

CHAPTER 2

28 **Molly LaRue and Geoff Hood:** Earl Swift, "Murder on the Appalachian Trail," *Outside*, September 2, 2015, www.outsideonline.com/2011326/murder-appalachian-trail.

30 **homicides in our national parks:** International Association of Chiefs of Police, *Policing the National Parks: 21st Century Requirements*, National Park Service History eLibrary, October 2000, npshistory.com/publications/ranger/iacp-policing-np-2000.pdf.

31 **rangers revealed:** US Department of the Interior, Office of the Inspector General, *Disquieting Disorder: An Assessment of Department of the Interior Law Enforcement* (Washington, DC: US Department of the Interior, 2002), 36.

31 **"not worth the paper":** Ibid.

31 **In the case:** Government Accountability Office, *Federal Lands: Adopting a Formal, Risk-Based Approach Could Help Land Management Agencies Better Manage Their Law Enforcement Resources* (GAO-11-144, Washington, DC, December 2010), www.gao.gov/products/gao-11-144.

32 **ad hoc programs:** Multiple inquiries by the Government Accountability Office corroborated these findings, stating that the actual threats and assaults on federal land remain difficult to assess for many of the same reasons. According to the GAO, available evidence suggested an increase in illegal activity on federal lands, including serious crimes. Meanwhile, the number of Department of Interior law enforcement officers, including NPS rangers, has decreased by more than 20 percent in the last decade, while wilderness usage has increased by about the same percentage, making it all the more likely that violent crimes won't be recorded at all.

32 **toward male victims:** According to the FBI's Uniform Crime Report, 78 percent of all murder victims are male. Federal Bureau of Investigation, Criminal Justice

Information Services Division, *2019 Crime in the United States*, ucr.fib.gov/crime-in
-the.u.s/2019/crime-in-the-u.s.-2019.

33 **"You gotta remember":** Cox News Service, "Hiker Never Gave Up Fight, Her Killer
Said," *Blue Ridge Times*, March 24, 2008, www.blueridgenow.com/article/NC/20080324/
News/606044574/HT.

CHAPTER 3

36 **provide their DNA:** Michelle Hibbert, "DNA Databases: Law Enforcement's
Greatest Surveillance Tool?" *Wake Forest Law Review* 34 (Fall 1999): 767–825.

40 **protocols for homicide investigation:** National Medicological Review Panel,
Death Investigation: A Guide for the Investigator (US Department of Justice, Washington,
DC, 1996).

41 **a murder weapon:** Charles Wellford and James Cronin, *An Analysis of Variables
Affecting the Clearance of Homicides: A Multistate Study* (Justice Research and Statistics
Association, October 1999), www.jrsa.org/pubs/reports/Clearance_of_Homicide.html.

44 **rules for the latter:** "The Evolution of Enforcement in the Service," *Ranger: The
Journal of the Association of National Park Rangers* 1, no. 2 (1985): 7–12.

44 **agents outnumber rangers:** "Park Rangers' Jobs Increasingly Dangerous,"
Seattle Times, January 2, 2012, https://www.seattletimes.com/seattle-news/park-rangers-
jobs-increasingly-dangerous.

CHAPTER 4

50 **promised her roommate:** As told to me by her parents, Tom and Patsy Williams.

54 **already thin resources:** "Battle for the Blue Ridge," *Washington Post*, October 31, 1993.
www.washingtonpost.com/archive/lifestyle/magazine/1993/10/31/battle-for-the-blue-
ridge/f2654e4a-075b-4607-ab41-37b855439aa4/.

54 **cutting back on seasonal:** In the twenty-five years since, this problem has only
worsened. The Government Accountability Office currently estimates the NPS maintenance backlog exceeds eleven billion dollars.

55 **the Fraternal Order:** Ned Burks and Chris Fordney, "Battle for the Blue
Ridge," *Washington Post*, October 31, 1993, www.washingtonpost.com/archive/lifestyle/
magazine/1993/10/31/battle-for-the-blue-ridge/f2654e4a-075b-4607-ab41-37b855439aa4/.

55 **"patently illogical":** Cyril T. Zaneski, "The Thin Green Line," *Government
Executive*, May 1, 2003, www.govexec.com/magazine/2003/05/the-thin-green-line/14088/.

55 **trees and other hazards:** GAO Report to Congressional Requesters, *National Parks:
Difficult Choices Need to Be Made about the Future of the Parks* (T-RCED-95-124 [GAO/
RCED-95-238], Washington, DC, August 1995), www.gao.gov/assets/rced-95-238.pdf.

57 **previous two weeks:** My narrative of the initial investigation is based on a combination of first-person interviews with the agents, archival documents obtained from the
NPS, and court records.

69 **"He was so nice":** Pamela Gould, "Link Probed in 29 Stalker Cases," *Free Lance–
Star* (Fredericksburg, VA), May 12, 1996.

71 **"It's very important":** Leef Smith, "Fatal Fantasy: Police Profile Rt. 29 Stalker,"
Washington Post, November 13, 1996.

CHAPTER 5

76 **"I was very surprised":** Associated Press, "Investigators Search for Clues," *Free Lance–Star* (Fredericksburg, VA), June 13, 1996.

CHAPTER 6

83 **Rigor mortis exits:** Kori Shivpoojan, "Time since Death from Rigor Mortis: Forensic Prospective." *Journal of Forensic Science and Criminal Investigation* 9, no. 5 (July 2018): 555771, doi.org/10.19080/JFSCI.2018.09.555771.

84 **press conference was tense:** Rajiv Chandrasekaran and Tod Robberson, "2 Women Slain in Shenandoah National Park," *Washington Post*, June 4, 1996.

85 **twelve to fifteen hours:** Ibid.

86 **"This is ridiculous":** A. J. Plunkett, "Probe of Deaths Oddly Quiet," *Times-Dispatch* (Richmond, VA), June 23, 1996.

CHAPTER 7

89 **"It took us":** "Questions Remain in Shenandoah Case," *Virginian-Pilot* (Norfolk, VA), June 6, 1996.

89 **"Spokesperson Paul Pfenninger":** Rajiv Chandrasekaran and Tod Robberson, "Throats of Shenandoah Hikers Were Slashed, Authorities Say," *Washington Post*, June 5, 1996, www.washingtonpost.com/archive/local/1996/06/05/throats-of-shenandoah-hikers-were-slashed-authorities-say/e89a30d7-dd2f-4bcc-a50b-ecc803c2e603/.

89 **"We can't pin down":** "Lesbian Hikers Slain," *Washington Blade*, June 7, 1996.

89 **"shocked" to hear:** David Rered, "Murders Spark Fear among Hikers," Associated Press, June 5, 1996.

89 **"We'll feel safer":** John Rivera, "Hikers Are Uneasy after Two Slayings along Path," *Baltimore Sun*, June 8, 1996.

CHAPTER 8

95 **discover her body:** As it turned out, Largay became lost after following the Appalachian Trail Conservancy's mandate that hikers go at least two hundred feet off the trail to relieve themselves. Largay, who was on a Maine section of the trail at the time, hiked in vain for several days, hoping to find cell reception. She eventually set up camp near a small stream. She survived for at least fourteen days on three days of food. During that time, she kept a journal that recorded her attempts to be found and, eventually, farewell letters to her family. Working with them, I detailed the search for Largay and the eventual discovery of her body and the remaining journal in a series of articles for the *Boston Globe* from 2014 to 2016.

CHAPTER 10

109 **"endless woods":** William Wordsworth, "An Evening Walk," *Wordsworth's Poetry and Prose*, ed. Nicholas Halmi (New York: W. W. Norton, 2013), 443.

110 **"absolute freedom and wildness":** Henry David Thoreau, "Walking." *Thoreau: Collected Essays and Poems* (Washington, DC: Library of America, 2001), 225.

111 **"How womankind":** Ibid., 231.

111 **"a dropping out of "**: Edward H. Clark, *Sex in Education; or, A Fair Chance for Girls* (Project Gutenberg eBook; first published 1875), accessed July 14, 2020, www.gutenberg .org/files/18504/18504-h/18504-h.htm.

112 **"outdoor pursuits":** Ibid.

112 **duties and timetables:** John M. Gould, *How to Camp Out: Hints for Camping and Walking* (Project Gutenberg eBook; first published 1877), accessed July 14, 2020, www. gutenberg.org/files/17575/17575-h/17575-h.htm.

112 **schoolhouses or sawmills:** Ibid.

113 **"nativism and masculinity":** Ben Jordan, "'Conservation of Boyhood': Boy Scouting's Modest Manliness and Natural Resource Conservation, 1910–1930," *Environmental History* 15, no. 4 (2010): 612–42, 617.

113 **remain wholly separate:** Wilma Miranda and Rita Yerkes, "The History of Camping Women in the Professionalization of Experiential Education," in *Women's Voices in Experiential Education,* ed. Karen Warren (Dubuque, IA: Kendall/Hunt, 1996), 63–77.

113 **Military-inspired language:** Silas Chamberlin, *On the Trail: A History of American Hiking* (New Haven, CT: Yale University Press, 2016).

113 **veteran Paul Petzoldt:** McKay Jenkins, *The Last Ridge: The Epic Story of America's First Mountain Soldiers and the Assault on Hitler's Europe* (New York: Random House, 2004).

114 **"There was a strong":** Qtd. in Joshua L. Miner and Joseph R. Boldt, *Outward Bound USA* (Seattle: Mountaineer Books, 2002), 289.

114 **practice emotional stoicism:** Jay Kennedy and Constance Russell, "Hegemonic Masculinity in Outdoor Education," *Journal of Adventure Education and Outdoor Learning,* April 2020, doi.org/10.1080/14729679.2020.1755706.

116 **sexist and exclusionary programming:** For more on this research, see Karen Warren, Denise Mitten, Chiara D'Amore, and Erin Lotz, "The Gendered Hidden Curriculum of Adventure Education," *Journal of Experiential Education* 42, no. 2 (June 2019): 140–54; Alison Lugg, "Women's Experience of Outdoor Education: Still Trying to Be 'One of the Boys?,'" in *Whose Journeys? The Outdoor and Adventurous Social and Cultural Phenomena: Critical Explorations of Relations between Individuals, 'Other' and the Environment,* ed. Barbara Humberstone, Heather Brown, and Kaye Richards (London: Institute for Outdoor Learning, 2003); and Sheryl Clark, "Running into Trouble: Constructions of Danger and Risk in Girls' Access to Outdoor Space and Physical Activity," *Sport, Education and Society* 20, no. 8 (2015): 1012–28.

116 **A recent study:** Jamie N. McNiel, Deborah A. Harris, and Kristi M. Fondren, "Women and the Wild": Gender Socialization in Wilderness Recreation Advertising," *Gender Issues* 29 (November 2012): 1–4.

CHAPTER 11

129 **for its missteps:** The dialogue that follows is taken verbatim from the hearing transcript: US Senate, "Hearing before the Subcommittee on Parks, Historic Preservation, and Recreation of the Committee on Energy and Natural Resources on S.1703 to Amend the Act Establishing the National Park Foundation," 104th Cong., 2nd Sess. (June 6, 1996).

129 **"Can you tell":** Ibid.

130 **"Obviously, neither"**: Ibid.

130 **"It's safe to assume"**: Lisa K. Garcia, "Hikers' Killer Going Home," *Roanoke (VA) Times*, September 25, 1996.

132 **"Finding their killer"**: Associated Press, "Parents Visit Crime Scene," *Daily Press* (Newport News, VA), September 19, 1996.

132 **"One [reporter] asked"**: Sue Fox, "FBI Deflects Questions in Hiker Slayings," *Washington Blade*, September 20, 1996.

133 **and ready access:** NCAVC, *National Center for the Analysis of Violent Crime Affidavit: Considerations Regarding Homicides—Julie Williams and Lollie Winans* (report, Department of Justice, Washington, DC, 1996).

CHAPTER 12

136 **"You'd really have"**: Associated Press, "As Latest Bodies Identified, Fear Pervasive in Hamlet," Virginian-Pilot (Norfolk, VA), September 26, 1996.

137 **"The glaring factor"**: Michael D. Shear, "Body Found, Renewing Town's Fears," *Washington Post*, September 24, 1996.

137 **"Offenders like this"**: Associated Press, "Who Is the 29 Stalker?" *Free Lance–Star* (Fredericksburg, VA), September 22, 2002.

137 **"The likelihood"**: Associated Press, "Slayings Have Similarities, Expert Says," *Free Lance–Star* (Fredericksburg, VA), September 25, 1996.

139 **"seventy-seven million"**: "Thousands of Hikers Take Back the Trails," *Daily Press* (Newport News, VA), May 30, 1997.

143 **"There have been"**: "Serial Killer Fears Renewed after Mistake Handling Evidence Revealed," *News Leader* (Staunton, VA), June 4, 1997.

CHAPTER 13

157 **cues and norms:** Associated Press, "Slayings Have Similarities, Expert Says," *Free Lance–Star* (Fredericksburg, VA), September 25, 1996.

158 **hold down regular jobs:** John Douglas, Ann W. Burgess, Allen G. Burgess, and Robert K. Ressler, *Crime Classification Manual: A Standard System for Investigating and Classifying Violent Crimes*, 2nd ed. (San Francisco: Jossey-Bass, 2006).

158 **collection of pornography:** Jeffrey Rinek, *In the Name of the Children: An FBI Agent's Relentless Pursuit of the Nation's Worst Predators* (Dallas: BenBella Books, 2018).

CHAPTER 14

168 **"flaunting their sexuality"**: Qtd. in H. L. Polman, *The Whole Truth? A Case of Murder on the Appalachian Trail* (Amherst: University of Massachusetts Press, 1999), 198.

169 **After six hours:** David Margolick, "Lorena Bobbitt Acquitted in Mutilation of Husband," *New York Times*, January 22, 1994.

169 **"You opened up"**: Abbe Smith, "On Representing a Victim of Crime," in *Law Stories: Law, Meaning, and Violence*, ed. Garry Gellow and Martha Minow (Ann Arbor: University of Michigan Press, 1998), 151.

169 **"A man could get"**: Pohlman, *The Whole Truth?*, 318.

172 **crimes against Muslims:** Human Rights Watch, *We Are Not the Enemy: Hate Crimes Against Arabs, Muslims and Those Perceived to Be Arab or Muslim after September 11* (report, Human Rights Watch, New York, 2002), https://www.hrw.org/reports/2002/usahate/.

175 **"Informant: They didn't":** This passage is taken verbatim from defense motions filed in federal court. Any alterations or emphasis added was done by that legal team.

CHAPTER 15

178 **performed on LaRue:** Earl Swift, "The Stranger in the Shelter," *Outside*, November 5, 2018, www.outsideonline.com/2359316/appalachian-trail-shelter-first-murder-1974.

CHAPTER 16

190 **logic and inquiry:** Kim D. Rossmo and Jocelyn M. Pollock, "Confirmation Bias and Other Systemic Causes of Wrongful Convictions: A Sentinel Events Perspective," *Northeastern University Law Review* 11, no. 2 (2019): 790–835.

193 **do so undetected:** Blaine Harden, "The Banality of Gary: A Green River Chiller," *Washington Post*, November 16, 2003, www.washingtonpost.com/archive/life-style/2003/11/16/the-banality-of-gary-a-green-river-chiller/2d9575c7-6843-4ec3-9517-72cd3ecdd9bo/.

CHAPTER 17

196 **"patriarchal law and order":** Kate Manne, *Down Girl: The Logic of Misogyny* (New York: Oxford University Press, 2018), 74.

CHAPTER 18

206 **the state altered:** Margaret Edds, *An Expendable Man: The Near Execution of Earl Washington Jr.* (New York: New York University Press, 2003).

CHAPTER 20

224 **Jeff and Amy:** At their request, I have changed their first names.

235 **"serious problems":** Qtd. in Paul Berkowitz, *The Case of the Indian Trader: Billy Malone and the National Park Service Investigation at Hubbell Trading Post* (Albuquerque: University of New Mexico Press, 2011), Kindle location 1607 of 7041.

236 **corruption remains rampant:** *Legacy of the Yosemite Mafia: The Ranger Image and Noble Cause Corruption in the National Park Service* (Waltherville, OR: TrineDay, 2017).

237 **crimes ever occurred:** Ibid.

237 **deficiencies in training:** Office of the Inspector General, *Assessment of the Department of the Interior's Law Enforcement Activities* (GAO 2002-I-0014, Washington, DC, January 14, 2002), www.govinfo.gov/content/pkg/GPO-DOI-IGREPORTS-2002-i-0014/html/GPO-DOI-IGREPORTS-2002-i-0014.htm.

238 **part of law enforcement:** Samuel R. Gross, Maurice J. Possley, Kaitlin Jackson Roll, and Klara Huber Stephens, *Government Misconduct and Convicting the Innocent: The Role of Prosecutors, Police and Other Law Enforcement* (report, National Registry of Exonerations, Washington, DC, 2020).

CHAPTER 22

248 **"known and respected":** Mike German, *Disrupt, Discredit and Divide: How the New FBI Damages Democracy* (New York: New Press, 2019), 27.

249 **"unmanageable, unaccountable":** Ibid., 53.

258 **"Most experienced":** Ibid., 78.

CHAPTER 24

276 **load of laundry:** Erin Murphy, *Inside the Cell: The Dark Side of Forensic DNA* (New York: Bold Type Books, 2015).